CENTRAL ASIA

Also from *M.E.* Sharpe

CENTRAL ASIA IN TRANSITION
Dilemmas of Political and Economic Development
Boris Rumer, Editor

CENTRAL ASIA
The Challenges of Independence
Boris Rumer and Stanislav Zhukov, Editors

**CENTRAL ASIA
AND THE
NEW GLOBAL ECONOMY**
Boris Rumer, Editor

CENTRAL ASIA
A Gathering Storm?
Boris Rumer, Editor

**CENTRAL ASIA
AT THE
END OF THE TRANSITION**
Boris Rumer, Editor

CENTRAL ASIA
Views from Washington, Moscow, and Beijing
*Eugene Rumer, Dmitri Trenin, and Huasheng Zhao
with an Introduction by Rajan Menon*

CENTRAL ASIA

Views from Washington, Moscow, and Beijing

Eugene Rumer, Dmitri Trenin,
and Huasheng Zhao

With an Introduction by
Rajan Menon

M.E.Sharpe
Armonk, New York
London, England

Library of Congress Cataloging-in-Publication Data

Rumer, Eugene B., 1958–
Central Asia : views from Washington, Moscow, and Beijing / by Eugene Rumer,
  Dmitri Trenin, and Huasheng Zhao; with an Introduction by Rajan Menon
    p. cm.
  Includes bibliographical references and index.
  Contents: Introduction: Central Asia in the twenty-first century / Rajan Menon — The
United States and Central Asia : in search of a strategy / Eugene Rumer — Russia and Cen-
tral Asia : interests, policies, prospects / Dmitri Trenin — Central Asia in China's diplomacy
/ Huasheng Zhao.
  ISBN 978-0-7656-1994-5 (cloth : alk. paper) — ISBN 978-0-7656-1995-2 (pbk.: alk. paper)
  1. Asia, Central—Foreign relations—1991– 2. Asia, Central—Politics and government—
1991– I. Trenin, Dmitri. II. Zhao, Huasheng. III. Title.

DK859.57.R86 2007
327.58--dc22   2006028580

Printed in the United States of America

| BM (c) | 10 | 9 | 8 | 7 | 6 | 5 | 4 | 3 | 2 | 1 |
| BM (p) | 10 | 9 | 8 | 7 | 6 | 5 | 4 | 3 | 2 | 1 |

Contents

Acknowledgments

This volume, like the preceding works in this series published by M.E. Sharpe under the general editorship of Dr. Boris Rumer, was written within the framework of a long-term project on the post-Soviet countries of Central Asia and the South Caucasus sponsored by the Sasakawa Peace Foundation, the leading Japanese nongovernmental organization in the sphere of international affairs. The authors would like to express their gratitude to the Foundation and, especially, to Dr. Akira Iriyama, Dr. Akinori Seki, and Dr. Lau Sim Yee, who have given considerable attention to the organization of the project and to its conferences and seminars. This volume owes much to Professor Gregory L. Freeze, who has been an active participant in the project and to Bruce Acker for his careful copyediting. Sincere thanks are also due to the expert staff at M.E. Sharpe and, in particular, to Vice President and Editorial Director Patricia Kolb, who has strongly supported this publishing venture on behalf of the Sasakawa Peace Foundation.

CENTRAL ASIA

Introduction

Central Asia in the Twenty-First Century

Rajan Menon

The disintegration of the Soviet Union in December 1991 transformed Central Asia's political landscape—rapidly, utterly, and irrevocably. Situated between the Russian Federation and Afghanistan, with some states also bordering China and Iran, the region accounts for 50 million people distributed across five sovereign states: Kazakhstan, Kyrgyzstan, Tajikistan, Turkmenistan, and Uzbekistan. All of them are Turkic in cultural and linguistic background except Tajikistan, which in both respects is closer to Iran. Long an imperial domain of Russia, Central Asia was catapulted into the world suddenly—and for the most part against the will, and certainly against the expectations of the Communist Party officials who ruled what had been autonomous republics within the Union of Soviet Socialist Republics (USSR).

Post-Imperial Challenges

The new leaders immediately faced cosmic questions—ones they never imagined having to confront. Among them were: What should the form of government be in their newly born countries, and what were the appropriate institutional mechanisms for making and implementing policies while also ensuring regime survival? What should be the relationship between the state and the citizenry, particularly regarding representation and accountability? How should Soviet-style economies be transformed to establish private property and markets (capitalism, in other words) without generating dislocations and hardships that could produce popular protests? How should policies regarding language, culture, historiography, and citizenship be framed to build a new, post-Soviet identity reflecting popular aspirations, while also offering a sense of belonging to ethnic minorities, particularly to Russians (and other Slavic people), in Kazakhstan and Kyrgyzstan, where they constitute a significant portion of the population? What should be the role of Islam in a historically Islamic part of the world; more specifically, what were the best ways to accommodate its inevitable rise as a religion and as a source of identity while preventing it from inspiring radical political movements? What principles should underlie foreign policy: in particular, what was the proper balance between maintaining ties to Russia (which considers the region its sphere of influence, Central Asia's formal independence notwithstanding) while also reducing the dependence on it by engaging other states and organizations from beyond the region?

Although the specifics were obviously different, these same vexed questions relating to state formation, national identity, economics, and statecraft had confronted other new states and so were hardly unique to Central Asia. The difference was that, in the West at any rate, they had been worked out over centuries and in stages—and even then the changes had been disruptive, even violent (consider, for example, the enclosure system in Britain, the French Revolution, and the American Civil War). Central Asian countries are in a different circumstance entirely. They do not have the luxury of gradualness and must face these historic challenges in a far more compressed period of time, and simultaneously. Their situation is more like that of the Asian and African countries that emerged after World War II, following the dissolution of the nineteenth-century European colonial empires. But even there, India being a case in point, colonial institutions offered a base on which to build. Nor was it necessary to engineer a new economic order from the ground up.

In Central Asia, addressing these various tasks of state creation and nation-building simultaneously is especially complicated, because progress on one particular front can create problems in other areas. For example, the passage from socialist-style command economies toward market-driven alternatives can create disruptions that increase the chances for instability. And the concomitant redistribution of wealth and power (that typifies rapid economic change) can make it harder to create cohesive societies based on harmony among different nationalities. Likewise, the creation of a new identity based on the history and cultural values of the majority nationality can make minorities feel marginalized and apprehensive and everything from historiography to the renaming of streets and cities can stir controversy because even the past, which shapes people's sense of identity in the present, is being redefined. These momentous tasks are even more daunting for another reason. There are no manuals or theories to guide the construction of post-socialist political and economic orders. Amidst the flurry of books that Marxist intellectuals wrote predicting the emergence of socialism from the debris of capitalism, no one thought to write a good book on the reverse process, which roughly speaking is what confronts the leaders of the post-Soviet states today.

It is safe to say that Central Asian presidents, who have reinvented themselves from Communist Party functionaries to presidents of independent states, had spent little, if any, time pondering these matters and were therefore unprepared to deal with them. Their education, life experiences, and political inclinations had prepared them to the Soviet imperial order, not to govern sovereign states. But history, which does not conform to timetables or allow us to prepare for the changes it brings, thrust independence upon Central Asia's leaders, despite their preferences or lack of preparation. The population at large may have had a somewhat different attitude—although even that is debatable given the lack of empirical evidence—and many ordinary Central Asians may have welcomed independence. Nevertheless, they were scarcely better prepared than their rulers in figuring what to do with it once they had it, and many have found themselves poorer and economically less secure than in the Soviet era, and for this reason, and despite the tyrannical nature of the USSR, they tend toward nostalgia. In sum, at the beginning of 1992, Central Asians faced a vacuum in politics and economics, and no one in a position of power knew quite how to fill it.

The Imperial Legacy

History was part of the reason for this lack of preparedness. From the point at which Tsarist Russia's conquest of Central Asia was completed in the late nineteenth century until the fall of the USSR, the region was ruled by two successive empires, those of the Romanovs and the Bolsheviks. Although each imperial system was different in the means through which it controlled Central Asia and the ends for which it exercised that control (for one thing, the degree of social engineering applied by the Soviet regime was incomparably greater than what the Romanovs were capable of or indeed wanted to apply), there was one common denominator. As with other imperial structures the vertical connections between the imperial metropole (St. Petersburg under the Tsars, Moscow under the Commissars) and its Central Asian periphery superseded, even preempted, horizontal connections between the units of the periphery, not to mention links between the peripheral entities and other metropoles. As Alexander Motyl has shown, this asymmetry is the defining structural feature of empires, and it allows day-to-day governance and control while making the resort to force unnecessary by enabling the cooptation of peripheral elites rather than coercion of peripheral peoples to serve as the quotidian means of control. (Resorting to force is also costly in that it entails dispatching troops and maintaining them in the field for prolonged periods and counterproductive in that it risks backlashes.)[1] The vertical connections tying periphery to metropole covered the gamut of transactions: political dealings, economic exchanges, communication links (by rail, road, and air), cultural and educational currents, and flows of information. The imperial order managed political life in the periphery on terms that it defined and, when necessary, enforced, and with little regard for local welfare. To say the least, such a system was not an ideal training ground for peripheral elites who would suddenly be forced to take the reins of independent states following a sudden and unanticipated imperial collapse.

This north-south imperial structure, which endured for over a century, has been shattered and seems highly unlikely ever to be recreated again. Rhetoric aside, even the most nationalistic of Russian politicians do not seriously entertain the possibility of re-gathering this former domain, and few if any ordinary Russians want that responsibility, and certainly not the costs that will accompany it. Yet while Russia will never again "own" Central Asia, it will certainly remain a strong force in the region, and for many reasons. It shares a vast border with Kazakhstan and a much smaller one with Kyrgyzstan; some 6.5 million ethnic Russians (as well as other Slavs and Germans) continue to live in Central Asia, the overwhelming majority in Kazakhstan, where they account for a majority in some of that country's northern provinces. The Central Asian elite remains Russified in language and cultural orientation (although that will slowly change as the first post-Soviet generation comes to adulthood starting in about 2009) and thousands of Central Asians still work and study in Russia. Russia has an overriding stake in the region's stability and, for their part, Central Asian leaders realize that, by virtue of sheer geography, it is to Russia that they would turn—and where they would most likely flee—should upheaval threaten their grip on power. Finally, despite the stress placed today on Russia's multifarious problems and its decline, let us not forget that on virtually all dimensions of power, Central Asian states are even weaker and less stable. In the end, power is a relative concept, and although Russia is falling further behind the West and China (and perhaps India before long) it remains a power to be reckoned with in Central Asia, which is in fact the only place in the world where it can still be regarded as a great power.[2]

The Opening of Central Asia

Yet the days of Russian exclusivity are gone forever, a point that each contributor to this volume makes clear. The United States and Europe have established a political presence in Central Asia; so have China, India, Iran, Israel, Pakistan, and Turkey among other states. In addition to establishing a political presence, these states have also become sources of trade and investment, with the latter particularly visible in Kazakhstan's oil and gas sector. China, in particular, has established a strong position, not least because it regards the region as critical to the stability of its Xinjiang Autonomous Region, where the indigenous Turkic-Muslim Uighurs, cultural kin to Central Asians, continue to chafe under Chinese control. In addition, new connections are being established in the form of tourism, educational exchanges, military training programs, and transportation links. The Baku-Ceyhan oil pipeline and the pipeline-in-progress that will connect Kazakhstan's oilfields to China exemplify the emergence of east-west flows in people and goods that has eroded the dominance of the north-south axes of the imperial age. And these new connections are but the beginning of an unstoppable process.

States are not alone in entering what was long a Russian preserve. Multinational corporations (again, principally those specializing in energy) have established themselves in the region: Kazakhstan alone, the regional leader in foreign investment intake, witnessed an increase in investment from $1.8 billion in 1999 to $2.4 billion in 2004, chiefly in its energy sector.[3] NATO, through its Partnership for Peace program, has forged ties with regional states in the domain of security, stoking Russian and Chinese suspicions in the process. The Organization for Security and Cooperation in Europe (OSCE) has become active in conflict resolution and human rights monitoring in this part of the post-Soviet world, as it has in others. The European Union (EU) has extended its political and economic reach into Central Asia, as have various non-governmental organizations specializing in conflict resolution and human rights, among them International Crisis Group, Freedom House, and Amnesty International. In the realms of religion and culture, Iran, Turkey, Arab-Muslim states, and various Islamic organizations are helping to build mosques, making instructional material on Islam available, and providing educational opportunities to students, whether for secular or religious education. Then there is the Internet, that great transformational technology. It has given Central Asians, no matter how repressive their governments, an alternative source of information and a mechanism to transmit to the outside world news of what is really happening in their countries and to establish contacts with international groups. Were it not for that, news of the bloody crackdown that occurred in Uzbekistan's Andijon region in May 2005 would have reached the outside world far more slowly and in forms suited to the needs of Uzbek president Islam Karimov's dictatorial regime. Last but not least, transnational networks have become part of the Central Asian scene, and are diverse in nature, ranging from Hizb ut-Tahrir, which seeks to create a pan-Islamic caliphate, to organizations that traffic in narcotics and the global sex trade. These forces enter and operate in the region with ease because poorly patrolled borders have become porous, which also means that what happens in Chechnya, Afghanistan, and the Persian Gulf matters to the security of Central Asian regimes as never before. Central Asia is now part of the world—for good or ill.

The overall picture, details of which are provided in the chapters that follow, should be clear: in a remarkably short period of time, a constellation of states, companies, nongovernmental organizations (NGOs), and transnational organizations has moved into a region in which Russia exercised near-total control or in which, at the very least, it served as gatekeeper. For 100 years, imperial Russia was able to shape (but not totally control) the terms under which the "outside" world influenced Central Asia's politics, economics, culture, and security. The vertical lines that bound metropole and periphery together were dominant and excluded, or at minimum strictly regulated, horizontal connections. What we have witnessed since 1991 is the demolition of the imperial edifice and the emergence of multiple and multifarious horizontal lines connecting Central Asia to regions to its west, south, and east. The former overlord is now one of many players, and in several respects, because of its economic and military decline, is competing against newcomers from a position of inferiority. This overarching theme unites the chapters in this book.

In an effort to capture this historic shift in a catchy yet pithy formulation, some have called it the "new Great Game," harking back to the terminology Rudyard Kipling offered in *Kim* to describe the contest that the British and Russian empires waged in the latter part of the nineteenth century in this part of the world. But the old label, colorful though it is, does not capture the new reality. There are, to begin with, no empires vying for influence in Central Asia any longer; states are the principal participants in the rivalry. Nor does the current contest involve the possession of people or the annexation of land. We have transcended the age of empire (once a mark of prestige, imperialism is now a badge of dishonor), and in our day, the conquest and annexation of territory in the name of empire is neither feasible nor legitimate: Any attempts to repeat this past practice would elicit condemnation and resistance. Moreover, the competition of two great empires has been supplanted by a rivalry for influence (as opposed to control) by a multiplicity of states, whose cultural characteristics cannot be subsumed under the category Christian/European, as witnessed by the presence in Central Asia of China, India, Pakistan, Turkey, Israel, Iran, and various Arab states. China, India, Pakistan, and the Muslim world, themselves largely under imperial control or domination in the nineteenth century, are important now as participants in the quest for influence in twenty-first century Central Asia; and so is Israel, which emerged from the processes of empire. The cast of characters in the current Central Asian drama is more colorfully variegated than in Kipling's day. Non-state organizations were not entirely absent during the Great Game, but there certainly were no analogues, either in structure or purpose, to the EU, NATO, the OSCE, and the International Crisis Group. Moreover, the nineteenth-century competition between Britain and Russia was settled by a combination of conquest and negotiated spheres of influence. No such arrangement is possible in Central Asia today. As a result, the jockeying for advantage will be fluid, with some participants wielding a comparative advantage in some areas, while having to settle for little, or even no, influence in others. Kipling's formulation, although catchy and convenient, is, for all of these reasons, misleading in the extreme.

Central Asia's opening to the wider world will obviously have the greatest consequences for the peoples and regimes of the region. The former will, on the one hand, have new and unimagined choices. They can travel to destinations that would have been forbidden or allowed only to a select few that the Soviet regime deemed trustworthy; they will, as a result, be exposed to new ideas and to living conditions beyond their borders. And this will make a difference even if, as a practical matter, only a small segment of the population in Central Asian countries will have such opportunities. The exposure to the world will breed envy, create frustration with conditions at home, and offer up new political ideas that serve as means to understand and change politics; and governments will have to face a citizenry that is less subject to intellectual control than in Soviet times. They also will have to be prepared for the bad press and adverse consequences of mistreating their people. Consider for example the fallout from the Andijon massacre and its effects on the already poor reputation of Karimov's regime, or the effect that the so-called colored revolutions in Georgia and Ukraine had on the mass protests that occurred during Kyrgyzstan's Tulip Revolution. Yet the news is not all bad for Central Asia's leaders. As their region becomes a new arena for competition, they will have room to maneuver, to seek advantage, and to resist influence by playing off competitors—be they states or corporations—against each other.

Islam and Politics

Islam's appeal, as a religion and as a political force, will surely increase as contact between Central Asia and the Islamic world increases—through travel to the Muslim world, programs offered by Muslim governments and NGOs, the construction of mosques with foreign assistance, and the dissemination of information about Islam. But it would be an oversimplification, and an uncritical acceptance of the formulations widely used by the Kremlin and by the most repressive Central Asian regimes, to conclude that the inevitable result will be an upsurge of "fundamentalism" or "Wahhabism." To be sure, the rise of revolutionary movements influenced by specific forms of Islam can hardly be ruled out; indeed they have made their appearance as exemplified by the Islamic Movement of Uzbekistan (which seems to have been suppressed following the fall of the Taliban regime in Afghanistan) and the continued presence of Hizb ut-Tahrir.

Yet there are many variants of Islam in the vast expanse stretching from the Maghreb to Malacca, and the world's 1.3 billion Muslims are diverse. One cannot, therefore, speak with any confidence about how Islam will most affect Central Asia's politics. What can be said with certainty is that what should have happened long ago from the historical-cultural standpoint will now certainly happen. The nineteenth-century Russian conquest interrupted what would otherwise have been a symbiosis between Muslim Central Asia and the wider Islamic world. That process will now resume, the pace will be far faster than was possible under the technological conditions of previous centuries, and Islam will be among the important shapers of thought and conduct in Central Asia as a result. Precisely what form Islam will take will depend on the political circumstances and cultural features of each country—for example, Islam has traditionally had greater traction in regions of Central Asia that have a sedentary as opposed to a nomadic tradition—and on the contest between various forms of that religion. Nevertheless, Central Asians will have at their disposal, in the form of Islam, a new intellectual framework to understand prevalent problems such as corruption, inequality, ethnic strife, and repression—and to mobilize against regimes for failing to address them.

The Perils of Repression

The hegemony of Marxism-Leninism is over. Totalitarianism's time has come and gone. Try as they might, Central Asia's governing elites have been unable to proffer any alternative that stirs hearts and minds. Even the most repressive regimes—Turkmenistan and Uzbekistan—to emerge from the ashes of the USSR lack the capacity for mass indoctrination, and the institutional weakness that comes from dependence on the longevity of individual strongmen prevents them from acquiring any lasting form of it. The discourse of a particular dictator is limited in its appeal to his lifespan.

Moreover, globalization makes openness an indispensable ingredient for economic development and competitiveness, and that, in turn, increases the costs of repression while also making it harder to apply. Punishing boldness of thought or controlling access to information through such means as censoring the Internet is a recipe for stagnation. So is enforcing a curriculum designed to ensure the survival of the regime rather than to educate and train people suited to functioning in the modern world (an extreme case in point being the Turkmenistan school curriculum with the late President Saparmurad Niiazov's primitive tract, the *Rukhnama*, "Book of the Soul," as its centerpiece). The iron law that is inescapable is this: the more dictatorial the regime, the less that country's prospects for economic development. Local dictators, for whom the retention of power is the prime imperative, may be unperturbed by this, but it surely matters to the fate of Central Asia's people.

There are three additional outcomes that can be expected with a high degree of confidence based on a country's political and economic characteristics. First, political systems that are institutionally weak because they pivot on the personality of an all-powerful leader are bound to face succession crises, because the rules of the game and the procedures for transferring power are unclear. Succession therefore threatens to become an occasion for contestation outside formal institutional channels and, as a result, to create uncertainty, perhaps even turmoil. Obviously, the regimes most vulnerable to this dynamic are Turkmenistan and Uzbekistan, but the others are not entirely safe. Second, the more political institutions preclude genuine participation and stifle representation and aggregation of societal interests, the fewer the chances for moderate political forces to emerge, and the greater the possibility that oppositionist movements will be subterranean and radical. This pattern is already observable in Uzbekistan, particular in the Fergana Valley, which is more densely populated and poor compared to the rest of the country and where Islam has greater traction both as a religion and as a means for mobilizing and expressing dissent. Third, oil-based economies, like their counterparts elsewhere, may experience rapid economic growth rates, but they will invariably breed pathologies associated with other hydrocarbon-based economies. For example, the concentration of power in the hands of the state, pervasive and high levels of corruption, the loss of competitiveness in non-oil energy sectors (owing to the so-called Dutch disease), and a resistance to economic reform because revenues from energy are considered by the leadership to be a cure-all and an alternative to making tough choices.[4]

Beijing and Moscow: Present vs. Future

Taken together, these characteristics augur ill for Central Asia's developmental prospects. They also create deeply rooted sources of instability. The latter problem—upheaval—matters most among neighboring countries to Russia, and then to China. Not only is Russia heir to an empire in Central Asia, the ex-empire is continental (resembling those of the Ottomans and Habsburgs) and not a maritime one (such as those of Britain, France, Spain, and Portugal). The distinction is a critical one from a strategic standpoint. In principle, the metropole of maritime empires can disengage from its periphery, even though the process may be prolonged and bloody, as shown by the French departure from Indochina or Algeria. The former metropoles of continental empires, by contrast, remain joined at the hip to their ex-peripheries, and it becomes difficult to separate their security from turmoil in their former domains, which remain connected to them, and not just as a consequence of geography.[5] This is Russia's lot. It is fated to be deeply involved in Central Asia, and the region is destined to deal with that reality; no divorce is possible. Similarly for China, Central Asia has become a western strategic flank. China's role in trade and investment is growing; the region is becoming important (even if at the margins) for it as a source of energy to keep the booming Chinese economy running; and it is a corridor to Xinjiang, a restive region far removed from China's centers of power to the east. Given these stakes, the efforts of Beijing to increase its influence in Central Asia and its creation of institutional mechanisms to do so (the Shanghai Cooperation Organization [SCO], which China and Russia have sought to strengthen), is unsurprising.

For now, there is an intersection of interests between Russia and China because of the shared suspicion of the American military presence in the region, symbolized by U.S. access to the Kyrgyz airbase at Manas; the common concern about Islamic radicalism in Central Asia; and "the strategic partnership" formed in response to a U.S.-dominated unipolar world. But this could change, and probably will. In time, the U.S. military presence is bound to be scaled back, perhaps even eliminated; Central Asia is quite unlikely to become a region of abiding strategic centrality in Washington's eyes; indeed, absent 9/11 it would not have. An American disengagement and the continuing shift in the balance of power between Russia and China in the latter's favor in the decades ahead could alter the calculations of Beijing and Moscow.

The relevant question is whether convergence will give way to sharp rivalry or whether Russia, realizing the limits of its power, will slowly accommodate Chinese hegemony in the region, creating in the process a historic change wherein Moscow moves from accepting competition in its long-standing sphere of influence from an array of states (which it is doing now, albeit out of necessity) to ceding supremacy to one state. For the moment, with Russia retaining its base in Kant (Kyrgyzstan), gaining access to Uzbek bases (in the wake of Uzbekistan's post-Anidjon break with the United States), and operating within SCO as China's co-equal, this outcome does not seem likely. But in the long run, the probability that China will displace Russia as the predominant external power in Central Asia is quite high. What bears watching is whether this happens seamlessly or contentiously.

The chances that a state other than China will occupy the position of hegemony in Central Asia are slim. In the immediate post-Cold War years, there was much breathless talk about Turkey's ambitions and supposed natural advantages in Central Asia (by virtue of religious, cultural, and linguistic similarities with the Turkic republics of Central Asia). But Turkey's preoccupation with internal problems, its economic limitations, and its lack of direct geographical access to Central Asia have demonstrated that its reach in the region exceeds its grasp. And Central Asian regimes have come to expect less from Turkey the more they have come to know it. Iran, for its part, may have some advantages in Tajikistan, but even there, it acted as Moscow's partner in fostering the 1997 power-sharing accord that ended the Tajik civil war. In any event, Tehran has shown little inclination to sacrifice its beneficial relationship with Russia on the altar of its Central Asian ambitions, where it has maintained a steady but low-key presence.

A Preview

Many of the overarching themes that I have sketched here are illustrated with the aid of considerably more detail in the chapters that follow of Eugene Rumer, Dmitri Trenin, and Zhao Huasheng. Apart from the expertise that each scholar brings to the table and the judicious combination of analysis and specificity that marks their contributions, what is remarkable is the degree to which three authors—from the United States, Russia, and China—have reached similar conclusion on many key issues, even as they have looked at this complicated and rapidly changing part of the world from three different locations and three distinct vantage points. Without stealing the authors' thunder, in the rest of this introduction I will highlight the principal arguments contained in their chapters.

Eugene Rumer reminds us of a fact worth bearing in mind given that the United States has been actively engaged in Central Asia since late 2001: for most of the 1990s, Washington attached little importance to the area. To be sure, the United States encouraged economic reform based on markets and private property; spoke of the importance of human rights, elections, and civil society; encouraged Turkey's political and military forays into the region, viewing them as a counter to Iran; and promoted Central Asia's links with NATO via the Partnership for Peace. More important, it funded the removal and destruction of Soviet strategic nuclear weapons from Kazakhstan under the so-called Nunn-Lugar initiative. But compared to its role in Europe, the Persian Gulf, or the North Pacific, American strategic engagement in Central Asia was measured; indeed, the region's largely undemocratic regimes were judged to be potential liabilities, and the concern that their repressive character could foster turmoil was very much present in American official and academic assessments (and that has hardly disappeared).

September 11, 2001, changed this pattern of (relative) neglect entirely. Central Asia became a key center of logistical support for conducting America's war against the Taliban and for its efforts to create stability and to conduct counterinsurgency operations against Taliban remnants. No one would have predicted in the 1990s that the United States would establish military bases in Kyrgyzstan and Uzbekistan. Washington had been cool toward insistent Uzbek efforts to propose an anti-Russian alignment. Similarly, while hailing Kyrgyzstan's budding democracy, Washington nurtured it with only modest material support. Concerns about Karimov's dictatorial ways and disregard for human rights gave way to Realpolitik after 9/11, and Central Asia was elevated in American strategic calculations.

Yet with increased engagement has come misplaced hopes on both sides. The Andijon events amounted to a cold shower of reality for both countries. On May 13, 2005, a protest that drew some 10,000 people occurred in the Fergana Valley town of Andijon, in response to the trial of twenty-three local businessmen accused by the Karimov regime of being Islamic extremists linked to the pan-Islamic organization Hizb ut-Tahrir. Uzbek troops arrived on the scene and opened fire, killing hundreds of people (the precise figures are not known). Karimov claimed that only 189 people had died and that the so-called extremists had killed them, a claim that is patently false. After some hesitation the United States condemned the killings and called for an outside investigation. In response Karimov ended U.S. access to the Karshi-Khanabad base in July. Karimov learned that America's Realpolitik had its limits, and the summary eviction from the Karshi-Khanabad base showed Washington that the American presence rested on an unreliable foundation and that Russia, while down, was hardly out. The historical legacy of empire, enduring north-south communication links, the importance of Russia as a trading partner, Russified local elites, and the fear of Central Asian autocrats that American-backed democratic movements could arise—all of these factors enabled Russia to retain a significant presence in Central Asia, and the wealth that rising oil prices have given the Kremlin provides the basis for increasing it.

For its part, the United States, in Rumer's account, must balance at least three competing considerations. First, it must reconcile the commitment to democracy with the continuing need to deal with the region's undemocratic regimes, which, like it or not, are now important to American security. Second, Washington must both compete and cooperate with Russia and China. On the one hand, both states are seeking to expand their influence in the region while reducing America's but, on the other hand, they are important players without whose cooperation the United States can accomplish little of lasting value. Third, the

United States must weigh the costs and benefits of deepening its involvement in a region that contains plenty of pitfalls, is ripe for upheaval, and could offer unpleasant surprises as a result. Andijon was a stark reminder of this hazard.

Dmitri Trenin's chapter begins by reminding of a most basic fact: proximity. The Russian term of art for the post-Soviet states has been "the near abroad." It is clear from Trenin's analysis that Central Asia is something of a "near-near abroad": the Russian-Kazakh border, the world's longest, spans 7,500 kilometers, and the Volga Muslim Republic of Bashkortostan is merely 50 kilometers away at its nearest point. The lesson is that despite the slogan that globalization has reduced the relevance of distance, cheek-by-jowl propinquity still matters—a lot. Moreover, the strategic significance created by geography is strengthened by the role of demography. Russia has some 25 million Muslims (the precise number is in dispute and depends on who is counted and who is excluded), and though it is facile to posit some automatic affinity between them and Central Asia's Muslims—not all of whom are believers in any event, given the Soviet legacy—it would also be foolish to dismiss the significance of this connection: much depends on the political evolution of Russia and Central Asia, and on that, the jury remains out. Trenin shows also ways in which Central Asia matters to Russia: a case in point is the drug trade, which moves north into Russia from Afghanistan through Central Asia. Given the soaring problem of drug use in Russia, which in turn boosts the spread of HIV/AIDS, it is clear why the Kremlin frets about this unconventional security threat.

Trenin—quite correctly in my view—rejects apocalyptic scenarios of Russian irredentism (Kazakhstan, with its Slavic majority or plurality in several northern provinces, has elicited the most speculation about this) or reconquest. Moscow, he emphasizes, seeks a sphere of influence, but is not in the business of repossession; nor will it be. This is no trivial distinction. Russia's desire for predominance in Central Asia can be decried, but as a matter of historical patterns and political realities it is hardly unusual: consider the longtime policy of the United States toward Central America, or Britain's effort to retain its influence in its former colonies through the Commonwealth.

The desire for a sphere of influence explains Russia's growing ambivalence toward the U.S. military presence in Central Asia, an important element in Trenin's assessment. On the one hand, Moscow—however reluctantly—realized that the American military emplacement was an inevitable consequence of its post-9/11 campaign to topple the Taliban and the subsequent, and ongoing, effort to establish a stable, friendly successor regime in that country. Moscow may have even welcomed the American presence to a degree, given its antipathy toward the extremist, anti-Russian Taliban. Indeed, Trenin believes that the Kremlin by and large still sees America's military campaign as a far better alternative to a political breakdown in Afghanistan that would lead to a resurrection of Taliban.

Nevertheless, Trenin shows that Russia, joined by China, has become suspicious of America's long-term plans and is determined to thwart any permanent U.S. presence, and this sentiment has been deepened by the testiness that has come to characterize relations between Moscow and Washington. The SCO, the Russian bases at Kant, Kyrgyzstan, and Aini, Tajikistan, and the Kremlin's quick and opportunistic rapprochement with wayward Uzbekistan all testify to this. What Russia wants above all, in Trenin's eyes, is not democratic governments, but stable ones, and the scenario it dreads above all is prolonged instability in its vast southern periphery. Russia is comfortable with the Soviet-era elites that govern in the region. The problem for Moscow is that leadership transitions are in the offing in all Central Asian regimes (Kyrgyzstan's Tulip Revolution has produced one already, and the dust has yet to settle) and the probability that upheaval, or prolonged uncertainty, could accompany the transfer of power remains strong. For Moscow, then, increasing engagement involves the danger of entrapment.

Contrary to the commonplace view that the Chinese leadership is staking out a major position in Central Asia with the aid of a cunning strategy, Huasheng Zhao maintains that it is precisely the lack of a clear and comprehensive plan and the absence of consensus among policymakers that marks China's policy, which he finds to be an unsystematic mix of the reactive and the active. Yet anyone who considers the methodical way in which Beijing has entered the Central Asian energy market—investing effort and money to buy equity in Kazakhstan's oil firms and launching pipelines—can be forgiven for concluding that, in this area at least, China is motivated by a deliberate, well-conceived goal. And it is not just about economics. Beijing's oil diplomacy in Central Asia is clearly driven by the aim of securing sources of oil that flow through interior lines of communication that are not vulnerable to turmoil in the Persian Gulf or to disruptions—whether by accident or deliberately created by an adversary—in the long maritime passages that connect it to the Gulf oil suppliers. Central Asia is not a cure-all for such problems, but it certainly helps. Despite this methodical approach to the energy sector, Zhao makes an important point, especially given the tendency of those of the Realist persuasion to paint China as an adversary that should be contained. He alerts us to the difficulties China faces in Central Asia; and to support his argument that Beijing lacks a coherent Central Asia game-plan, he points out that Chinese scholars are still coping with a lack of information and research materials. If this observation applies to the government as well, we should not assume that Beijing has a master plan and is surefooted while its competitors in Central Asia are stumbling and bumbling along.

An irreducible reality that China must deal with—and one that Zhao stresses—is that although Central Asia is no longer a hostile front, as it was for most of the post-World War II era when Soviet forces were ensconced there and the Kremlin was able to make mischief by stirring up the Uighur population, the region presents new challenges. To begin with, all told, China's border with Kazakhstan, Kyrgyzstan, and Tajikistan is over 2,250 kilometers long, and as it has become open thanks to the reopening of rail and road connections—and there are plans for additional routes—China must now contend with the fact that what happens in Central Asia can wash over the border into Xinjiang.

Zhao leaves us with little doubt about Beijing's biggest worry: Uighur nationalism and the prospect that it could increase as the China-Central Asia border becomes more permeable and exiled Uighur nationalist groups in Central Asia are able, as a result, to extend their activities eastward into Xinjiang. Quite apart from Uighur nationalism, Beijing is also keeping watchful eyes on Islamist movements in Central Asia. It knows that a Taliban resurgence could set off waves of turmoil that travel across Central Asia and influence events in Muslim Xinjiang, where, despite the systematic effort by Beijing to settle Han Chinese, the Uighurs have not lost their sense of cultural distinctiveness. The slow growth of interdependence between China and Central Asia is, therefore, something of a double-edged sword.[6] China's influence in Central Asia is growing, but so is its vulnerability to developments there. And that, as Rumer and Trenin show, is true for America and Russia as well.

Notes

1. Alexander J. Motyl, *Imperial Ends* (New York: Columbia University Press, 2001).

2. I develop this argument in detail in "After Empire: Russia and the Southern 'Near Abroad,'" in *The New Russian Foreign Policy*, ed. Michael Mandelbaum (New York: Council on Foreign Relations Press, 1998), ch. 3.

3. See "The EU's Relationship with Kazakhstan," http://ec.europa.edu/comm/external_relations/kazakhstan/intro/index.htm.

4. On the problems that afflict oil-rich states, see Robert Ebel and Rajan Menon, eds., *Energy and Conflict in Central Asia and the Caucasus* (Lanham, MD: Rowman and Littlefield, 2000); and Terry Lynn Karl, *Paradox of Plenty: Oil Booms and Petro-States* (Berkeley: University of California Press, 1997).

5. On variations in the processes of imperial disengagement, see Hendrik Spruyt, *Ending Empire* (Ithaca, NY: Cornell University Press, 2005).

6. The slowness must be emphasized; Zhao notes that as a proportion of total volume, bilateral trade between the two sides is small, and even optimistic projections predict that China will obtain no more than 10 percent of its total oil imports from Central Asia.

1

The United States and Central Asia
In Search of a Strategy

Eugene Rumer

A Rude Awakening

The fall of the Soviet Union was rapid and unexpected, both inside and outside the country that for nearly half a century the United States had perceived as the defining influence on its foreign policy. By the time the Soviet Union broke up, the stand-off between Washington and Moscow had acquired the quality of a permanent feature of American policy toward a country that occupied nearly one-sixth of the earth's landmass. Few in the U.S. foreign policy and national security community, whether inside or outside the government, could conceive of the vast Eurasian landmass in terms other than those dictated by Cold War competition. The rise of five new independent states in what used to be Soviet Central Asia therefore caught most, if not all, of the American foreign policy experts by surprise.

There were good reasons for that surprise. Remote, isolated, and land-locked, Central Asia had no prior history of American involvement. Moreover, the five Central Asian states had had no modern experience of independence and statehood; nor had they any record of diplomatic relations with the United States. And indeed they were little known outside a relatively narrow circle of experts in the United States. These newcomers to the international arena had few cultural ties to the United States, and American economic involvement in this region was virtually nonexistent.

Focused on Cold War nuclear competition with the Soviet Union and the military stand-off in Europe, the foreign policy community in Washington had relatively little interest in developments in the Soviet heartland. The Cold War focus on competition with Soviet Communism did not leave much room to explore—and exploit—ethnic, religious, and cultural differences inside the Soviet empire. The fact that the Soviet Union was not a monolith and that it was crisscrossed by multiple fissures and fault lines was marginalized by the U.S. foreign policy community and its approaches to the study and understanding of the USSR.[1] An analytic approach built on the premise of such tensions and fissures inside the Soviet Union carried with it the risk of departing from worst-case planning assumptions and, conversely, the risk of underestimating the Soviet threat. Treating the Soviet Union as a monolith[2] therefore was a more prudent course for understanding and dealing with the USSR.

This view of the Soviet Union and the lack of appreciation for possible cracks in the monolith underwent little change even after the Soviet invasion of Afghanistan in 1979—next door to Central Asia—and the ensuing U.S. campaign to support the resistance movement in that country.[3] That conflict and U.S. involvement were also viewed largely in the context of the Cold War, with Europe as its epicenter and with little attention to the immediate regional context of the war in Afghanistan.

The rapid unraveling of the Soviet Union presented U.S. foreign policymakers with a whole host of new challenges that had to be addressed urgently and left little time to consider American interests and policies—save the most urgent issues requiring immediate resolution and response. The attention of the policy community focused on such issues as Soviet nuclear weapons deployed in far-flung, newly independent former Soviet republics, or the conventional weapons and troops deployed in Eastern Europe and the Baltics. Hence most of Central Asia was once again marginalized.[4]

The U.S. policy in neighboring Afghanistan was acclaimed a success and the American mission there considered accomplished when the Soviet Union withdrew its troops in 1989. It was a major milestone for U.S. policy in the whole region.[5] American policymakers then turned to other, more pressing issues—the revolutions in Eastern Europe; German unification; the unraveling of the Soviet Union and the future of Russia; Iraq and the first Gulf War; the breakup of Yugoslavia; interventions in Haiti and Somalia, to name just the most urgent items on the post-Cold War agenda. To that must be added issues raised by the emergence of China as the sole potential peer competitor of the United States.

Indeed, in the midst of these crises—China's Tiananmen Square events in 1989, the war in the Gulf in 1991, and the conflict within Yugoslavia—the breakup of the Soviet Union greatly exacerbated the challenges facing policymakers in Washington. They had to contend with the potential for destabilization that would ensue from the Soviet Union's breakup, the threat of ethnic conflict, the proliferation of weapons of mass destruction and the loose control over vast conventional arsenals, coupled with incomplete Soviet withdrawal from Eastern Europe. The Soviet breakup undoubtedly promised more challenges than opportunities, at least in the near term.

Moreover, the breakup appeared especially troubling given the positive changes already taking place in the Soviet Union—proliferation of free speech, the opening of the political system, and the Communist Party's loss of political monopoly. There could be little doubt that American interests were already quite well served by changes in Soviet foreign policy—the INF treaty, the CFE treaty, Soviet withdrawal from Eastern Europe, and support for key U.S. positions during the Iraq crisis. Thus the breakup of the Soviet was not only an unexpected, but in many ways even an unwelcome, development.[6]

The fact that American policymakers were not loath to leave is abundantly clear from the memoirs of former top U.S. officials. Thus, former Secretary of State James Baker provided an interesting insight into the mindset of senior U.S. officials after the failed August 1991 coup that led to the Soviet Union's rapid dissolution: "With the victory of the Center (Gorbachev) and the Republic leaders (Yeltsin) who were committed to reform . . . we should expect the political leadership to move aggressively on reform now."[7] Baker's analysis of the situation suggests that Washington was still not prepared to give up on the idea of salvaging arrangements for peaceful coexistence and cooperation between the federal government of the Soviet Union and its constituent republics even after the failed August coup and well after events on the ground had moved past the point of no return.

The most that Baker's team would devise as guidelines for U.S. policy in the former Soviet Union consisted of five general principles:

1. peaceful self-determination consistent with democratic values and principles;
2. respect for existing borders, with any changes occurring peacefully and consensually;
3. respect for democracy and the rule of law, especially elections and referenda;
4. human rights, particularly minority rights;
5. respect for international laws and obligations.[8]

What was good enough for Germany at the time of its unification—almost the same time as the Soviet Union was falling apart—was good enough for the USSR's constituent republics, including those of Central Asia.

Beyond that, who could pay attention to Central Asia in the midst of all these crises? The region's remoteness, novelty, and lack of familiarity to U.S. policymakers, combined with a multitude of other pressing issues, virtually guaranteed that it would not rise to the top tier of the U.S. foreign policy agenda, except if it were to become a problem that could no longer be ignored.

After the End of History

The prevalent mindset of the post-Cold War era worked to prevent the elevation of Central Asia to the top tier of Washington's foreign policy concerns. The end of Cold War also ended the great ideological confrontation between liberal democracy and communism. The famous "end of history" thesis articulated by Francis Fukuyama held out the prospect of the universal spread of liberal democracy as the only legitimate form of political and social organization, as well as a guarantee of long-term stability in many countries that otherwise would be threatened by internal turmoil.[9]

Along with the "end of history," market capitalism triumphed over central planning as the sole practical principle for organizing economies, especially those emerging from the ashes of the Soviet Union. Combined with rapid technological change, free market principles became the bedrock of the new phenomenon of globalization that opened doors for the worldwide flow of ideas, people, goods, capital, and technology. The rules of globalization would not tolerate government interference in the workings of free markets, which, in any event, cannot be fooled.[10]

The "end of history"—the triumph of liberal ideas—prophesied a wave of democratization that, in turn, would lead to greater accountability on the part of governments and better understanding of national self-interest on the part of citizens. And that, in turn, would promote the spread of free markets required for successful navigation of the tides of globalization. Any deviation from these basics would be detected and elicit reactions from the ever-watchful markets, with a consequent impact on the fortunes of erring nations and governments. Hence nations interested in long-term stability and prosperity—and which nations are not?—had no choice but to pursue markets and democracy. It was simply a matter of their self-interest.

Moreover, globalization appeared to have upended many previously accepted ideas about international relations and security. Access to resources would not matter as much as it formerly did, since markets would punish those who interfered with the flows of goods, capital, and services; war, especially major war, had become obsolete. And the rise of the Internet and instantaneous global communications would ensure the free flow of ideas that could be neither monitored nor interdicted.

Ironically, for Central Asia this meant its marginalization on the U.S. foreign policy agenda. As globalization, free markets, and liberal democracy eclipsed other approaches to international relations (including balance of power and geopolitics), Central Asia presented neither the primary opportunity for the dissemination of liberal, market ideas, nor the primary obstacle to their progress. Certainly, within the framework of its immediate neighborhood, Central Asia paled in significance to Russia, which was struggling with its own transition to a market economy and democracy. Russia's size and potential, to say nothing of its nuclear weapons, guaranteed its dominant position on the U.S. foreign policy agenda. If Russia made good on its post-Soviet transition, its neighbors would stand a fair chance of succeeding in theirs—such, at least, was the thinking then prevalent in U.S. foreign policy circles. If Russia failed, it could, and most likely would, drag down its neighbors as well.

In 1991, therefore, Central Asia appeared on the U.S. foreign policy agenda chiefly in the context of the post-Soviet region. The State Department's European Bureau assumed responsibility for conducting relations with and formulating and implementing U.S. foreign policy toward this region. The same bureau that had previously formulated and implemented U.S. policy toward the Soviet Union now dealt with all of its successor states. In 1993 the State Department created a provisional structure to deal with Russia and other former Soviet states (a de facto bureau), thereby consolidating policy formulation toward Central Asia and the rest of the Soviet Union in a single, separate bureaucratic structure.[11]

The passage of the Freedom Support Act in 1992 and the Cooperative Threat Reduction program in 1991 (the so-called Nunn-Lugar legislation) provided funding—under a common financing umbrella—to support the development and independence of the former Soviet states and to help these new states secure and eliminate weapons of mass destruction and components left over from the Soviet Union on their territories.[12] As a result of these important but incremental steps, American policy toward the former Soviet states tended to overlook their connections to other neighboring countries and regions—South Asia, Iran, and China. All this seemed to be a matter of distant historical memories, recognized in the abstract, but rarely if ever treated as a specific policy concern.

For much of the 1990s, Central Asia did not constitute a topic of intense, focused thinking in U.S. foreign policy community. Therefore, Washington did not devise a strategy to ensure coherent, determined actions in the region. Rather, American policy toward Central Asia, especially in the early stages, was driven more by inertia, convenience, and attention to other factors deemed to be of greater significance. On the whole, Central Asia became an element of U.S. policy toward the former Soviet lands, but one where the agenda was dominated by America's relations with Russia and concerns about developments in that country.

Yet Russia was not the sole factor in shaping U.S. policy toward Central Asia in the 1990s. There were several others—for example, de-nuclearization of the former Soviet lands and nonproliferation, energy, promotion of democracy, counterterrorism, and Iran, to name just a handful of the principal factors.

The problem for Central Asia then, as well as now, fifteen years into its independence, is the lack on the part of the United States of a clear vision of its interests in this remote and unfamiliar region. That lack of clarity is hardly unique to Central Asia and American policy toward this region, but it is certainly manifest there. Inertia still weighs heavily on Washington's approach toward Central Asia. The certitudes of the Cold War and the defining influence of competition with the Soviet Union bequeathed a distorting legacy for U.S. foreign policy: in the post-Cold War era the United States has had to operate in a world that is no longer binary—indeed, one where partners, adversaries, and interests are far more complex, and difficult to define.

How important is Central Asia to the United States? Should this region be seen as a strategic beachhead in the heart of Eurasia, a stepping-stone to Iran, Russia, China, and Afghanistan? Or be regarded primarily as a source of hydrocarbon reserves? Or be seen as a target of American efforts to promote democracy? None of these concerns alone merits inclusion of this region in the top ranks of American foreign policy and national security concerns. Still, if taken together, these considerations do provide a rationale for a strong U.S. interest in Central Asia.

In the post-Cold War era dominated by other, more pressing events in Europe and in Asia, this complex combination of interests and concerns did not become immediately evident. Rather, they emerged sequentially; their combined importance took more than a full decade to be fully perceived and appreciated.

Despite the aggregate weight of U.S. interests, Central Asia neither offers major opportunities (like early post-Cold War Russia) nor ranks as a rising peer competitor (like China); it is neither an ally (like Europe or Japan) nor an adversary (like Saddam Hussein's Iraq or Iran). As a result, Central Asia falls in the vast middle tier of regions and countries that are important, but its relative significance on the U.S. foreign policy agenda is a product of many, often competing interests. American policy toward the region therefore reflects multiple interests and principles; it is not set in stone, but varies according to other U.S. concerns, as well as current ideological preferences and relationships.

In the case of Central Asia, a region deeply rooted in its Soviet experience, this newfound fluidity and ambiguity has represented a stark departure from the certitudes that characterized Soviet-American relations during the Cold War. Moreover, in the early post-Soviet years, uncertainty and ambiguity stood in stark contrast to what appeared to be a well-defined strategy with clearly set priorities that guided U.S. relations with Russia. The uncertainty and ambiguity posed a challenge both to U.S. policymakers seeking to devise a sustainable course for American relations with Central Asia, and for the leaders of Central Asia, who sought unequivocal international recognition and a clear geopolitical orientation.

First Steps

Central Asia as a region of considerable importance in its own right for U.S. policymakers did not come into focus for a considerable period of time after the dissolution of the USSR. In the 1990s the policy passed through several stages, with Washington's predominant concerns in the region changing every few years. American policy was more a product of events in and around the region than a predetermined strategy driven by a clear vision of U.S. interests in that part of the world. As those events evolved, so did U.S. policy.

Loose Nukes

The first and most urgent condition on the ground requiring immediate attention after the breakup of the Soviet Union was the remaining nuclear arsenal and weapons of mass destruction (WMD) components—both of which were found on the territory of post-Soviet Central Asia in large quantities. Securing, removing, or eliminating this extremely dangerous legacy of the Soviet era was priority number one—given the high risk of proliferation, the proximity of Central Asia to the Middle East and South Asia, and the large potential market for such merchandise (whether in the Middle East, North Korea, or elsewhere).

The American focus on nuclear weapons (viz., their security, removal, and consolidation in Russia, which was designated as the sole nuclear successor state to the Soviet Union) cast the spotlight on Kazakhstan, home to a large arsenal of both nuclear-armed missiles as well as large production facilities that were poorly guarded and maintained. Although other Central Asian countries had various WMD components and related technical and scientific facilities, Kazakhstan was the only Central Asian country, and one of four (along with the Russian Federation, Ukraine, and Belarus) post-Soviet states, to possess a substantial nuclear arsenal within its borders. The Soviet WMD patrimony in Kazakhstan included 104 SS-18 intercontinental ballistic missiles (ICBMs) with some 1,400 warheads.[13] In addition to this ICBM arsenal (which, at least on paper, made Kazakhstan a nuclear superpower), Kazakhstan inherited a collection of heavy bombers, ICBM launchers, launch control centers, and test silos, all of which had to be secured, destroyed, or removed.[14]

Although the prospect that Kazakhstan would retain possession of its nuclear inheritance never seemed realistic and few, if any, ever gave it serious consideration, it nevertheless required a significant diplomatic effort to secure this arsenal and extract a commitment from Kazakhstani authorities to join the Treaty on the Nonproliferation of Nuclear Weapons (NPT) as a non-nuclear state. Kazakhstan signed the NPT as a non-nuclear state in 1994, with all nuclear weapons being withdrawn from its territory by May 1995.[15]

In addition to these accomplishments, in 1994 the United States collaborated with Russia to remove 600 kilograms of weapons-grade, highly enriched uranium from a poorly guarded plant in Ulba, Kazakhstan. The operation, known as Project Sapphire, was considered one of the brightest success stories in American efforts to prevent nuclear proliferation in Central Asia, or anywhere else for that matter.[16]

The apogee of Washington's nuclear diplomacy in Central Asia came in the mid-1990s. A variety of U.S. programs designed to eliminate or, at a minimum, to reduce significantly the threat of the different types of WMD—chemical, biological, radiological, and of course nuclear—have continued in the region until the present day. However, with the elimination of the problem of "loose nukes"—unsecured ex-Soviet nuclear weapons and the risk of their falling into the wrong hands—nuclear diplomacy receded into the background, leaving room for other issues to dominate the American policy agenda in Central Asia.

The Reform Agenda

Parallel with the nonproliferation agenda, the United States undertook an ambitious effort to help the five Central Asian states implement political and economic reforms as the centerpiece of a post-communist transition. This effort was the logical next step in the nascent American relationship with Central Asia, following Washington's recognition of the five states as independent and sovereign. U.S. policymakers believed that Washington could not just leave these new countries to their own devices and must act to ensure their survival.

The reforms promoted by the United States laid a heavy emphasis on market institutions and democratic governance. They were the product of two factors: the continuing resonance of James Baker's five principles for recognizing the newly independent states of the former Soviet Union (including the prominence of democratic values); and, simultaneously, the widespread belief in the U.S. policy community in Fukuyama's "end of history." [17]

The strong emphasis on the development of a market economy and privatization reflected an equally widespread belief in the so-called Washington consensus, a set of liberal economic principles that include free trade, unimpeded movement of capital, fiscal discipline, and market-driven interest rate policies deemed essential for any state to survive in the rough waters of globalization. The basic recipe proffered by American advisers to Central Asian governments essentially encapsulated these principles.

The political reforms promoted by U.S. advisers sought to follow a similar pattern. This included a well-established policy of providing support for the development of nongovernmental organizations (NGOs), independent media, political parties, and free elections.[18]

The results of U.S. policy in promoting economic and political reform varied greatly across Central Asia, depending on individual countries and their internal conditions.[19] Kazakhstan and Kyrgyzstan embarked on ambitious political and economic reform programs; Turkmenistan and Uzbekistan stalled; and Tajikistan descended into civil war. Nevertheless, Washington's basic approach to political reform was essentially the same across the board, local conditions permitting.

But this reform agenda offered little guidance as to the objectives of American policy in Central Asia. Was this reform for the sake of reform? Was the United States committing itself to the modernization of Central Asia in order to expand the zone of democracy and prosperity, both as a gesture of good will and as an act of enlightened self-interest, on the assumption that once these five nations of Central Asia become democratic, they would not go to war with each other, their neighbors, or the United States (on the long-held premise that democracies do not go to war with each other). Or, alternatively, did Washington have an ulterior motive—namely, developing future markets for U.S. exports through economic reform and development in Central Asia?

Neither of these two explanations seemed plausible to skeptics seeking a concrete, tangible motive behind American support for Central Asia. Neither explanation seemed likely to provide a compelling—strategic—rationale for sustained U.S. involvement in this region. Responding to the "loose nukes" threat certainly made for a compelling rationale for U.S. policy; political and economic reforms as good will gestures did not.

The Security Agenda

In addition to political and economic reform, the United States also adopted a new foreign policy orientation toward this region. This effort too—much like the political and economic reform agenda—reflected a general American preference for familiar structures and principles. In this instance, Washington encouraged Central Asia to establish and develop relations with the Euro-Atlantic security institutions—the North Atlantic Treaty Organization (NATO) and the Organization for Security and Cooperation in Europe (OSCE). Both Cold War-era institutions were adapting to new times and new frontiers, figuratively and literally; and both welcomed the challenges that relations with Central Asia, far beyond their traditional perimeters, would pose.[20]

Although not European, the five states of Central Asia were "grandfathered" into the OSCE as successor states to the Soviet Union. NATO extended to them membership in the Euro-Atlantic Partnership Council (EAPC)—a forum designed specifically for dialogue among allies and partners in Eastern Europe and Asia. Membership in the Alliance's Partnership for Peace (PfP) program was also offered—and accepted by—the five Central Asian nations.

This program of security assistance promoted by Washington (both through the Euro-Atlantic institutions and bilaterally) followed the pattern of cooperation being pursued in Eastern Europe. The goal was to promote overall compatibility with NATO, even if that did not entail offering the Central Asian states membership in the alliance. The approach entailed reform in the security sector; a new model of civil-military relations to ensure civilian control of the military and accountability; as well as development of the so-called niche capabilities (enabling partner states lacking the budget resources to maintain large military organizations to "plug into" the coalition formations comprised of allies and other partners).

The prospect of large-scale or even small war immediately impacting any of the NATO member countries was deemed remote. The Alliance was preoccupied with the so-called out-of-area contingencies, especially the Balkans, a region that was part of Europe, but where the conflict did not involve directly any member of the Alliance. But not with Central Asia, which presumably was too far out of area. Accordingly, efforts by the United States and NATO to provide security assistance concentrated on the development of peacekeeping capabilities, disaster relief, and regional and NATO interoperability. Increasingly in the 1990s, American concerns about illegal trafficking in drugs, weapons, and people led Washington to provide assistance to Central Asia to improve border security.

Admittedly, this assistance would address some of the challenges facing Central Asia. But it appears in retrospect that its primary goal was to help Europe make itself more secure from Central Asia or get Central Asia to help address the challenges facing Europe elsewhere, rather than help Central Asia proper secure itself from any threats facing it.

Security assistance programs of the United States and NATO were driven by European and Eurocentric, not Central Asian, security assessments and perceptions. In effect, these programs sought to enable Central Asia to plug into Europe's security architecture, not create a gateway whereby Europe would provide for security in this region. The U.S. Government issued the single most important official statement on its Central Asia policy in July 1997. The statement referred to the upcoming regional exercise that would bring together Uzbek, Kazakh, Kyrgyz, American, Turkish, and Russian troops in a joint exercise to "practice together their skills in minesweeping and distributing humanitarian aid."[21] But that declaration did not contain a single reference to the Taliban—at the very time that this new radical regime in Afghanistan was consolidating its power on the southern borders of Central Asia.

But when it came to sufficient grounds to anchor America's engagement in Central Asia, security cooperation and assistance programs did not provide a compelling rationale to warrant a sustained, long-term commitment to the region. Central Asia proved to be among the least enthusiastic regional PfP partners. And for the entire decade of the 1990s, the region seemed to be hopelessly remote from the issues that stood at the top of the American and Euro-Atlantic security agenda.

A Policy in Search of a Rationale

Other explanations and rationales were also advanced. Some of them proved quite esoteric. The breakup of the Soviet Union exposed to the outside world countries that, for more than a century, had been outside the international system and cut off from countries and regions with which they had once had close cultural, ethnic, economic, and religious ties. Iran and Turkey in particular were poised to capitalize on this common heritage. They shared Persian and Turkic linguistic and cultural legacies with Central Asia, and that made them, respectively, a source of concern and a source of opportunity. Iran's recent revolutionary past and antagonistic posture vis-à-vis the United States naturally made it a source of concern for U.S. policymakers. The opposite view obtained for Turkey. As a strong U.S. ally, ethnic kin of Central Asia's nations, and a secular Islamic nation with democratic governance, Turkey seemed like the natural partner for the United States to promote Central Asia's re-emergence into the international arena and domestic modernization. Moreover, for Turkey, long spurned by the European Union in its aspirations for membership, the chance to expand its sphere of influence in Central Asia and to serve as a bridge between that region and Europe seemed an irresistible opportunity. The United States, eager to support its ally, encouraged closer relations between Central Asia and Turkey as a role model for the region and as a conduit for U.S. interests.[22]

However, these and other rationales did not suffice to justify a robust American involvement in Central Asia. As Turkey sought to address its own internal challenges (political crises, the role of Islam, civil-military relations, economic modernization, and the Kurdish rebellion), it had neither the resources nor a strong interest to play the role of a patron to a region looking for security and stability in the post-Soviet world.

For Central Asia, while Turkey may have been an attractive partner, it was hardly a substitute for the United States in its capacity as the only superpower, and the only global power. The region was unlikely to accept a substitute. But the United States, still unaccustomed to its role as the sole remaining superpower, or its global interests and responsibilities, remained ambivalent about its stake in these remote lands.

Protecting Independence or Professing Indifference?

Nothing encapsulated American ambivalence about Central Asia more than the statement of U.S. policy since James Baker's five principles: a speech in 1997 by Deputy Secretary of State Strobe Talbott, the chief architect of the Clinton Administration's policy toward the former Soviet Union.[23] In effect, Talbott's address was the first focused attempt by a senior American official to articulate a broad strategic vision for Central Asia, to clarify U.S. interests there, and to chart a course for U.S. policy.

Ironically, the most authoritative U.S. Government statement about its strategy for the region made quite clear that the United States had no compelling interest in the region, that Central Asia was not a region of critical strategic importance to American interests, and that hence Washington effectively did not have a specific strategy for Central Asia. The title of Talbott's speech, "Farewell to Flashman," was telling in its own right—as a repudiation of the fictional Victorian-era character and the atavistic "Great Game," in which the swashbuckling adventurer ostensibly played such an active role.

The United States, Talbott made clear, had no interest in planting its flag in Central Asia and becoming another player in the Great Game. The Great Game itself was a relic of the past; Talbott stressed that "overcoming old prejudices and predispositions . . . needs to be a constant theme in our own diplomacy in the region."[24] This was certainly a far cry from the "boots-on-the-ground" approach that appeared just a few years later. For the time being, at least, American interests in Central Asia were defined in terms of conflict avoidance, building democracy, market reform, and cooperative security arrangements. And these presupposed not an outdated zero-sum (we-win-you-lose approach), but on the modern post-Great Game, post-Cold War geopolitics that abjured the zero-sum, win-lose perspective.

Hidden beneath the allegorical use of Flashman's fictional character was an important message to all those suspecting the United States of engaging in yet another land grab in the heart of Eurasia. The message was clear: the United States did not have a compelling interest in the region. Its goal was not to become dominant in Central Asia, but to avert either the domination of others or the competition for influence there. Unlike Europe or East Asia, where a well-defined American footprint (maintained through a web of alliance relationships) was essential for U.S. interests, Central Asia was of secondary importance. Hence no immediate United States presence was required. American interests would be served just as well if the region continued, in effect, as a no-man's land outside the sphere of influence of any other power.

From Washington's perspective, the worst imaginable turn of events would be a geopolitical wrestling match between Russia, China, Iran, India, Pakistan, and Turkey to gain control over Central Asia since that would upset too many *other* interests that the United States might have *elsewhere*. The best approach for all concerned, Talbott suggested, would be to make Central Asia a "great-power-free zone" and to allow it to develop its natural resources and achieve stability through economic development. Hence the unspoken but obvious conclusion: the United States was willing to help with economic development and democratization, but above all did not want the region to become an American problem.

Talbott's rejection of the Great Game approach was neither understood nor accepted by the most important audience of all—in Central Asia proper. The win-lose, zero-sum approach was dominant in the region, especially among the five Central Asian states themselves. Their late twentieth-century borders were a product of nineteenth-century imperial competition between Russia and Britain and early Soviet experimentation with the "nationalities policy" of the Stalin era. They were dependent on each other for water, energy, key commodities, and communications. Surrounded by major Eurasian powers (China and Russia) and unpredictable regional actors (Iran and Afghanistan), they needed to cooperate as a simple matter of survival. But for such cooperation they lacked both tradition and interest; rather, they sought to exploit their advantages against neighbors or to hedge against retaliation; they generally sought to undermine, not strengthen, each other. In a word, Central Asian solidarity was an oxymoron.

Although a stampede of major powers vying for influence could not have been a welcome prospect for the Central Asian states, some competition among Russia, China, and the United States must have been a desirable development. After all, the contrary—a total lack of interest in their affairs—would have left them vulnerable to an increasingly volatile neighborhood and no realistic recourse to outside help.

Significantly, Central Asia's great-power neighbors—Russia and China—also spurned Talbott's appeal for a Central Asia free from the competition and domination of major powers. From the perspective of Moscow and Beijing, the notion of a region free of great-power competition was tantamount to a power vacuum in their strategic backyard. That prospect was singularly unwelcome, given the growing volatility of Central Asia's neighborhood after Taliban forces seized Kabul in 1996. The Shanghai Five (Russia, China, Kazakhstan, Kyrgyzstan, and Tajikistan), established in 1996, was initially a border management organization, but it increasingly turned into a regional forum where China and Russia could showcase their influence in Central Asia—to the exclusion of the United States.

The United States had yet another, tacit interest with respect to the role of the major powers (especially Russia) in Central Asia. Within the American foreign policy community, Russia was widely perceived as too weak to intervene effectively in the region in the event of a crisis or a provocation, whether domestic or external. However, its weakness was not viewed as an insurmountable obstacle to its intervention, even if that would lead to disastrous consequences for Russia itself, to say nothing of its Central Asian neighbors. Thus, saving Russia from another Afghanistan or Chechnya-type war (as tragic mistakes) was an important, albeit rarely articulated, American objective in Central Asia; it was deemed to be in the interest of all concerned—the United States, Russia, and Central Asian states themselves.

Nonetheless, Russia and China must have been suspicious of American statements about new rules for cooperation in Central Asia. First, these suspicions stemmed from doubts about Washington's efforts to assert leadership in a region half-way around the world and its right to determine the rules for Central Asia. Second, new win-win rules must have had a hollow ring because of Washington's explicit desire to keep Central Asia free from Chinese and Russian—but not American!—influence. Third, statements by the United States about its own lack of ulterior motives must have seemed disingenuous to Russian and Chinese observers, given the efforts by Washington to develop and market Caspian oil and gas deposits, including those in Kazakhstan and Turkmenistan.

Oil and Pipelines

If political and economic reforms, independence from major Eurasian powers, and integration in the Euro-Atlantic security structures did not provide a weighty rationale for active, strategic American engagement in Central Asia, oil—in the view of many observers—certainly did. Needless to say, U.S. officials strenuously contested the notion that American policy in the region was about oil; rather, they insisted that in the overall concept of policy oil was *instrumental* to all other concerns—reforms, integration, and security. Deputy Secretary of State Talbott addressed the issue in his 1997 speech:

> For the last several years, it has been fashionable to proclaim, or at least to predict, a replay of the "Great Game" in the Caucasus and Central Asia. The implication, of course, is that the driving dynamic of the region, fueled and lubricated by oil, will be the competition of the great powers to the disadvantage of the people who live there.
>
> Our goal is to avoid and actively to discourage that atavistic outcome. In pondering and practicing the geopolitics of oil, let's make sure that we are thinking in terms appropriate to the 21st century and not the 19th. Let's leave Rudyard Kipling and George McDonald Fraser where they belong—on the shelves of historical fiction. The Great Game, which starred Kipling's Kim and Fraser's Flashman, was very much of the zero-sum variety. What we want help bring about is just the opposite: We want to see all responsible players in the Caucasus and Central Asia be winners.[25]

Despite such unequivocal pronouncements, press accounts of American policy in Central Asia in the 1990s lead to the inescapable conclusion that oil was not just a subsidiary factor, but the principal objective. This dimension of U.S. policy in the region attracted the most attention, even when the price of oil was dropping below twenty U.S. dollars a barrel.

The presence of oil in Central Asia was not a new discovery. Kazakhstan, Turkmenistan, and Uzbekistan had been known to contain substantial hydrocarbon reserves. According to the Energy Information Administration of the U.S. Department of Energy, Kazakhstan—home to the largest oil reserves in Central Asia—has proven combined onshore and offshore hydrocarbon reserves with a range of 9 to 40 billion barrels. At the low end, this estimate is comparable to Algeria's oil reserves, and at the high end to Lybia.[26]

Kazakhstan has the largest natural gas reserves in the region with estimates ranging from 65–100 trillion cubic feet. Turkmenistan has the region's second largest reserves estimated at 71 trillion cubic feet. Uzbekistan's gas reserves are estimated at 66 trillion cubic feet.[27] Turkmenistan and Uzbekistan each has proven oil reserves of approximately half a billion barrels.[28]

Although the hydrocarbon reserves of Central Asia have long been known, they were not considered priority targets for investment and exploitation by the Soviet government. The fall of the Soviet Union and the emergence of independent states in Central Asia opened the region's oil and gas reserves for exploration. A number of companies, including U.S. energy companies, were soon knocking on the doors of the new countries' governments in order to secure contracts.

Caspian oil deposits generated a great deal of speculation and enthusiasm in the oil industry, as well as in the general policy community. The 1997 Caspian Region Energy Development Report (produced by the U.S. Department of State at the request of the United States Congress) estimated potential oil reserves in the Caspian basin to be as high as 200 billion barrels, which would—if accurate—rank it second only to the Middle East.[29] A more conservative estimate of 90 billion barrels contained in the same report compared Caspian oil reserves to those of Iran—still a significant amount.

However, proven reserves were estimated to be considerably less—just over 15 billion barrels of oil. Nevertheless, 200 billion barrels was the figure that captured the imagination of many observers inside and outside the region. The figure that was even more impressive was four trillion U.S. dollars in potential revenues that, if the high estimate of 200 billion barrels of oil proved true, would be generated at what was then the market rate for oil—20 dollars a barrel. The report for Congress further noted: "Since the dissolution of the Soviet Union, the benefits from these vast resources have been constrained by limited export routes and regional conflicts—issues that must be addressed in order to develop Caspian resources to the advantage of all participants."[30]

Indeed, the absence of pipelines to transport oil from this land-locked region to international markets was the major obstacle in the whole Caspian energy scheme. At certain points in the 1990s, the intensity of Caspian pipeline diplomacy could have made one think that the lack of pipelines was the major barrier to development of the entire region.

American policy on Caspian pipelines was a product of many considerations, among which energy and economics were only two and not the most significant ones. There were also numerous legal, political, and strategic issues to address.[31]

None of the options for building pipelines from the Caspian was simple. To the north, the Russian pipeline system was already carrying limited amounts of Caspian oil. However, to carry more (significantly more, as predicted by the Caspian Basin Energy Development Report), the Russian pipeline system would have to build more capacity. It would then be in a position to accommodate additional Caspian oil volumes and deliver them to markets in Europe and beyond.

However, the idea of building additional pipeline capacity through Russia made little strategic sense, since the goal of U.S. policy was not simply to pump as much oil as possible from the Caspian, but to leverage that oil into better prospects for independence, sovereignty, and prosperity for the newly independent states of the region. From that point of view, it made little sense to give Russia further control over Caspian energy exporters in addition to its already considerable sway over the neighborhood. The idea of building further pipeline capacity through Russia made even less sense given the fact that Russia too was an oil exporter. If given virtually monopolistic control over rival Central Asian oil exports competing—in an era of low oil prices—for the same markets, Russia would be given an unfair competitive advantage over its Caspian neighbors.

But excluding Russia from Caspian pipeline schemes was not an attractive option either. Aside from economic and commercial considerations, the exclusion of Moscow from future pipeline schemes would, by default, paint it as an adversary, discourage the development of cooperative commercial relations between Russia and its neighbors, and antagonize it unnecessarily.

The southern route—through Iran—to the Persian Gulf appealed to some analysts as an attractive option. Its advantages included the relatively short distance and the possibility of linking up with the existing pipeline network in Iran, which would enable Caspian oil producers to swap their shipments to northern Iranian markets for Iranian oil to be shipped from terminals in the south of the country in the Persian Gulf.

However, this southern route through Iran was fraught with legal, political, and strategic considerations—quite apart from issues of economic viability. For American policymakers, the Iranian route was illegal and counterproductive: Iran was and is the target of U.S. sanctions designed to penalize private and state entities that invest in Iran's energy sector, regarded as the critical enabler for Tehran's suspected pursuit of WMD and missile capabilities as well as its support for terrorist activities.[32] Nor, from the standpoint of energy security, did it make much sense to ship Caspian oil through Iran to the Persian Gulf. Not only would this option have put Iran—an oil exporter itself—in control of Caspian exports, but it would also send more oil to the Persian Gulf and through the already congested bottleneck, the Strait of Hormuz. Hence the southern route did nothing to diversify global energy supplies. In short, from the standpoint of American interests and policy in Central Asia, there was no reason to encourage projects that would only augment Iran's influence in the region.

Other pipeline options were vaguely under consideration. These routes included a gas pipeline from Turkmenistan that would traverse Afghanistan and deliver natural gas to Pakistan and possibly even India. Another possibility was a pipeline running across Kazakhstan to western China, possibly continuing across China to the Pacific. Neither of these proposals, however, seemed even remotely plausible at the time. Afghanistan was engulfed in factional warfare and ruled by the radical Taliban regime—hardly an attractive environment for a major investment project. The Chinese pipeline proposal carried a huge price tag; its undetermined end point also gave it an air of uncertainty.

That left the United States with only a western-bound option, albeit with two different pipelines. One route would traverse Kazakhstan and southern Russia and end at the Russian Black Sea port of Novorossiisk. This route would encourage Russia's cooperative stance vis-à-vis Caspian energy development, but would not leave Russia in total control of the region's oil exports. This pipeline, ultimately completed in 2003, became known as the Caspian Pipeline Consortium. The second pipeline would carry Caspian oil from Baku, Azerbaijan, via Tbilisi, Georgia, to the Turkish port of Ceyhan in the eastern Mediterranean. That route would accomplish several goals: it would provide a new outlet for Caspian oil, bypass both Russia and Iran, avoid the Black Sea (with the highly congested and environmentally vulnerable Bosporus Strait), and provide a much-needed boost to Turkey, which had lobbied hard for the project. The pipeline was completed in 2005.

Although ultimately successful and the most visible aspect of Washington's engagement in Central Asia during the 1990s, the pipeline policy nonetheless did not provide a strategic rationale for the United States to rank Central Asia among the top concerns of its foreign and national security policy. Despite the vast amounts of high-level attention given to the pipeline issue, Central Asia had to compete with numerous other demands on the time and resources of policymakers.

Human rights in Central Asia have always been a problem area from the standpoint of American observers. Human rights advocates argued that American support for Central Asian pipelines came at the expense of human rights and democratic development in the region, that the governments in the region should face penalties for human rights violations, and that the United States should make its support for pipelines conditional on adequate human rights performance.

Moreover, Washington's relations with Iran sometimes came into conflict with American support for particular pipeline routes and their advocates. The prospect of a thaw in American-Iranian relations in 1999 generated widespread speculation among Caspian-watchers that the United States would relax its policy of firm opposition to pipelines through Iran. Such a shift, however, would have undermined the commercial and economic rationale for the Baku-Tbilisi-Ceyhan pipeline.

The U.S. Caspian pipeline policy was challenged by critics arguing that Washington was overly involved in a project that should be decided on commercial, not strategic, merits. The Caspian region, charged these critics, is unlikely to produce more than a small fraction of the world's total oil supply and only if its full production potential is realized. Hence in their view U.S. policy exaggerated the significance of this region and laid too much emphasis on the energy factor.

As oil prices dropped below twenty dollars a barrel in the second half of the 1990s and the attractiveness of Caspian oil deposits as a source of revenue for economic development faded, the interest of the U.S. policy community and general public in Central Asia diminished as well. The notion that the Caspian region had the potential of becoming "another Middle East" was not necessarily even a welcome one, since the Middle East seemed to be the source of never-ending trouble for the United States; in an increasingly globalized world economy, oil seemed to be more an obstacle to economic development, a crutch that would keep the newly independent nations of Central Asia from standing on their own two feet.[33]

A Period of Disillusionment

For the remainder of the 1990s, U.S. policy was beset by growing disillusionment with Central Asia. By the end of the second Clinton administration, its relations with the region reached a difficult stage. The image of Central Asia had become tarnished in Western media by widespread reports of corruption, growing authoritarianism, and lack of progress on economic reform.

Increasingly, the policy community came to view the "stans" not as the next generation of Asian tigers but as the next wave of failing states. The region's energy wealth—once thought to be the engine of its economic recovery—had come to be viewed as the source of rampant, debilitating corruption that would eventually place these countries in the ranks of Nigeria or the Congo—resource-rich nations that had failed to take advantage of their natural wealth. As a result, American strategic discourse about Central Asia came increasingly to question whether Central Asia was "strategic quicksand" or a "mission too far."[34] A 1999 monograph about NATO and Central Asia concluded that the United States and other Western nations had very limited interests and leverage in Central Asia; the wise and prudent course for the alliance would be to provide modest assistance to reform the security sector and to promote restructuring and professionalization of Central Asian armed forces, but to avoid new security commitments and responsibilities in the region.[35]

As the prospects for Central Asia overcoming its growing pains appeared increasingly remote, American policymakers began to lose interest in this region as an area of significant opportunities. Corruption, undemocratic governance, and sputtering economies were widely seen as prevalent throughout the region, and Central Asia came to be viewed as fraught with the risk of destabilization.

Central Asian leaders also began to fear that the stability of the region was endangered by domestic unrest and threats from abroad.[36] Their human rights records gradually deteriorated.[37] In response, then-Secretary of State Madeleine Albright visited Central Asia in the spring of 2000 and argued that adherence to international human rights norms would serve as a hedge against further destabilization and radicalization of the population. That argument was firmly rejected by President Islam Karimov of Uzbekistan, who feared that such a policy would have precisely the opposite effect.[38]

The United States also viewed Central Asia as a potential target for the radical Taliban regime that ruled Afghanistan.[39] U.S. concerns about the Taliban were widely shared in Central Asia. Once again, however, the leaders in Central Asia roundly rejected the American strategy to address the Taliban challenge—namely, political reform, observance of international human rights practices, and economic liberalization—for fear of unleashing domestic instability.

Despite growing American concerns about the Taliban government, U.S. policymakers had few tools at their disposal to counter its threat to regional stability. Although specialists on Central Asia widely recognized the gravity of the Taliban threat, they generally held that the main vulnerability of the Central Asian regimes was domestic, not external. In their view, the fundamental sources of instability in the region derived from poverty, social inequality, underdevelopment, unrepresentative political systems, and corruption. Specialists on the region generally perceived the Taliban as a potential beneficiary of these conditions, a force that could exploit and aggravate the situation. Still, the Taliban regime was not seen as the primary factor in undermining Central Asian instability.

The U.S. policy tool kit had little beyond recommendations aimed at addressing the "root causes" of instability. These included the familiar stand bys—political liberalization, economic reform, and the rule of law. Although indispensable, these were tools that even the most optimistic observers of the Central Asian scene considered unlikely to work in the short-, medium- and possibly even long-term.

Moreover, American policy toward Central Asia and Afghanistan focused on the threat of terrorism, not regional destabilization. Following the embassy bombings in Nairobi, Kenya, and Dar-es-Salaam, Tanzania, in 1998 (and Osama bin Laden's role in them), Washington's counterterrorist policy with regard to Central Asia focused increasingly on the threat posed by Al Qaeda, its leader, and the Taliban, not regional destabilization. Occasional Taliban pronouncements about establishing a Central Asian caliphate were seen as far-fetched saber-rattling, not an immediate, realistic threat. The threat of terrorist attacks, however, was deemed to be much more real.

The U.S. Department of Defense undertook a low-level program of military cooperation with Uzbekistan following a secret 1998 intelligence "finding" by President William Clinton. The program involved joint U.S.-Uzbek covert operations to counter the Taliban regime, training for Uzbek military personnel by

U.S. Special Forces, and intelligence sharing.[40] These activities, little-known outside a relatively small circle of policymakers, became one element of the short-term vs. long-term dichotomy that came to define U.S.-Uzbek relations and American policy in Central Asia more broadly. From Washington's perspective, Central Asia (and, in particular, Uzbekistan) emerged as part of a short-term solution because of its operational significance, but as part of the long-term problem because of fundamental differences over how to fight what would soon become the "war on terrorism." This dichotomy would become a recurrent theme in American policy toward Central Asia.

The 2000 presidential election in the United States and the change of administrations in Washington initially appeared to bring few changes in this attitude of general indifference. Prior to 11 September 2001, the new Bush administration had little time to reconsider American policy toward Central Asia and to articulate a different vision for the region. Central Asia did not figure prominently in reports of the Bush administration's review of foreign policy priorities; these focused primarily on the major powers—China, Russia, and India. Perhaps the only exception was the region's energy potential; the May 2001 report of the National Energy Policy Development Group[41] identified the region as a promising source of hydrocarbons that could help diversify the world's energy supply and reduce global dependence on the Persian Gulf.

Overall, the first post-Soviet decade ended on a sour note for American relations with Central Asia. From Washington's perspective, the region was falling far short of its potential and failing to cope with the mounting challenges of post-Soviet transition. Central Asia was backsliding on democracy, even in the two countries that had made some progress toward liberalization—Kazakhstan and Kyrgyzstan. Those two nations had implemented market reforms, but both were tainted with a heavy dose of corruption and had acquired a reputation as kleptocratic, undemocratic regimes. The image of Uzbekistan and Turkmenistan—as brutal dictatorships that had altogether stalled market reforms—was still worse, raising concerns about their long-term stability.[42] All this was taking place against the backdrop of Washington increasingly losing interest in nation-building.

Even the region's oil wealth came to be viewed as an obstacle to development. It was seen increasingly not as a stimulant for trade and a source of economic development, but as a cause of pervasive corruption and distortions in Central Asia's relations with its neighbors.

Central Asian leaders likewise had cause for disillusionment in the United States. Washington never seemed to take the region seriously and make it a major concern. Instead, the United States always treated Central Asia within the context of complex U.S. relationships with China, Russia, Iran, and even

Turkey. Nor was Washington's tool kit for security and development—through economic and political reforms—acceptable; Central Asian leaders viewed such reforms as a source of destabilization, not the precondition for long-term stability.

On the security front, Washington failed to appreciate Central Asia's predicament of living in a tough neighborhood surrounded by China, Russia, Iran, and the unraveling Afghanistan. Reform of the security sector and Euro-Atlantic integration—an agenda driven by Eurocentric security assessments—had little to do with the real, day-to-day security concerns of Central Asia's leaders living in the shadow of a Taliban-ruled Afghanistan. Their concern was further exacerbated by the security vacuum that resulted from the breakup of the Soviet Union and the subsequent Russian withdrawal. The Central Asian regimes were offered a "great-power-free zone" as the solution and non-zero sum approaches to their security, even as the American policy community debated the rationale for a more robust engagement in the region. As seen from the capitals of Central Asia, a great-power-free zone would make them less, not more, secure—especially when the United States seemed to avoid responsibility for Central Asia. In the words of one senior Central Asian official, asked in 2000 why the United States should be concerned about Central Asia, "the United States had global interests from which flowed global responsibilities."[43] The unspoken part of the message was that the United States had yet to fully appreciate those responsibilities and act responsibly to meet them.

A New Battlefield

The terrorist attacks of 11 September 2001 swept away much of the uncertainty about Central Asia's importance to the international system and its relationship with the major powers, especially the United States. Indeed, Tajikistan, Uzbekistan, Turkmenistan, Kazakhstan, and Kyrgyzstan became among the most important frontline states in America's war on terrorism.

Central Asia Redefined

The war on terrorism, however, did not alter many basic long-term trends that have complicated the conduct of American policy in the region and profoundly affected Central Asian perceptions of the United States. Beyond the immediate demands of the war on terrorism, many fundamental questions remain unanswered. How important is Central Asia to the United States? What is the nature of U.S. interest in the region? What role should the United States play in Central Asia—security manager, hegemon, or limited partner?

As the experience of the 1990s demonstrated, defining the right role for the United States in Central Asia is no easy task. The region is still geographically remote, still unknown to much of the American public, still not easily accessible, and still has few obvious connections to the United States.

U.S. interests in Central Asia—beyond the most basic ones articulated in the 1990s, such as peace, stability, and alleviation of human suffering, as well as those associated with counterterrorism—are still not easy to identify in ways that the American public or even senior policymakers would readily embrace. Moreover, given that the early record of American engagement in Central Asia after the breakup of the Soviet Union was not a positive one, mutual perceptions in Washington and in the Central Asian capitals bear a good deal of disappointment and a certain amount of mistrust. The record of the 1990s offers important lessons that merit closer consideration.

After 9/11 the United States became the principal actor in the regional security affairs of Central Asia. With the presence of American military forces in Kyrgyzstan, Tajikistan, and Uzbekistan, with the defeat of the Taliban government in Afghanistan, and with an explicit commitment for a long-term U.S. military presence in the region, Washington in effect became Central Asia's security manager. After ten years of maintaining a distance from Central Asia (to avoid making the region an American responsibility and headache), the United States now found itself squarely in the middle of Central Asian politics.

The most significant elements of the U.S. presence in Central Asia after 9/11 were two air bases—one at Karshi-Khanabad (K2) in Uzbekistan and the other at Manas in Kyrgyzstan. Both played important roles in the military operations against the Taliban regime in Afghanistan.

Overnight, Uzbekistan became an indispensable strategic ally of the United States in the war that the United States committed itself to fight over the long haul. The Uzbek government's decision at the time to open its facilities and airspace to U.S. military personnel proved enormously important; it recast Uzbekistan on the U.S. foreign policy agenda from a second-tier problem state to a crucial partner in the war on terror.

The crucial factor here was Uzbekistan's proximity to Afghanistan, especially at a time when Pakistan was viewed as an uncertain ally because of its sponsorship of the Taliban regime and domestic political fragility. Uzbekistan offered unique capabilities for staging combat search-and-rescue operations and Special Forces operations from facilities near the Afghan border.[44] Karimov's lack of concern for domestic public opinion and his ability to make decisions about partnership with the United States without having to solicit grassroots political support made his country an even more attractive partner. That was especially true immediately after 9/11, when the ability to act quickly and resolutely was critical to Washington's decision to overthrow the Taliban regime.

The special quality of this rapidly transformed relationship was reflected in the "United States-Uzbekistan Declaration on the Strategic Partnership and Cooperation Framework," signed by then-Secretary of State Colin Powell and President Karimov in March 2002.[45] According to Point I of that document,

> Uzbekistan reaffirms its commitment to further intensify the democratic transformation of its society politically and economically. The United States agrees to provide the Government of Uzbekistan assistance in implementing democratic reforms in priority areas such as building a strong and open civil society, establishing a genuine multi-party system and independence of the media, strengthening non-governmental structures, and improving the judicial system.[46]

The second point in this document provided the following:

> The U.S. affirms that it would regard with grave concern any external threat to the security and territorial integrity of the Republic of Uzbekistan. The two countries expect to develop cooperation in combating transnational threats to society, and to continue their dynamic military and military-technical cooperation.[47]

The document did not specify any penalty for failure to comply with the terms of the agreement.

The declaration was an extraordinary commitment on the part of the United States—unique for any of the former Soviet lands and de facto amounting to a security guarantee for the country that just a few months previously had been relegated to the second tier of American foreign policy priorities. The gravity of the threat posed by terrorism in general (and Al Qaeda in particular) and Washington's determination to prosecute the war on terror left little doubt about the seriousness of the American commitment to Uzbekistan's security. Tashkent's record in the 1990s and the experience of the United States with reform in Central Asia (and especially in Uzbekistan), however, left serious doubts about Karimov's pledge to carry out extensive political reforms.

Nevertheless, the long-standing U.S. reform agenda was given a new boost. It acquired new significance in the aftermath of 9/11; reform promotion was now seen not as a mere act of international charity, but as an essential national security tool—which could serve to prevent failing and failed states from becoming international security threats.

Washington's renewed interest in Central Asia was a definite gain for the

Central Asian regimes. The Russian withdrawal from Central Asia in the early 1990s, paradoxically, made life difficult for area leaders, who now found themselves without a regional security manager. Mutual suspicions and intraregional rivalries effectively thwarted hopes for region-wide cooperation and consolidation. Too weak to provide for their own security, the Central Asian states have had to contend with domestic insurgencies, cross-border incursions, fears of militant Islam, and such serious transnational threats as the illicit trade in narcotics and arms.

The American reluctance to fill the power vacuum in the 1990s drove the states of Central Asia to assume uneasy relationships with Russia and China. Neither had the requisite muscle and will to become effective regional hegemons, but both were more than willing to assert themselves at the expense of indigenous regimes. The American arrival in Central Asia changed that, displacing both Russia and China as the region's preeminent powers and giving local leaders room to maneuver vis-à-vis Moscow and Beijing.

The aftermath of the 11 September 2001 attacks had further benefits for Central Asian countries. At long last, the United States would take their security in the regional context seriously, deal with the Taliban threat, and redesign American security policy to address regional concerns.

As Washington prepared to launch its military campaign against the Taliban, it assumed a commitment to maintain a military, political, and economic presence in Central Asia in an unprecedented way. The size and composition of the U.S. presence would vary depending on specific circumstances and country needs, but driven by its pledge to liberate and secure Afghanistan and to fulfill its counterterrorism mission, the United States finally made a long-term commitment to the region.[48]

Moreover, the pledge by President George Bush and then-Secretary of State Colin Powell—"the United States will not abandon the people of Afghanistan"[49]—left no doubt that the American presence in Afghanistan would be a long-term proposition. It was reiterated by General Tommy Franks, who compared the U.S. presence in Afghanistan to its presence in Korea. Given Afghanistan's land-locked position and America's dependence on such volatile neighbors as Pakistan (to say nothing of Iran) for access, Central Asia was bound to play a critical role in Washington's counterterrorist strategy. Pakistan's volatility underscored the importance of Central Asia as an alternative staging area for operations in Afghanistan.

In the aftermath of 9/11, however, it would have been shortsighted to define American interests in Central Asia merely in terms of operational counterterrorism requirements and ongoing military operations in Afghanistan. The events of 11 September 2001 gave a new and very different meaning to a notion first articulated by U.S. policymakers in the 1990s and enunciated by Strobe Talbott in 1997—namely, U.S. interests in Central Asia would be adequately served by averting geopolitical competition and thus keeping the region free of the "Great Game." In the benign post-Cold War atmosphere of the 1990s, it was natural to interpret this simply as a formula of U.S. disinterest and desire to avoid a new entanglement. As long as Central Asia was free of great-power competition, the United States had little interest in the region. That logic would no longer apply.

A Challenge Recast

Whether the United States was prepared to take on the challenge of maintaining security and stability in Central Asia was a moot point: in the eyes of most powers interested in the region, it already had done so. After 9/11, U.S. actions and statements in this regard left little room for doubt.

Such an undertaking would require the United States to commit substantial financial resources and political capital. Whereas the initial U.S. military operation in Afghanistan appeared an ambitious undertaking, the real challenge in the region is certain to be not military but political, not short term but long term. The challenge of stabilizing and securing Central Asia over an extended period would require an almost open-ended commitment of military, economic, and political resources. Far more than funding for the acquisition of military capabilities and for bailouts of insolvent regimes, the United States would have to take on the challenge of the modernization and integration of the region into the international community and economy.

Reforms—both political and economic—made up a large portion of the American agenda for this region in the 1990s. Political liberalization, deregulation, and the introduction of market-based economies were deemed an integral element of post-communist transition. America's assistance to these former Soviet states during that transition was seen as consistent with U.S. interests, given the general objective of expanding the circle of democratic nations with a market economy.

The war on terror imposed new requirements on U.S. policy toward Central Asia and dramatically recast the mission of transforming the region. Democratization and market transition would no longer be simply a matter of preference; they would be an integral part of the campaign toward victory in the war on terror.

According to the National Strategy for Combating Terrorism[50] that the Bush administration released in February 2003, the United States would wage the global war on terror in accordance with a new blueprint. The new strategy would consist of four goals, referred to by the shorthand designation of the "4Ds"— Defeat, Deny, Diminish, and Defend. The 4D strategy in longhand meant:

1. Defeat terrorists and their organizations;
2. Deny sponsorship, support, and sanctuary to terrorists;
3. Diminish the underlying conditions that terrorists seek to exploit;
4. Defend U.S. citizens and interests at home and abroad.

The new strategy called not merely for defeating terrorists militarily and defending innocent civilians from terrorist attacks, but for eradicating the underlying conditions that produce or contribute to the emergence of terrorism. In effect, the new strategy made political and economic reform, along with support for good governance, a precondition for winning the war on terror:

> The third component of the 4D strategy is made up of the collective efforts to diminish conditions that terrorists can exploit. While we recognize that there are many countries and people living with poverty, deprivation, social disenfranchisement, and unresolved political and regional disputes, those conditions do not justify the use of terror. However, many terrorist organizations that have little in common with the poor and destitute masses exploit these conditions to their advantage. The September 11 terrorists, for instance, came predominantly from the ranks of the educated and middle-class and served in an organization led by a millionaire murderer.
>
> These efforts to address underlying conditions have material as well as intangible dimensions. Ongoing U.S. efforts to resolve regional disputes, but also to foster economic, social, and political development, market-based economies, good governance, and the rule of law, while not necessarily focused on combating terrorism, seek to address underlying conditions that terrorists often seek to manipulate for their own advantage. It also meant that the United States, with its friends and allies, must win the "war of ideas"—that is, support democratic values and promote economic freedom.[51]

Unlike U.S. efforts to promote reforms in Central Asia in the 1990s, this was no longer an act of international charity or a legacy of the Cold War, albeit undertaken fully in conformity with U.S. interest in expanding the ranks of market democracies. Reform was now a wartime imperative. From the standpoint of U.S. policymakers, only political and economic reforms leading to liberalization would ensure long-term stability and security in Central Asia, in turn guaranteeing that the region would never again encounter the prospect of state failure and the threat of ungoverned spaces that could be exploited by radical movements and regimes. Given the heightened urgency that U.S. policymakers now assigned to political and economic modernization in Central Asia, it is hardly surprising that the first point in the bilateral American-Uzbek declaration on strategic partnership was devoted to these areas.

After 9/11: Boots on the Ground

Despite the new urgency attached by U.S. policymakers to long-term reform in Central Asia, the principal and most visible changes in the strategic landscape of the region were military and near-term. Aside from overthrowing the Taliban regime in Afghanistan, the military campaign there triggered a new geopolitical dynamic in the entire region, which in turn produced new winners and losers.

In the near term, the most prominent victim of the post-9/11 security order in Central Asia was the Shanghai Cooperation Organization (SCO) and, by extension, China. In the face of an existential threat from the Taliban, the SCO member states and its two principal sponsors—China and Russia—did little except to continue their long-practiced meddling in Afghan factional politics. The decisive defeat of the Taliban by U.S. forces with the help of the Russian- and Chinese-backed Northern Alliance demonstrated that the United States could do in Central Asia what Russia and China had failed to accomplish for nearly a decade—return Afghanistan to a path leading to stability, reconstruction, and security. The net effect was to marginalize the SCO, which had aspired to play the role of regional security organization.

Furthermore, with its new military deployment to Central Asia, the United States established itself as the main power broker in China's strategic backyard. The United States succeeded in diluting the Russian-Chinese partnership in Central Asia and reinforced its relationship with Russia, without compromising its strategic objectives in Central Asia or elsewhere. For example, U.S.-Russian relations did not suffer as a result of U.S. withdrawal from the Anti-Ballistic Missile treaty—undoubtedly a setback for China as it sought to forge a partnership with Moscow and oppose American missile defense plans.

The United States also sought to establish a new strategic relationship with India—China's long-term competitor. Simultaneously, Washington resumed a patron-client relationship with Pakistan, which had long been a Chinese partner. None of this was to be taken lightly by the national security establishment in Beijing, especially given the tensions in U.S.-Chinese relations early in the new decade and the long-standing concerns of some senior national security officials in the Bush administration that China was the rising peer competitor of the United States.

In the near term, China's reversal of fortune in the heart of Eurasia was significant. A regional power broker prior to 9/11, China found itself marginalized, displaced, and virtually isolated, pondering the unenviable (for Beijing) role of playing second fiddle to the United States and a host of its newfound best friends in and around the region. No matter how much China stood to gain from the U.S. military campaign (and there can be little doubt that it benefited from the campaign against the Taliban and the consequent blow to operations by its own Uighur militants), American preponderance in the region must have been a serious setback to a government aspiring to become the Asian superpower.

Russia's position in Central Asia after 9/11 was more bittersweet. Undoubtedly, few among Moscow's foreign policy and military elite cherished the idea of having American forces stationed in their strategic backyard; this military presence was an awkward reality for Russia's national security establishment. After all, the Russian government acquiesced to the United States using facilities that the Russian military had controlled only a decade ago. At least, some must have thought resentfully, the United States had the decency to consult with Russia before moving into the region.

Still, Putin's uncompromising public support of U.S. actions yielded important advantages to Moscow. The United States tacitly acknowledged a certain Russian *droit de regard* in Central Asia. Russia's own military campaign in Chechnya ceased being a barrier to Moscow's relations with the West and instead became something of a bridge on the strength of the argument that both Russia and the United States were fighting the same militant Islamic enemy. Russian claims of Osama bin Laden's complicity in Chechnya's separatist (Moscow preferring to label it "terrorist") movement were perceived in a different light after 11 September 2001. The issue of human rights violations in Chechnya was effectively relegated to the back burner in favor of the more immediate concerns about terrorism and other issues in relations with Washington.

Furthermore, after 9/11 Russia received a major boost in its standing in relation to China, whose growing economic, military, and strategic might had become a source of concern among Russian politicians and foreign policy specialists.[52] New regard for Russia in Washington, as well as prospects for continuing improvements in U.S.-Russian relations, had to send an important signal to Beijing, further contributing to its suddenly diminished importance, relatively speaking.

In Central Asia proper, the new spirit of accord and cooperation in U.S.-Russian relations had important implications as well. Central Asian leaders had learned how to play off Washington and Moscow against each other. The fact that there was now less light between respective Russian and American positions on a number of important issues left Central Asian governments less room to maneuver and exploit their differences, whether in regard to pipeline routes, Caspian boundaries, or security ties to rogue regimes.

In practical terms, Russia could do little other than offer the United States unimpeded access to Central Asia. It lacked the military muscle to play a significant role in the Afghanistan military campaign, whether in the air or on the ground. In the short and medium term, the best that Moscow could do to support the U.S. war on terror was to provide unfettered access to Central Asia, to share intelligence, and to do all it could to put its own house in order (by securing the weapons, materials, and expertise for its nuclear, chemical, and biological weapons).

Russia's contribution to the war in Afghanistan suggested its likely role beyond the near term. Geography would ensure its continuing importance for years to come, if only as an outlet for oil and gas. Alternatives to existing shipping routes would take years to build, and even then they would complement, rather than substitute for, the routes crossing Russia.

In addition to geographic proximity, Russia was bound to stay involved in Central Asia in the long run because of its residual ethnic population there. Despite considerable emigration from Central Asia, the region is still home to some 8 million ethnic Russians (the largest populations residing in Kazakhstan and Uzbekistan—5.1 million and 1.4 million, respectively).[53] No Russian government can ignore this issue, especially in the event of regional destabilization.

However, Russia's military weakness, lack of adequate power projection capability, and limited resources (already under pressure from multiple domestic demands) would eliminate it as a realistic candidate for becoming the region's security manager or hegemon for years to come. The future of Russian-American relations would have little bearing on this. Even so, given the congruence of U.S. and Russian interests in combating radical Islamic terrorism, Moscow's military weakness means that in the interim the American military presence in Central Asia brings important benefits for Russian security interests, however difficult it might be for the Russian elite to accept this turn of events.

By contrast, Iran (Russia's long-time partner in Central Asia and ally in the anti-Taliban cause) found itself among the losers in the regional realignment after 9/11. Long the pivotal member of the anti-Taliban coalition and loyal backer of the Northern Alliance, Iran was squeezed out of its key foothold in Central Asia—Tajikistan—with which it shares strong cultural, linguistic, and ethnic ties.

The speed and eagerness with which the Tajik government made its facilities available to the U.S. military must have seemed the ultimate betrayal to Tehran. The opening of Turkmen airspace to American overflights (even if limited to humanitarian purposes) and the deployment of allied troops to Central Asia must have impressed Iran's political establishment that, in a confrontation with the United States, it would have to worry about the American presence not only in the Persian Gulf but also to its north in Central Asia and the Caucasus, to say nothing of its eastern and southern neighbors, Afghanistan and Pakistan.

To be sure, Iran (like China) was an immediate beneficiary of the military defeat of the Taliban regime, which had been on hostile terms with Tehran. But the aftermath of the military campaign and the de facto establishment of an American protectorate in Afghanistan must have been seen as a blow to Iranian interests, adding to a growing sense of encirclement by the United States.

In the time immediately after 9/11 and during the military campaign in Afghanistan, American-Iranian relations had showed signs of slight improvement. Both the United States and Iran had long been opposed to the Taliban regime. Iran's expression of sympathy over 9/11, its pledge of cooperation in delivering essential humanitarian aid to Afghanistan, and its offer of assistance to American airmen in cases of emergency further fueled hopes for better American-Iranian ties. After the overthrow of the Taliban regime, however, the United States and Iran found themselves on opposite sides of the Afghan divide. Iranian attempts to play factional politics in Afghanistan to its benefit threatened to undermine the fragile U.S.-backed government of Hamid Karzai.

In addition, Tehran rejected Washington's invitation to join the war on terrorism and continued to support terrorist attacks against Israel. That was most notable in the so-called Karine-A incident of January 2002, when Israel Defense Forces intercepted a major clandestine shipment of Iranian-supplied weapons and munitions to the Palestinian Authority.[54] The episode sent a powerful signal that hopes for an imminent American-Iranian thaw were premature indeed. This in turn must have sent a signal throughout Central Asia, where a new "sheriff"—the United States—was now in charge.

New Landscape, Old Problems

The meaning of these developments—the establishment of an American military presence in Central Asia, a stark departure from the detachment prevalent in the 1990s—did not elicit a uniform assessment. In retrospect, there apparently existed a broad gap between the United States and its Central Asian partners as to how they viewed the war on terror and the changed circumstances in the region.

The United States viewed the situation in Central Asia through the prism of the war on terror. With the short-term military problem of defeating the Taliban addressed through the military campaign in Afghanistan, U.S. policymakers took on the challenge of long-term political and economic change in the region as an integral part of their National Strategy for Combating Terrorism. The reforms that the United States had promoted in Central Asia—with variable success at best—constituted basic elements in its assistance to the ex-Soviet states. These reforms now acquired still greater urgency as a matter of national security for the United States and as a precondition for long-term stability in the region. The reforms, therefore, now came to comprise an element of the global war on terror.

From the standpoint of Central Asian elites, the situation looked entirely different. For over a decade their region had struggled with a host of challenges. These included difficult neighbors, internal instability, impoverishment, political uncertainty, demanding aid donors, and a lack of interest on the part of the sole remaining superpower. After 9/11 the United States finally showed a serious interest in the region and its problems. But Washington's solution is the diametrical opposite to what local elites want to see.

Both American policymakers and Central Asian elites concurred that stability must be a common goal. For the United States, however, a virtually uniform consensus view holds that long-term stability in the region will require Central Asian governments to abandon the status quo and embark on a program of broad, sustained, and systemic change that would encompass the economy, society, and political order. In other words, it would be the kind of change envisioned by U.S. policymakers, pledged by local elites after the breakup of the Soviet Union, and codified in James Baker's five principles.

For local elites, however, "stability through change" appeared to be an oxymoron. This seemed like a contradiction in terms, a source of insecurity and multiple challenges to what they treasured the most—the status quo and the security and well-being of their regimes. Having survived in a tough neighborhood, having watched the destruction of Afghanistan through internecine warfare among former freedom-fighters, having seen neighboring Tajikistan implode in a bloody civil war in the 1990s (from which it is still recovering), having witnessed the Soviet Union disintegrate under the weight of liberalization and reforms, these Soviet-schooled leaders were not inclined to accept U.S. assurances about long-term benefits of freedom.

Moreover, with the passage of time and growing entrenchment of their regimes, Central Asian leaders must have become genuinely convinced that they themselves are essential to stability and security in their own countries and in the region as a whole. Even leaders like President Askar Akaev of Kyrgyzstan, who came to power with respectable democratic credentials, were overstaying their constitutionally mandated terms and seeking ways to extend their tenure with the help of amendments, legal loopholes, and staged elections.

For the United States the situation presented a difficult and familiar predicament: relying on compromised regimes for the sake of achieving its strategic goals. The situation was further aggravated by the fact that this was an integral part of a new U.S. existential struggle—the war on terror. The reform agenda had constituted the basis for U.S. engagement in the region following the breakup of the Soviet Union. But during that decade the entire Central Asian region had fallen far short of the goals of that reform agenda.

In the terms of the U.S. National Strategy for Combating Terrorism, this predicament sounded even more ominous. The regimes the United States had to rely on as partners to defeat terrorists in the near term were the same regimes the United States would have to challenge in the long run in order to remove the conditions that terrorists could exploit. In short, a broad consensus of U.S. policymakers and analysts believed that, without reform and change in Central Asia, near-term partners in the war on terror would become long-term adversaries.

For local elites, top priority was and is stability of their regimes, both short term and long term.

Succession: The Tip of the Iceberg

Nothing brought the difference between U.S. policymakers and Central Asian elites into sharper focus than the problem of political succession. From the American perspective, succession was necessary and healthy; by contrast, the Central Asian elites wanted to avoid this issue at all costs. The Rose Revolution in November 2003 not only resulted in the overthrow of Georgia's long-serving leader Eduard Shevardnadze, but also unleashed a wave of "colored revolutions"—the Orange Revolution in Ukraine and the Tulip Revolution in Kyrgyzstan. The colored revolutions sent a powerful shock wave throughout the former Soviet lands, Central Asia included.

Political succession and the colored revolutions emerged as the most important political issues in Central Asia. A change in leadership, after all, is bound to happen sooner if not later. When Central Asia's leaders first pondered the implications of the Rose Revolution, all but one (Tajikistan's Emomali Rakhmonov) had exceeded life expectancy in the region (approximately 60 for men). Political succession was a matter of when, not if. The question was how. The threat of colored revolutions was unnerving to leaders who came of age in the Soviet era and who, for the most part, had ruled their countries even before the breakup of the Soviet Union.

The Tulip Revolution in Kyrgyzstan in March 2005 only reinforced the leaders' nervousness and determination to bolster their hold on power. Ironically, during the tenure of Kyrgyzstan's first president, Askar Akaev, that country was arguably the least oppressive of Central Asian regimes. Akaev had tolerated political opposition as well as considerable independence in the media; elections there were not completely staged or falsified, as was often the case elsewhere in the region. A former academic, Akaev had the reputation of being a relatively tolerant and enlightened leader in a region where former Communist Party apparatchicks turned autocrats.

The wave of popular unrest in March 2005 that swept Akaev from power must have been seen in the region as a failure to exercise proper control over his country. The revolution was triggered by charges of fraudulent parliamentary elections. That Akaev had allowed the opposition to carry its campaign into the streets and gain popular support must have struck other Central Asian leaders as a sign of fatal weakness. The lesson of the Tulip Revolution for Central Asian leaders was the need for more control, not liberalization and tolerance of opposition.

Leadership succession is not a new issue for the post-communist states of Central Asia. The fact that the incumbent Soviet-era generation of leaders has been in power for more than a decade does not mean that these leaders have not considered or laid plans for succession. Indeed, succession appears to be the main preoccupation of these leaders, who have put the well-being of their personal regimes above all else and have done everything within their means to avert a transfer of power.

This monopolistic pursuit of power has produced stable political regimes, but has left prospects for their continuity and long-term stability in doubt. As incumbents accumulated power and shaped institutional and constitutional arrangements to secure the authority to match their aspirations for political longevity, they eliminated potential successors and thwarted mechanisms that would make succession a predictable and transparent process.

But the lack of emergency preparedness cannot guarantee that emergencies will not occur. To the contrary, it increases the likelihood that such emergencies will bear even more destructive consequences. Thus, when succession becomes inevitable, the absence of planning or rules for succession in a country like Uzbekistan, with a highly personality-dependent regime, could lead to country-wide destabilization. Given the nature of borders in Central Asia, drawn by Russian and Soviet rulers without respect to ethnic populations and historical traditions, destabilization could be region-wide, exceeding the arbitrarily established confines of a single country.

Succession is also an issue that divides the United States from its Central Asian partners and allies in the war on terror. From the perspective of U.S. policymakers, the status quo—if unaltered—is fraught with dire consequences for the region, its neighbors, and U.S. interests there. Moreover, succession is the most contentious issue on the reform agenda pursued by the United States in Central Asia; it is the tip of an iceberg with a submerged mass of recommended political and social changes that Central Asian ruling elites have generally avoided.

For the United States, political succession in Central Asia presents a difficult challenge, and one associated with very unpleasant choices. The United States, through its political involvement and military presence in the region, has run the risk of becoming the security guarantor of existing regimes that are retrograde, corrupt, and resistant to the political and economic reforms propounded by the United States and much of the rest of the international community. The chances that the United States can use its military presence and political influence to advance economic and political reform there are not encouraging. Hence, the danger that regional regimes would use their role in fighting terrorism as an excuse to resist change has become increasingly salient.

The crisis in U.S. policy toward Central Asia was precipitated by violent clashes in May 2005 in the city of Andijon—with government troops and security personnel on one side and residents and protesters on the other. The violence followed a series of peaceful protests in support of local business-men put on trial on charges of Islamic extremism; the protests subsequently escalated and resulted in a seizure of the local prison by antigovernment forces. The Uzbek government's use of force to restore authority is reported to have caused hundreds of deaths, including of unarmed civilians. The U.S. Government charged that Uzbek authorities used excessive force, and called for an independent inquiry with international involvement.[55] The Uzbek government countered that force was an appropriate response to an upris-ing by terrorists; that there was no need for an international commission to investigate the incident; and that the Uzbek authorities would conduct the investigation on their own.[56]

The Andijon uprising triggered a full-fledged crisis in U.S. policy toward Central Asia. For Washington, the sharp deterioration in relations with Uz-bekistan that followed mutual recriminations in the summer of 2005 had tangible and far-reaching consequences. In July 2005 the Uzbek Government formally requested that the United States military personnel vacate the base at Karshi-Khanabad, which had played an important role in the military cam-paign in Afghanistan in 2001 and which continued to support U.S. operations there. The United States returned the base to Uzbek control well before the six-month deadline set by Tashkent.

The loss of K2 was a most unwelcome turn of events for U.S. interests in the region. The base was one of only two that the United States had established in the heart of Eurasia as stepping-stones to Afghanistan. Land-locked and blocked from the Indian Ocean by Iran and Pakistan, Afghanistan has no rail network, a road network heavily damaged by decades of neglect and civil war, and a limited airport capacity to accommodate the resupply and other transportation requirements generated by U.S. and allied military and recon-struction operations. Access to additional airfields in the region is important to the U.S. ability to continue its operations in Afghanistan.[57]

That the United States would sacrifice its interest in K2 and its ties with Uzbekistan (a frontline state in the war on terror) for the sake of human rights and democracy struck Central Asian elites as astonishingly naïve. Such a turn of events sent powerful shock waves throughout the region. That the United States would act in this manner almost immediately after the Tulip Revolution in Kyrgyzstan—host to the other U.S. base in the region and itself profoundly destabilized by unrest—sent a definite message about U.S. priorities.

The message was made all the more potent by the fact that throughout the 1990s Kyrgyzstan had been promoted by the United States as the poster child of reform and progress for the entire region. Washington had also portrayed Uzbekistan as a key ally in the war on terror and one that had provided indispensable assistance in the aftermath of 9/11. Nevertheless, there could be no ambiguity: the United States would not compromise its principles and its determination to promote the spread of democracy and reform.

For Central Asian rulers, it was troubling that the United States would support—some say, even encourage—the wave of generally peaceful revolutions that swept across Georgia, Ukraine, and Kyrgyzstan. American endorsement of these revolutions and promotion of democracy constituted a signal to Central Asian elites that Washington was not a pillar of security, but an agent of change; that they could not count on American support in the event of domestic upheavals; and that if unable to cope with the risk of turbulence, Central Asian regimes would have to look for support elsewhere.

They would not have to look very far.

New Geopolitical Realities Since 2005

Renewed American interest in Central Asia, prompted by the terrorist attacks of 11 September 2001 and the military campaign in Afghanistan, was matched by the growing interest of several neighboring states. This interest, in turn, has triggered a new round of competition for influence in the region. Unlike the previous phase, when U.S. policymakers professed to be content with a superpower-free zone in Central Asia, the distinguishing feature of the new stage in Central Asian geopolitics was the military presence of the United States and the central role played by the sole remaining superpower. In an action-reaction chain of events, regional powers, most notably Russia and China, hastened to counter U.S. influence. India too has sought to establish a presence in the region. The scramble for influence opened new opportunities for Central Asian leaders to pick and choose partners and shift geopolitical orientations.

In a relatively short time (between 2001 and 2005), the geopolitical environment around Central Asia changed significantly. Russia, long the principal contender for the role of regional security manager, underwent a significant positive transformation in its domestic conditions, international outlook, and capabilities, both mobilized and latent. China, long recognized as a likely future major player in regional affairs, assumed a much more visible role in Central Asia. Together, these two regional heavyweights have reenergized their exclusive forum for Central Asian regional affairs, the Shanghai Cooperation Organizations, which also assumed a much higher profile for Central Asian leaders. The renewed SCO has added further to the range of geopolitical choices for the countries in the region.

Russia Resurgent

In 2001 Russia was still recovering from the shock of its 1998 financial and political crisis. Its recovery was uncertain and the memories of the 1990s were still fresh in the minds of elites and the general public. Putin's foreign policy course was still uncertain as he sought integration in the community of major industrialized democracies and partnership with the United States. His country's strategic position appeared weakened, at least relative to that of the United States, as a result of U.S. military deployment to Central Asia and the rapid victory in the military campaign in Afghanistan—a country that the Soviet Union had failed to conquer in a ten-year war. Moreover, Russia's own inability to bring stability and security to its rebellious province of Chechnya underscored its weakness relative to the United States—the power with global interests and presence.

By 2006 U.S.-Russian dynamics had changed significantly, with consequences for a wide range of issues, including Central Asia. Russia had experienced seven years of uninterrupted growth; its foreign currency reserves exceeded 200 billion dollars. Putin consistently enjoyed domestic approval ratings of 70 percent and higher. His administration was busy developing and articulating a strategy for becoming an "energy superpower" as the price of oil soared past 70 dollars per barrel. Russia projected an image of confidence, and memories of the 1998 implosion gradually faded away.

In a related development, Russia expanded its influence within its own neighborhood, most notably in Central Asia. Indeed, that influence had been significant even in the turbulent 1990s; like it or not, Central Asian states found it hard to sever their links to Russia. Geography alone was enough to thwart their best efforts. The most important links were in the spheres of energy and transportation. Russia controlled much of Central Asia's access to the outside world—railroads, pipelines, airspace, and even some of the ports that gave these new states access to global markets.

In addition, Russia retained a good deal of soft power in Central Asia. Russian remains the *lingua franca*, a condition that is likely to continue for a considerable period of time. For the elites and the educated classes, English will serve as the language connecting them to much of the outside world. But for the common folk, Russian has yet to lose its importance. Even the Central Asian elites are to a large degree still the product of the Soviet Russian-dominated education system. Many attended universities in Russia, sent children to study there, and have been deeply immersed in Russian life and culture. This connection is likely to fade over time, but only slowly, as generational change takes hold in the region's political and cultural elites.

Russian economic growth, furthermore, has created a huge market for exports from Central Asia, including for agricultural goods that are unlikely to find markets elsewhere. Russia's economic growth combined with demographic decline has also created an insatiable appetite for migrant labor. This too has generated a mutual dependency between Russia and Central Asia. The former, lacking its own manpower, has come to rely on foreign workers. The latter sends hundreds of millions of dollars in remittances back home, where Russian-generated revenues represent a major building block of economic welfare and political stability. Through its regime of visa-free travel, Russia holds considerable sway over its former colonies, but it can cut off the flow of labor to its internal market only at its own peril.

Recently, Russia has acquired yet another cache vis-à-vis some of its neighbors. In contrast with American policy of promoting democracy, Russia has forged close ties with former Soviet republics irrespective of internal conditions. It has thus pursued its own form of Realpolitik, emerging as a counterweight to the United States and potentially the last refuge to rulers fleeing from unrest in their own countries.

The former president of Kyrgyzstan, Askar Akaev, overthrown by mass protests in March 2005, found refuge in Moscow. Uzbekistan's president Islam Karimov, criticized repeatedly by the United States and European officials for human rights violations, sought and secured political backing from Russia. His family has reportedly acquired real estate and business interests in Moscow. Banned from travel to Europe and the United States, Karimov is likely to view Moscow as his safe haven in case of a domestic emergency.

Whether Russia will honor this alleged commitment or renege (playing the ultimate Realpolitik card in pursuit of a more attractive bargain) remains to be seen. However, for the time being, Russia's nonjudgmental approach to its neighbors represents a powerful card in dealing with regimes that feel threatened by the American promotion of democratic objectives.

Russian interest in Central Asia was recast in a new light during the winter of 2005. The crisis surrounding gas exports to (and through) Ukraine and the decision by Gazprom (the Russian state-owned monopoly) to cut gas deliveries because of increased domestic demand due to cold weather underscored the importance of Central Asia for Russia and its energy future. With growing doubts about Gazprom's ability to sustain and expand domestic gas production and exports because of high costs and long lead times associated with development of remote fields in difficult climactic conditions, Central Asian reserves represent the key strategic growth capacity, which Gazprom could control by virtue of its lock on export routes.[58]

Gazprom's increased interest in Central Asian policy, however, does not fundamentally alter Moscow's outlook on the region. It merely underscores the importance of the region for Russia and makes it all the more obvious that Moscow is now both willing and able to assert itself in Central Asia in pursuit of its interests.

China's Growing Presence

The other important change in 2005–6 with far-reaching consequences for the geopolitical balance in Central Asia was the vast increase in the presence of China. The latter's rise there is hardly surprising. It directly borders the region; it has ethnic minorities that straddle the boundaries with Kazakhstan and Kyrgyzstan. Beijing also has had concerns about the stability of its western provinces (populated by Turkic-speaking Moslem minorities) and about the prospect of instability in Central Asia.

China's role in Central Asia has taken on a new quality. This is the result of several factors: its overall growing role in Asia and international prominence; the expansion of its commercial ties to the region, which have steadily grown over the years; progress on oil pipelines from Kazakhstan to China (which, only a few years ago, were considered unlikely to see fruition); investment in oil exploration and development projects in Kazakhstan; a nonjudgmental approach to domestic political practices; and last but not least, the new-found prominence of the SCO in regional affairs.

Economic factors were undoubtedly critical in helping China expand its influence in Central Asia, just as they have been in other regions. In 2006, for example, bilateral Chinese-Kazakhstani trade is estimated to increase by 4 billion to 10 billion dollars.[59] China's economic dynamism is widely recognized as a given in the region, adding to its strategic heft.

Political and strategic considerations appear to have played an even more important role in altering the geopolitical balance in Central Asia in China's favor. Key among them has been the role that the United States has played since the defeat of the Taliban and the growing American insistence on democratic reforms and political liberalization. As already noted, Washington's break with Uzbekistan and its support for the Tulip Revolution in Kyrgyzstan must have had a deep impact on regional elites.

Mistrust and opposition to Washington's democratization campaign prompted Central Asian elites to look for partners elsewhere. Their choice was obvious: not only Russia, but also China opposed to the American campaign to promote democratic reform. Like Russia, China regarded U.S. support for revolutionary change as fraught with the specter of destabilization that might spill over into its own province of Xinjiang.[60] U.S. support for the Tulip Revolution appeared to Chinese leaders as naïve and irresponsible.

To demonstrate support for current Central Asian leaders, Beijing accorded a warm welcome to Uzbek president Karimov soon after the Andijon events. The gesture was mutually convenient, since it also demonstrated to all concerned that the United States was not the only significant power and that Karimov had other friends who would back him up.

Moreover, having accepted the U.S. military presence in Central Asia as a necessary evil to be tolerated as the price of getting rid of the Taliban threat, both Chinese and Russian observers began to raise questions and concerns about an open-ended U.S. military deployment in the region. Combined with the U.S. campaign to promote democracy, this military presence must have reinforced a perception of imbalance in a region that both China and Russia regard as their strategic backyard.

In response, both moved to energize the SCO, the key multilateral vehicle that they used to assert their influence in Central Asia. The SCO pointedly did not include the United States as either a member or an observer. The reinvigorated political role of the SCO was a convenient alternative for all—China, Russia, and the Central Asian states. Moscow and Beijing, unchallenged in their great-power aspirations within the SCO, welcomed this opportunity to diminish American influence in the region and to demonstrate that their voices still counted even against the sole remaining superpower. The Central Asian states welcomed an opportunity, if not to challenge the United States, then at least to demonstrate their independence and to send Washington a signal that they were appreciated by China and Russia, the two regional powers not to be trifled with.

The apogee in this competition for influence in the heart of Eurasia came in July 2005, when the SCO heads of state assembled in Astana (the new Kazakhstani capital) and urged the United States to clarify its intentions with regard to its military presence in Central Asia and to make clear when it planned to withdraw its forces. Although the appeal was mostly symbolic, with no binding legal import, it sent a strong message to observers inside and outside Central Asia that Russia and China were gaining influence in the region at the expense of the United States. Such a clear message could not have appeared a year or two earlier, when the United States was at the peak of its influence in the region.

The United States: Fighting the *Global* War

The message that the U.S. military presence was no longer welcome in Central Asia was made substantive by Uzbekistan's eviction of U.S. forces from its Karshi-Khanabad base. The loss of K2 left the United States dependent on a single base in Central Asia—Manas in Kyrgyzstan.

But the loss of K2 had a broader strategic meaning for the United States, its policy toward Central Asia, and its general strategy in the global war on terror. At stake was not only access to K2 (with the attendant logistical complications of supplying American forces in Afghanistan). It also represented a challenge to the entire American strategy of promoting democracy as a way to build stability and security in countries threatened by poor governance and terrorist movements. The crisis pitted Washington's global strategy (making democratization the focal point of U.S. foreign policy) against the operational requirements of the war on terror.

The deterioration in U.S.-Uzbek relations and Tashkent's reorientation toward Russia and China also dealt a blow to Washington's long-term war on terror. The discord between Tashkent and Washington undermined the notion that the United States could pursue a constructive relationship with a moderate, albeit undemocratic, Islamic country with a secular political culture and simultaneously promote a democratic transformation there.

Moreover, the eviction of the United States from K2 signaled Uzbekistan's neighbors and beyond that the United States could be told to leave, and that it would. It was a sign that the geopolitical balance in Central Asia had shifted in a relatively short period of time—and not in favor of the United States.

Although not the main theater in the global war on terror and a peripheral target of application of the U.S. strategy of democracy promotion, which focused heavily on the Middle East, Central Asia—quite unexpectedly— emerged as the key test for that strategy. Retreat from it appeared out of the question. The strategy was articulated by President Bush himself in his second inaugural address in January 2005 and reiterated by senior administration officials countless times thereafter.

But Central Asia has proven an infertile ground for democracy. The reasons for this include the new geopolitical environment in the region, the resistance of local elites to reforms, and the weakness of institutions needed to consolidate progress toward democracy. Kyrgyzstan—the one country where a grassroots movement was successful in challenging a corrupt, authoritarian leader—has been teetering on the brink of chaos since the days of its Tulip Revolution in March 2005.

Yet a strategy articulated with such forcefulness and from the highest levels on behalf of the United States cannot be easily changed, especially in the face of blatant challenges to it from Central Asia and the neighboring states. To do so would constitute retreat and an even greater loss of face by the United States at a crucial moment in its global campaign against terror.

Moreover, a retreat from the democratic agenda would be unacceptable for the many highly influential advocates of an even more dynamic U.S. posture to promote democracy abroad. In the absence of major ethnic domestic lobbies advocating American engagement in Central Asia, domestic constituencies for this area are limited to business interests and to NGOs promoting human rights and democratization. Another important constituency is Congress itself: this region has attracted considerable attention from a number of prominent members of both parties who are interested in a variety of public policy areas, such as nuclear nonproliferation; human rights and democracy; and energy security.[61]

The domestic constituency favoring the promotion of democracy is reinforced by those who advocate a more dynamic geopolitical posture in Central Asia to defend U.S. interests against the growing influence of Russia and China. The merger of Russian and Chinese opposition to the American promotion of democracy in Central Asia with their efforts to expand their influence there has helped to combine geopolitical and idealist interests on the American side into an even more dynamic policy to counter Russian and Chinese influence.

Geopolitical and idealist arguments concur on at least one part of their policy prescription for the region: The United States must counter Russian influence either to challenge Russia's undemocratic tendencies at home and abroad, or to offset Moscow's growing influence in Central Asia.

But there is considerable tension between the two approaches. The advocates of the geopolitical/Realpolitik approach want to defer the democracy agenda at least in the near term and to focus on the practical aspects of security cooperation in the region. The democracy/idealist approach does not allow such concessions and demands a full range of discussions and engagement with Central Asian governments, with no easing of the emphasis on democracy and human rights.

The choice before the United States has been made all the more difficult by broader considerations. Specifically, Central Asia is not the principal theater in Washington's war on terror and the battle of ideas. But U.S. retreat from its principled position with regard to domestic political trends in countries like Uzbekistan and Turkmenistan, for example, would reverberate far outside the region and undermine the credibility of the U.S. commitment to promote democracy as the centerpiece of its war on terror. This in effect could easily lend itself to an interpretation that the United States was abandoning its entire strategy for the war on terror.

But proceeding along the path of high moral principle also is fraught with unattractive consequences. The aftermath of the revolution in Kyrgyzstan has been chaos; the potentially destabilizing ripple effect could spread beyond its borders into neighboring Kazakhstan and Uzbekistan, neither of which is well-equipped to deal with displaced populations, civil emergencies, or popular unrest.

The experience of Kyrgyzstan gives credence to the argument that the real choice in Central Asia, at least in the near- and medium-term, is not between autocratic and democratic regimes, but between autocratic regimes and chaos. If so, the lesser of the two evils, serving the interests of all parties involved—the countries themselves, their neighbors, and the United States—may well be the status quo.

U.S. policy in Central Asia has apparently reached an impasse and now requires a thorough reassessment. It is unclear how long the status quo there can hold and how long U.S. policy toward Central Asia can proceed without major changes. Given the region's peripheral role in the war on terror (compared with Iraq, Afghanistan, and more broadly the Middle East), fundamental changes in U.S. policy do not appear imminent. However, American policy toward this important region does require a new direction. That reorientation may be forced on the U.S. policymakers by events on the ground in Central Asia. In that event, U.S. policy toward the region may follow the path already well trodden in the past fifteen years, one that is shaped by the need to respond rather than preempt.

What Next for U.S. Policy in Central Asia?

As U.S. policymakers ponder their next steps with regard to Central Asia, the question of American interests in Central Asia still lacks a clear answer. How important is the region to the United States? It is, after all, remote, land-locked, and virtually devoid of cultural or historical connections to the United States. Other than Afghanistan, what is the nature of U.S. interests there? The oil reserves are hardly of unique significance, even in these energy-hungry times. Its economic potential hardly matches that of many other regions and countries. And if Kyrgyzstan's government eventually yields to further Chinese and Russian pressures and evicts the United States from its base at Manas (thereby severing an important link between the United States and the region), why should the United States care any more? These are serious questions that must be the preamble to any further discussion of American policy in Central Asia.

The Backyard of Eurasia

To say that Central Asia is uniquely important (whereby its significance exceeds the size of its population, its geographic expanse, its natural wealth, and its economic potential) would be no exaggeration. It *is* uniquely important by virtue of its position at the heart of Eurasia. As such it is important for the Eurasian continent, as well as globally, since Eurasia as a geographic, rather than political concept, is, and for the foreseeable future will remain, the economic, political, and strategic center of gravity in the world.

Eurasia is home to the world's largest and most populous countries, the most important and abundant deposits of key minerals, and the most destructive arsenals. The most important conflicts of the world are in Eurasia. The world's principal religions have their holiest shrines in Eurasia. Central Asia is in the very middle of it all.

Central Asia is the strategic backyard of every major power of Europe and Asia. China, India, Russia, Iran, Turkey and Pakistan all either share borders with the region or have strong interests in it otherwise. Yet, for each and every one of them, this is a secondary strategic theater. Russia's interests historically are concentrated in Europe; China's key interests lie mainly in the Pacific; for India it is Pakistan, the Middle East, and Europe; for Pakistan it is India; and Iran's interests are focused on the Persian Gulf.

Notwithstanding their interests elsewhere, each of these powers is keenly aware of the negative consequences for their interests if the Eurasian heartland were to fall into hostile hands. The consequences could be severe.

For Russia, instability in Central Asia, or its domination by a hostile power, could leave the Russian heartland vulnerable to destabilization, disrupt trade flows, deny access to Central Asian gas reserves, and threaten its internal communications.

For China, instability in Central Asia could endanger the status quo in its restive western province, where the indigenous Turkic population has long resented Han Chinese domination and on occasion rebelled against it. Separatist contagion from Central Asia could be sparked by a spontaneous grassroots movement or instigated by a hostile power. In either case, Chinese security and territorial integrity would be at risk.

For Pakistan, Central Asia arouses concern with respect to its rivalry with India. The latter's growing influence in the region could pose a challenge to Pakistani interests and influence in Afghanistan, a country with which Pakistan shares a long and difficult border, deep ties of ethnic kinship, and a very complicated relationship. For Iran, Central Asia represents its strategic rear; domination by a hostile power or regime, as was the case during the Taliban rule, would therefore threaten Iran's northern frontier.

The coalition that emerged to confront the rise of the Taliban provided a clear example of regional mobilization against a power that threatened to destabilize or even seize major portions of Central Asia. Iran, Russia, China, all of the Central Asian states, and India joined to form an anti-Taliban coalition, putting aside any differences they might have had. Pakistan did not join the coalition because of its close relationship with the Taliban, but that did not diminish its interest in Central Asia.

The United States also joined the anti-Taliban coalition. Its stakes in Central Asia were then (and remain) less immediate and tangible, but important all the same. Had the Taliban destabilized or encroached on Central Asia, that would have damaged American interests as well.

But which interests? The answer to this question remains elusive. The United States has greater interests at stake in each of Central Asia's neighbors than in Central Asia itself. There is more oil in Russia and Iran; there are nuclear weapons in Russia and China; Russia could be decisive in resolving the crisis with Iran's suspected nuclear program, which poses a greater threat from the standpoint of proliferation than components or know-how that can be found in Central Asia. India and China are the two rising Eurasian superpowers that will play an ever increasing role in the international order and marketplace in the new century. And Pakistan is a critical ally in the war on terror.

Nevertheless, Central Asia is the stepping stone, the strategic rear, the soft underbelly to all of these states. As the experience in Afghanistan has shown, unfettered access to Central Asia is important for the U.S. capacity to operate in South Asia. Moreover, as a global power with global interests and global reach, access to Central Asia is of strategic importance for the United States. Indeed, that significance would rise were such access to be denied by one or more hostile powers.

Beyond access, the United States has a strong interest in Central Asia not becoming a collection of even weaker states—with shaky sovereignty and uncertain control over their lands. In that event, these territories could become a large ungoverned space, much like Afghanistan became after years of foreign occupation and factional infighting. Were Central Asia to slide to such a condition, that would be a major setback to the U.S. war on terror.

Absent active intervention from the United States, the possibility of Central Asia sliding toward chaos and anarchy is real, if not necessarily immediate. The mountainous regions of Kyrgyzstan and Tajikistan during its civil war have already experienced the loss of government control. A repetition of that scenario and the deterioration of existing conditions in the future cannot be ruled out. The United States has a strong interest in ensuring that this does not happen. To prevent such a course of events, however, the United States must become actively involved in state-building in the region.

But active involvement there will inevitably pit the United States against the other two major geopolitical actors in the region—China and Russia. The problem is that both are strongly inclined to regard American state-building efforts as inimical to their interests, which they identify with the status quo and close ties to the ruling elites of Central Asia. Neither China nor Russia is likely to encourage the systemic reforms that the United States deems essential for long-term stability in the region.

Some tensions between the United States, on the one hand, and China and Russia, on the other, are inevitable. Managing these tensions and keeping them from infringing on other important American concerns is important to U.S. interests. The United States has many other important interests—maintaining access to Afghanistan, delivering Caspian oil and gas to markets, securing gas supplies and energy independence for Ukraine, retaining access to the region in the event of future crises involving Iran or stepped up competition with China.

The region's proximity to China could be valuable in the event of rising tensions with Beijing. Although the main theater of Sino-U.S. tensions is likely to be the Pacific, access to Central Asia could prove helpful in that highly uncertain scenario.

Russian concerns about U.S. presence and influence in Central Asia are undoubtedly reinforced by suspicions of U.S. intentions vis-à-vis Russia. These range from destabilization to the promotion of democratization to the construction of anti-Russian missile defense systems. A rational look at the state of U.S.-Russian relations makes one question what advantages the United States might gain over Russia by establishing a prolonged presence in Central Asia. Nonetheless, Russian opposition to a continuing American presence in the region could become a contentious issue, especially if Russian influence in the region impedes or jeopardizes U.S. objectives in Afghanistan.

How to manage all these interests, resolve contradictions, secure primary U.S. objectives—all this will constitute important challenges for American foreign policymakers for the foreseeable future.

Economic Management: Big Steps, Small Changes

Given those stakes and the enduring nature of Central Asian resistance to political and economic modernization, the only sensible option for the United States is to cooperate with the region's ruling regimes even while, simultaneously, seeking incremental changes in their domestic political and economic environments. The watchwords in this context should be *continuity* and *gradualism.*

With respect to economic assistance, the United States should seek to alleviate widespread poverty and eliminate sources of political destabilization, such as high unemployment in rural and urban areas. Given the region's need for major improvements in basic infrastructure, the water supply system, and other labor-intensive projects, American and international assistance could provide much-needed jobs and income, defuse political tensions, and facilitate intraregional cooperation.

Furthermore, given the region's reluctance to yield to pressures for political liberalization, economic liberalization could prove to be more promising venue for change. Without question, the top priority for the region must be economic liberalization, which can be an important indicator to pace the rate of political reform. Although none of the countries in Central Asia is a paragon of political and economic reform, the country that has made the most progress in economic reform—Kazakhstan—also happens to be the one that has had the benefit of a relatively open (by Central Asian standards) political regime. The two countries that have accomplished the least economic reform—Uzbekistan and Turkmenistan—also have suffered from the most oppressive regimes in the region.

The strength of the regime in Uzbekistan, the pivotal state in Central Asia, makes the choice between political and economic liberalization in favor of the latter a relatively safe bet. The greatest threat to regime stability lies in the impoverishment of the population, unemployment, and the lack of commercial opportunities. A program of assistance designed to stimulate jobs and business would help defuse internal tensions and enhance stability in Uzbekistan and the region. The relative stability of the Karimov regime means that it has the strength and capacity to cooperate with U.S. assistance and to implement a development program that would bolster domestic political stability.

Another focus of U.S. assistance should be large infrastructure projects. Roads and water repeatedly have been mentioned as two critical weaknesses in the region's economic development. Projects sponsored by the United States and the international community to provide new highways to the Indian subcontinent, would generate new commercial opportunities, create jobs, and provide new strategic outlets for the land-locked region.

Domestic Politics: "The More It Changes . . ."

Domestic politics within the Central Asian states represents a far more challenging problem. The United States remains committed to promoting long-term stability through political and economic reforms in Central Asia. The region's elites are just as committed to oppose those reforms, if their hold on power is the price they have to pay for the region's long-term stability.

In Central Asia, the U.S. offer of economic and security assistance in exchange for democratization and economic reforms is no more likely to produce the desired effect in the next fifteen years than it did in the first fifteen years of the region's independence. A U.S. agenda of promoting democracy and human rights is unacceptable for local elites, who are more concerned about the survival of their own regimes and who have been frightened by the specter of revolutions—colored, democratic, Islamic, or other.

The entire experience of the first fifteen years of independence in Central Asia suggests that the region's political elites have not embraced the basic concepts of democracy and have only paid lip service—at best—to deflect admonitions from Western leaders and international organizations. Thus, given the inevitability of political succession throughout Central Asia, the fundamental challenge is to ensure that succession not lead to destabilization, as befell Tajikistan in the early 1990s, or Kyrgyzstan in 2005. Given the lack of stable domestic institutions and the presence of personality-based regimes (where the chief aim is to avoid political succession), succession remains the chief long-term threat to regional stability.

In the next decade, leadership succession will become the most critical political issue in Central Asia. The Soviet-era leaders in this region have proven to be neither competent reformers nor popular politicians. They are likely to be remembered for their firm hold on power, but they have not transformed that power into long-term stability. The challenge for the next generation of Central Asian leaders—to ensure stability and security through systemic change—promises to be greater than it is today.

Unpopular and mired in allegations of corruption, the current generation of Central Asian leaders has nonetheless proven its mettle. These leaders have maintained a measure of stability, which no one at the time of the Soviet breakup took for granted. As they did so, some leaders introduced significant economic reforms and tolerated limited political opposition. Others have accepted neither political nor economic reform and turned their countries into dictatorships.

While inevitable, succession does not mean that the new team of leaders —although a product of more than a decade of independence—will be fundamentally different from or better than its predecessors. It is not clear at this point that the successor generation will be up to the difficult tasks of maintaining a modicum of internal stability and sustaining complex diplomatic efforts abroad. Furthermore, there is no evidence that the next generation of leaders will prove capable of making up for the shortcomings of the incumbents. Although almost certain to have more exposure to Western culture and values and to be more urbane than their predecessors, the new leaders will remain part and parcel of a system riddled with nepotism and corruption and are unlikely candidates to lead their countries toward systemic change. Thus, change is likely to be very slow, and possibly painful, in Central Asia.

A further benefit of the Central Asian regimes' relative stability is that the United States has time to work with the new generation of leaders and to assist in the development of key institutions that could ultimately play the decisive role in securing the region and making it more stable. Therefore, education and training of new Central Asian elites must be given a high priority. Without harboring undue expectations and illusions about the impact of generational change on Central Asia's internal developments, the leaders who will come to the top of the political pyramid in next ten to fifteen years will have far more exposure to the outside world than their parents.

That difference alone is unlikely to be sufficient to alter the domestic political dynamics in Central Asia. The United States should undertake a sustained effort to educate and professionalize the next generation of Central Asian leaders—in business, government, military, and other areas—and to forge a shared understanding of what is likely to be at stake when they are ready to assume power. Such an effort, combined with a carefully targeted program of economic assistance, are the best options for U.S. policy to influence long-term trends in Central Asia and to help this region achieve sustainable security and stability.

U.S. policy options are quite limited and involve tradeoffs between stability and commitment to democratic principles. In some countries with troubled democratic traditions, such as Turkey, Pakistan, and South Korea, the military has taken an active role in domestic politics, claiming to be the last pillar of stability and savior of the nation. Regardless of the merits of those claims, the five Central Asian states do not yet have that option, however objectionable it may appear. Their militaries are small and new; they have no military traditions, given their short histories of independence and the Soviet practice of limiting Muslims in the officer corps. U.S. security assistance and military-to-military contacts could promote the development of professional military institutions in Central Asia. It is conceivable that in a future crisis in a Central Asian country, the military could indeed become the last pillar of stability, prompting its intervention in domestic politics.

Security Engagement

In the context of NATO's open door policy, the issue of the alliance's expansion beyond the geographic boundaries of Europe cannot be too far away. On the Western shores of the Caspian, Azerbaijan's leaders have expressed an interest in joining the NATO. Armenia maintains membership in the Partnership for Peace program, while Georgia is actively seeking membership as early as 2008. Kazakhstan too is participating in the PfP program. NATO troops deployed to Central Asia for the conduct of the war in Afghanistan against the Taliban. NATO plays an increasingly active role in securing, stabilizing, and rebuilding that country. In other words, NATO is already in Central Asia and will likely remain there for the foreseeable future.

The question then arises, even if only in principle: Should membership be extended to Central Asian states? If NATO is already in Central Asia, why not hold out the possibility of Central Asia in NATO? The answer is that even suggesting the possibility of future membership would be truly a "mission too far." While the South Caucasus may represent the natural next group of nations to be added to NATO's potential membership roster, the former Soviet states of Central Asia lie beyond it. These countries are well outside the geographic or political definitions of European or Euro-Atlantic regions, have shown little commitment to the alliance's fundamental shared values, and are oriented toward the major Asian powers—Russia, China, and India—that are certain to play important roles in the fate of Central Asia in the future. NATO can and, depending on its interests and concerns, should maintain productive security relations with Central Asia, as well as political dialogue through its already established fora—the Euro-Atlantic Partnership Council and the Partnership for Peace—but holding out the prospect of membership to these countries would be misleading and even counterproductive.

Toward a New Central Asia Strategy

None of these avenues for U.S. economic, political, and security engagement with Central Asia satisfy the demand for a new regional strategy. The events of 2005 and 2006 have made it clear that U.S. strategy in Central Asia—with its heavy emphasis on democracy promotion and support for peaceful revolutions —has backfired and that a fresh, new approach to the region is needed.

The policy community has three main options:

1. Stay the course and continue with present policy;
2. Abandon the idea of transforming Central Asia, concentrate on the security relationship and hard U.S. interests there from the position of pure Realpolitik, and let events on the ground determine the future of the region; or
3. Develop a new strategy that takes into account Central Asia's complex legacy and new geopolitical realities.

The first option is clearly unacceptable from the standpoint of U.S. interests, as outlined above. Aggressive promotion of democracy is likely to produce destabilization—as happened in Kyrgyzstan—not democratization. Moreover, this policy threatens to put the United States on a collision course with all regional governments, as well as with China and Russia, given their well-known opposition to this aspect of U.S. policy. Since Russia and China play important roles in the region and exercise considerable influence over its political, economic, and security affairs, such a policy would most likely be fraught with far-reaching adverse consequences for their overall relationships with the United States.

The second option is also unacceptable for the United States. Turning a blind eye to the nature of Central Asian domestic politics and limiting the relationship with the region strictly to security, energy, and U.S. access to military bases would contradict deeply held American values. Moreover, this course of action would ignore the very real need for reform that exists in Central Asia. The need for systemic transformation to underpin long-term sustainable economic development in the region and its healthy and productive integration into the international system, as well as progress to a more open and representative political system necessary for both domestic renewal and international integration, can be ignored only with dire consequences. For the United States to turn a blind eye to this crying need would be shortsighted and fraught with upheavals for its interests in the region not too far into the future.

Thus, the third option, development of a new strategy—the most challenging for the United States, the region and its neighbors—is the only viable policy if America is to achieve its objectives in Central Asia. To be successful, a new strategy for Central Asia could not be limited to an approach that is narrowly focused on the region alone. At the very least, given Central Asia's proximity to Russia and China and the role these two giant and influential neighbors are bound to play in the region's affairs, any new U.S. strategy must have a substantial component that will address various Russian and Chinese perspectives on developments there.

Thus, looking back at the first decade and a half of Central Asia's independence, one can say with confidence that the region has established itself on the map of the world as one of considerable importance. Its proximity to major powers is both a source of opportunity and vulnerability for it. It occupies a place on the international agenda as an important opportunity; its propensity to draw the attention of major powers is also a vulnerability, since it constrains the independence and impinges on the sovereignty of Central Asian countries. Although their independence and sovereignty are no longer in question, as they were a decade and a half ago, they still need help from the international community to carry the full burden of sovereign nations and secure their strategic independence in the international arena.

The United States is uniquely positioned to render assistance. Unlike Russia and China, it is remote, has limited interests in the region, and makes no claim to an empire in Eurasia. However, the United States is in no position to carry the burden of regional responsibility alone on its shoulders. In fact, given the region's location between China and Russia, to be successful the strategy would have to have the support and cooperation of both these Eurasian powers.

The successful experience after 11 September 2001 in establishing a substantial U.S. presence in Central Asia suggests that China's and Russia's support is necessary for the United States to attain its goals in Central Asia. To gain that support, however, both China and Russia need to see a clear self-interest in the U.S. presence. Both Russia and China had a clear self-interest in seeing the Taliban regime defeated and Afghanistan restored to the path of peace and reconstruction. Therefore, they acquiesced to U.S. military deployments in Central Asia.

At the moment, the United States appears to be retreating from Central Asia. It was evicted from K2; its support for the Tulip Revolution has backfired; the region's five countries backed by Russia and China have called for the United States to commit to a timetable for withdrawal of its military presence. However, this picture does not reflect the true correlation of forces in Central Asia.

The United States continues to hold the keys to regional security by virtue of its presence in Afghanistan. Success in Afghanistan would remove a dark cloud hanging over Central Asian security; failure in Afghanistan would cast a long shadow over it. The United States is the key actor in Afghanistan and by extension in Central Asia. It continues to perform a role that neither China, nor Russia, nor any other neighbor of Afghanistan could undertake, let alone accomplish. None of the Central Asian states, Russia, nor China has an interest in seeing the United States fail in its mission in Afghanistan. Their interests would be profoundly negatively affected by such an untoward turn of events. The United States has therefore powerful leverage and a critical point of departure for a conversation with Russia and China about shared stakes in the region.

Afghanistan's proximity and interdependence with the ex-Soviet Central Asian countries mean that the conversation has to be about that region as well. Because neither Russia nor China has a stake in its failure, Afghanistan could be the start of a conversation among Russia, China, and the United States about the future of the region their interests in Central Asia. This should not be a conversation behind the backs of Central Asian governments. They too should be participants in this process. But the conversation cannot exclude Russia and China, since both are involved, and Central Asia has proven to be in need of external help.

The second important source of influence and leverage at the disposal of U.S. policymakers is the fact that the United States is the most welcome great power in the region, even though at times it seems otherwise. It is welcome by Central Asian elites as the only global power, which is on the one hand quite remote and on the other hand able to balance Russian and Chinese influence in Central Asia, which at times can be too intrusive. As the sole remaining superpower, the United States is widely perceived in the region as the center of a global empire. A welcome reception in Washington or a high-level U.S. visit to the region still has a uniquely legitimizing quality in the eyes of local elites.

Moreover, China and Russia have an interest in the U.S. presence in Central Asia. For China, U.S. presence in Central Asia and Afghanistan, as well as the prospect of a continuing U.S. presence as a stabilizing force should be welcome, since it removes the threat of instability in Xinjiang, extends the U.S. security umbrella over Central Asia, and allows China to concentrate on economic development and expansion of its commercial and political ties to the region. For Russia, increasingly concerned about its relationship with China, the United States could emerge as a useful balancer against the rapidly growing eastern neighbor. Thus, while U.S. support for democracy in Central Asia and support for the Tulip Revolution was not welcomed in the region, the U.S. presence and security role there could well serve multiple interests for a long time to come.

The challenge is to engage China, Russia, and the region's elites in a conversation about U.S. interests, perceptions of key problems facing the region, and the best ways to resolve them. The United States and its partners in Central Asia need to bridge the gap in their perceptions. The United States views change as a prerequisite for success in the region; its interlocutors fear change as a recipe for disaster. They are committed to the status quo. The United States is committed to change it. It is a conversation that the region and its partners need to have as soon as possible.

The situation in Central Asia lends itself to a concept that U.S. policymakers have introduced in another, related area of U.S. foreign policy. The concept is that of a "responsible stakeholder," and it was enunciated with regard to China in a speech by U.S. Deputy Secretary of State Robert B. Zoellick.[62] The logic of stakeholder responsibility is self-evident: a major power invested in the international system has a compelling interest in seeing its investment protected and the rules of the international system defended against those likely to violate them:

> We now need to encourage China to become a responsible stakeholder in the international system. As a responsible stakeholder, China would be more than just a member—it would work with us to sustain the international system that has enabled its success.

Cooperation as stakeholders will not mean the absence of differences—we will have disputes that we need to manage. But that management can take place within a larger framework where the parties recognize a shared interest in sustaining political, economic, and security systems that provide common benefits.

The logic of stakeholder responsibility that applies to U.S. policy vis-à-vis China also applies to the task of building a cooperative regime for Central Asia. The five Central Asian states along with Russia, China, and the United States are in effect stakeholders in the region, albeit with different degrees of ownership and responsibility. Despite their differences, they have one shared interest—the region's stability and security.

It is not a fatal drawback if this framework does not ensure U.S. leadership in regional affairs. Moreover, it could be a substantial advantage, given the interest the United States has in generating self-sustaining capabilities for security and economic development, and especially given the multitude of demands on U.S. attention and resources elsewhere.

Central Asia is too important to be left to its own devices. It is also too important for the United States to leave it to Russia and China to manage on their own. They lack the resources and the vision to put the region on a path toward long-term stability and security. However, they have interests in Central Asia and capabilities that could either be part of the solution or part of the problem from the standpoint of U.S. efforts in the region. Enlisting their support in U.S. efforts in Central Asia has to be an integral part of U.S. strategy there, a strategy that must make clear to all shareholders in the remote and volatile region that success can benefit all involved, whereas failure could well be fraught with equally devastating consequences for those involved, as well as for those who are far removed from the heartland of Eurasia.

Notes

The views expressed here are those of the author and do not reflect the official policy or position of the National Defense University, the Department of Defense, or the U.S. Government.

1. See John Van Oudenaren, "Exploiting 'Fault Lines' in the Soviet Empire: An Overview" (Rand, P-7012, 1984).

2. Ellen Jones, "Manning the Soviet Military," *International Security* 7 (Summer 1982): 105–31.

3. Ibid.

4. This discussion draws on several accounts of U.S. policy toward the Soviet Union, some of them first-hand, including: Michael R. Beschloss and Strobe Talbott, *At the Highest Levels: The Inside Story of the End of the Cold War* (Boston: Little, Brown, 1993); George Bush and Brent Scowcroft, *A World Transformed* (New York:

Alfred A. Knopf, 1998); James A. Baker, III, with Thomas M. DeFrank, *The Politics of Diplomacy: Revolution, War, and Peace, 1989–1992* (New York: G.P. Putnam's Sons, 1995); Strobe Talbott, *The Russia Hand: A Memoir of Presidential Diplomacy* (New York: Random House, 2002); James M. Goldgeier and Michael McFaul, *Power and Purpose: U.S. Policy toward Russia after the Cold War* (Washington DC: Brookings Institution Press, 2003).

5. Stephen Coll, *Ghost Wars: The Secret History of the CIA, Afghanistan, and Bin Laden, from the Soviet Invasion to September 10, 2001* (New York: Penguin Press, 2004); George Crile, *Charlie Wilson's War: The Extraordinary Story of the Largest Covert Operation in History* (Boston: Atlantic Monthly Press, 2003).

6. Beschloss and Talbott, *At the Highest Levels*, 418.

7. Baker, *Politics of Diplomacy*, 523.

8. Ibid., 525.

9. Francis Fukuyama, "The End of History?" *National Interest*, Summer 1989.

10. See, for example, Robert Reich, *The Work of Nations: Preparing Ourselves for Twenty-First Century Capitalism* (New York: Vintage, 1992), and "Washington Consensus" (available at http://www.cid.harvard.edu/cidtrade/issues/washington.html and http://en.wikipedia.org/wiki/Washington_consensus).

11. Talbott, *Russia Hand*, 39.

12. Goldgeier and McFaul, *Power and Purpose*, 50–52, 80–81.

13. See http://www.fas.org/nuke/guide/kazakhstan/index.html.

14. Ibid.

15. Ibid.

16. Ashton B. Carter and William J. Perry, *Preventive Defense: A New Security Strategy for America* (Washington, DC: Brookings Institution Press, 1999), 65–91.

17. See the language of the White House press release on the occasion of the passage of the Freedom Support Act passed in 1992 that would for years constitute a key funding vehicle to support economic and political reforms in the former Soviet Union (available at http://www.fas.org/spp/starwars/offdocs/b920401.htm).

18. U.S. policy in Central Asia is well documented in testimony, speeches, and interviews by senior American officials, as well as in the press releases of the State Department (available at its website archive: http://secretary.state.gov/www/briefings/statements/index.html).

19. The record of individual countries in terms of democratic reforms is amply documented over time by the Freedom House survey, "Nations in Transit" (available at http://www.freedomhouse.org/template.cfm?page=17&year=2005).

20. This discussion draws on information available on the NATO website, http://www.nato.int, which covers its extensive network of relationships since the end of the Cold War; and the OSCE's website, http://www.osce.org, as well as the testimony and speeches of American officials during the 1990s, (available at http://secretary.state.gov/www/briefings/statements/index.html).

21. See http://www.treemedia.com/cfrlibrary/library/policy/talbott.html.

22. Ibid.

23. Ibid.

24. Ibid.

25. Ibid.

26. See http://www.eia.doe.gov/emeu/cabs/Region_ni.html.

27. See http://www.eia.doe.gov/emeu/cabs/Centasia/NaturalGas.html.

28. See http://www.eia.doe.gov/emeu/cabs/Centasia/Oil.html.

29. U.S. Department of State, *Caspian Region Energy Development Report (As Required by HR 3610)*, an undated report attached to a letter from Barbara Larkin, Assistant Secretary for Legislative Affairs, to Senator Robert Byrd (Democrat, West Virginia), dated 15 April 1997.

30. Ibid., 3.

31. American policy on Caspian pipelines has been addressed in numerous official statements by the U.S. Government, available at http://secretary.state.gov/www/briefings/statements/index.html.

32. See http://www.mipt.org/pdf/iranandlibyasanction104–172.pdf.

33. Martha Brill Olcott, "The Caspian's False Promise," *Foreign Policy*, Summer 1998.

34. Richard Sokolsky and Tanya Charlick-Paley, "NATO and Caspian Security: A Mission Too Far?" (Rand, MR-1074-AF, 1999); and Kenneth Weisbrode, "Central Eurasia: Prize or Quicksand? Contending Views of Instability in Karabagh, Ferghana and Afghanistan" (International Institute for Strategic Studies, Adelphi Paper 338).

35. Sokolsky and Charlick-Paley, "NATO and Caspian Security: A Mission Too Far?"

36. RFE/RL Newsline, vol. 3, no. 33, pt. 1, 17 February 1999, available at http://www.friends-partners.org/friends/news/omri/1999/02/990217I.html (opt,mozilla,un ix,english,,new).

37. Ibid.

38. Madeleine K. Albright, "Press Briefing on Plane En Route to Washington, DC from Tashkent, Uzbekistan," 19 April 2000 (http://secretary.state.gov/www/statements/2000/000419c.html).

39. Ambassador Michael A. Sheehan, Coordinator for Counterterrorism, U.S. Department of State, Testimony before the House International Relations Committee, 12 July 2000 (http://cryptome.quintessenz.at/mirror/mas071200.htm).

40. Thomas E. Ricks and Susan B. Glasser, "U.S. Operated Secret Alliance with Uzbekistan," *Washington Post*, 14 October 2001, p. A01; Elizabeth Sherwood-Randall, "Building Cooperative Security Ties in Central Asia," *Stanford Journal of International Relations* 3:2 (Fall–Winter 2002), available at http://www.stanford.edu/group/sjir/3.2.06_sherwoodrandall.html.

41. See http://www.whitehouse.gov/energy/Chapter8.pdf.

42. Their internal developments were amply documented by numerous nongovernmental organizations; the most comprehensive among them is the coverage provided by Freedom House, available at http://www.freedomhouse.org/template.cfm?page=5.

43. Author's personal conversation with a senior Central Asian security official, Washington, D.C., September 2000.

44. Tommy Franks, *American Soldier* (New York: Regan Books, 2004), 281, 286–87.

45. United States-Uzbekistan Declaration on the Strategic Partnership and Cooperation Framework, 12 March 2002 (http://www.state.gov/r/pa/prs/ps/2002/8736.htm).

46. Ibid.

47. Ibid.

48. See remarks by Tommy Franks in August 2002 that American troops will remain in Afghanistan "indefinitely" (accessed at http://www.usatoday.com/usatonline/20020826/4391202s.htm).

49. Colin L. Powell, remarks at International Conference for Reconstruction Assistance to Afghanistan, Tokyo, Japan, January 21, 2002, accessed at http://www.state. gov/secretary/rm/2002/7366.htm.

50. See http://www.whitehouse.gov/news/releases/2003/02/counter_terrorism/ counter_terrorism_strategy.pdf.

51. Ibid., 22.

52. See discussions of the Nikitsky Club in Moscow, "The Chinese Factor in the New Structure of International Relations and Russia's Strategy," available at http:// www.nikitskyclub.ru/article.php?idpublication=4&idissue=32.

53. See: CIA World Factbook (http://www.cia.gov/cia/publications/factbook/ geos/xx.html).

54. See Robert Satloff, "The Peace Process at Sea: The Karine-A Affair and the War On Terrorism," *National Interest*, Spring 2002, accessed at http://www.washingtonin-stitute.org/media/satloff/satloff-peace.htm; James Bennet, "Seized Arms Would Have Vastly Extended Arafat Arsenal," *New York Times*, 12 January 2002; and "President Bush, Prime Minister Sharon Discuss Middle East," *New York Times*, 7 February 2002, accessed at http://www.whitehouse.gov/news/releases/2002/02/20020207–15.html.

55. For a recent official U.S. statement on the Andijon events, see "The 2005 Country Reports on Human Rights Practices: Uzbekistan," released on 8 March 2006 by the U.S. State Department (available at the website of the U.S. embassy in Toshkent, http://www.usembassy.uz/home/index.aspx?&=&mid=594&lid=1). See also the letter to the editor by U.S. ambassador to Uzbekistan Jon Purnell (dated 15 June 2005) to the Uzbek newspaper *Narodnoe Slovo* (also available at the website of the U.S. Embassy in Tashkent, http://www.usembassy.uz/home/index.aspx?&=&mid=491).

56. Statement by the Uzbekistan Ministry of Foreign Affairs, 10 June 2005, available at the website of the Uzbek embassy in Washington, http://www.uzbekistan.org/ press/archive/220/); and the statement by President Islam A. Karimov of Uzbekistan at a press conference of 16 May 2005 (also available at the website of the Uzbek embassy in Washington, http://www.uzbekistan.org/press/archive/189/).

57. LTC Kurt H. Meppen, "U.S.-Uzbek Bilateral Relations: Policy Options," in *Anatomy of a Crisis: U.S.-Uzbekistan Relations, 2001–2005* (Silk Road Paper, February 2006), 17 (available at http://www.silkroadstudies.org/new/inside/publications/ 0602Uzbek.pdf).

58. Julie Corwin, "Central Asia: Experts Ponder Gazprom's Agenda," RFE/RL, 19 April 2006 (http://www.rferl.org/featuresarticle/2006/04/ce5c73e5-dee0–4b4b-ab3d-40f61be6fce5.html).

59. RIA Novosti, 10 January 2006, "Kazakhstan, China set to up trade by $4 billion" (http://en.rian.ru/world/20060110/42913602.html).

60. Stephen Blank, "Bishkek Reassures Beijing after Tulip Revolution," *Eurasia Daily Monitor*, 12 April 2005 (http://www.jamestown.org/publications_details. php?volume_id=407&issue_id=3297&article_id=2369581).

61. See, for example, the remarks by Senator John McCain at the Inter-Parliamentary Conference on Freedom and Human Rights in Central Asia, 1 May 2003 (available at http://mccain.senate.gov/index.cfm?fuseaction=Newscenter .ViewPressRelease&Content_id=941).

62. Robert Zoellick, "Whither China: From Membership to Responsibility?" Remarks to National Committee on U.S.-China Relations, New York City, 21 September 2005 (available at http://www.state.gov/s/d/rem/53682.htm).

2

Russia and Central Asia
Interests, Policies, and Prospects

Dmitri Trenin

Geographically, Russia connects with the outside world through three broad façades: to the west (Europe, the Atlantic and ultimately the eastern United States); to the east (China, Japan, Korea, the Pacific, and America's western seaboard); and to the south (which stretches from the Black Sea and the Caucasus across the Caspian to Central Asia). Russia has traditionally seen itself as a country situated between the West and the East. During Russia's early history (from the ninth to the sixteenth centuries), the principal security threats came from the East—that is, from the steppe nomads. For two-and-a-half centuries, Mongols of the Golden Horde dominated core Russian lands and made Russia part of an Asian empire. Once Russia freed itself from the "Mongol yoke" and the threat from the East abated, Russia entered the world of European power politics, and the West began to dominate Russian thinking—right up through the Cold War and its aftermath.

Until recently, the southern façade had been considered part of the East. Namely, the former Ottoman Empire was the Near East; Iran, Afghanistan, and the approaches to India were the Middle East; and China, Japan, Korea, and Mongolia were the Far East. "Oriental studies" in the Russian Academy of Sciences system covered everything from the Caucasus and the Arab-Persian world to India, China, and Japan. This broad concept of the Orient as non-Europe was born in the nineteenth century and unraveled in the twentieth century, when geographic Asia broke into two large pieces, with each having something akin to a broad common identity: East and South

Asia (or simply Asia) and the predominantly Muslim Greater Middle East, with the border between India and Pakistan dividing these two worlds.[1] For Russia, the arrival of the South as distinct from the East brought three major catastrophes: the Afghan war (1979–89); the Chechen war (1994–); and the developments unleashed by the terrorist attacks on the United States on 11 September 2001.

In retrospect, what we now call the South was, for Russia, a source of initial spiritual and cultural inspiration (Byzantium and Orthodox Christianity); an area of intense competition with the Ottomans, the Persians, the British, and—more recently, during the Cold War—the United States; and a vast borderland of the Russian and subsequent Soviet empires with a predominantly Muslim population. It was also the one area of the world where Russia could claim it was performing, from the second half of the nineteenth century, a *mission civilisatrice.*[2]

Today, from Moscow's perspective, the South looks like a sliced pie. On its outer periphery lie Egypt, Syria, Iraq, Israel (with the Palestinian Authority), Saudi Arabia, and the Gulf States. The core South consists of the former Soviet Union's direct neighbors—Turkey, Iran, Afghanistan, and Pakistan. Finally, the inner circle consists of the post-Soviet states in the Caucasus and Central Asia. The first group used to be the playground for Russia's wider geopolitical ambitions; that is now much reduced, but still raises energy-related considerations. Russia is much more closely involved with the countries in the second group. From political, commercial, and strategic perspectives, they cannot be safely ignored. Moreover, whatever internally happens there is likely to have a major impact further north. Lastly, the republics of the former Soviet South continue to have closest relations with the former imperial center.

What is now usually referred to as political Central Asia (the five post-Soviet states of Kazakhstan, Kyrgyzstan, Tajikistan, Turkmenistan, and Uzbekistan) is the biggest chunk of this immediate neighborhood. However, the term "Central Asia" requires some elaboration. It is not a single unit, either from a cultural or ethno-political point of view. From the beginning of the Russian colonization drive in the 1860s until the mid-1920s (the onset of Sovietization), the official Russian name of the mostly Turkic-speaking region was *Turkestan.* Throughout most of the Soviet period, the territory was known as "Middle Asia and Kazakhstan." Although the conservative military retained the term "Turkestan military district" until 1991, even it had to carve out a separate Middle Asian district at the start of the Afghan war.[3] The current name of Central Asia has been standard in Russia and the region since 1993. The purpose of renaming, which stemmed from the countries concerned, seems to have been twofold: to create a common regional identity and to drop the uninspiring description of "middle" in favor of a more uplifting "central."[4]

Whatever the advantages of renaming for the countries concerned, from the Russian perspective, the most fitting description now is still the Soviet one—which distinguished between Kazakhstan (the only country with which Russia has a border and whose population is one-third Slav) and the four other countries farther south.

In fact, however, the term "Central Asia" has been used by Russian geographers from the late nineteenth century to denote the landlocked areas of Turkestan, Afghanistan, western China, Mongolia, and parts of southern Siberia (Altai, Tuva, Buriatia). This overlaps with the concept of "Inner Asia" advanced by Robert Legvold.[5] According to Legvold, a "re-formation" is under way in a region that was initially enveloped by the Mongol empire of Genghis Khan. This vast region stretches from Mongolia and the Russian Far East to Central Asia, and further to northern Iran and the Caucasus. With the end of the Russian and Soviet empires, old links are being restored, new ones are emerging, and Islam is experiencing a revival. "Russia as Eurasia" is history; new geopolitical alignments, some with very old roots, are coming to the fore.

Historically, Central Asia was Imperial Russia's last territorial acquisition. Until the nineteenth century, Russia had taken only sporadic interest in the region. As late as 1800, it still lay outside of the empire's borders; it was only by 1895 that the acquisition was complete. The annexation of Central Asia took two main forms: more or less peaceful accession (for much of Kazakhstan) and military conquest (for the rest of Middle Asia). The Russian drive toward the south was motivated by a variety of reasons, from the need to protect against Khivan and other raiders (notorious for kidnapping Russian subjects and turning them into slaves) to the desire to create a land passage to India (seen as a market for Russian industrial goods).[6] Russia's expansion became especially intense after it suffered an ignominious defeat in the Crimean War (1853–56). Checked in the Black Sea and the Balkans, and its prestige shattered in Europe, St. Petersburg turned eastward and southward, where it was able to advance considerably in a short period of time. Bukhara, Khiva, and Kokand (the three Central Asian khanates in what are now Uzbekistan, Tajikistan, and Kyrgyzstan) were conquered in short order, in the 1860s and 1870s, the first two becoming Russian protectorates, and the last dissolved and annexed. Resistance of the Turkmen tribes was crushed in the 1880s, and the Tajik Pamir, the "Roof of the World," was added to the empire in the 1890s.

Throughout the nineteenth century, Russian moves on the Central Asian chessboard were closely monitored and usually countered by the British, who suspected St. Petersburg (not entirely without cause) of a secret intent to dislodge them from India. The Russians, for their part, were equally wary of British moves. The "Great Game" ended only in 1907 when Russia joined the Anglo-French (and anti-German) *entente cordiale.* By that time, what is now Central Asia was firmly in Russian hands; Iran was divided between Russian and British spheres of influence; and Afghanistan was a more-or-less neutral buffer between the two empires. As Russia was eyeing eastern (Chinese) Turkestan, also known as Kashgaria, Britain became dominant in Tibet. It should be pointed out, however, that for all the passion and fervor of the Great Game, from the Russian perspective the whole exercise was secondary to the all-consuming idea of capturing the Black Sea Straits and establishing Russia's hegemony in the Balkans, thereby resolving the "Eastern question" in its favor.

It is also interesting that in the second half of the nineteenth century Russia turned its attention to Central Asia to compensate for the defeats suffered in Europe, such as the Crimean War, and to demonstrate its ability to pose a serious challenge to the British position in India. It was not so much India itself that Russia was seeking, as it was diminishing Great Britain's world domination and gaining London's recognition of its own international importance.[7] Parallels could be drawn, of course, to the early twenty-first century.

After the Russian Revolution, the Bolsheviks not only consolidated the briefly defunct empire by force of arms, but used the borderlands as forward bases for further advances. Initially wrapped in revolutionary rhetoric, Moscow's policy objectives soon followed the traditional geopolitical precepts. In the new scheme of things, Soviet Central Asia first became a torch to ignite anticolonial movements in British India and Afghanistan; later, it served as a base to help install pro-Moscow regimes in neighboring countries and also functioned as a showcase of Soviet achievements for the Third World, supposedly validating the universal utility of the communist doctrine.

From the mid-1950s, the USSR embarked on a policy of bold geopolitical maneuvering in the Middle East, becoming, alongside the United States, a principal outside party to the Arab-Israeli conflict. Hoping to harness Arab nationalism for its global strategy, the Soviet Union challenged the West—first Britain and France, and ultimately the United States—for control of the world's principal oil-producing region. The superpower conflict in the Middle East had its ups and downs, but the seminal event that affected the fate of the Soviet Union was the invasion of Afghanistan and the subsequent withdrawal.

The Afghan war (1979–89) and the 1979 Islamic revolution in Iran first caused the ossified Soviet regime to realize the importance of the "religious factor" (which it previously ignored) and to adopt a policy that could effectively manage it. In the preceding six decades, Central Asia had been Russia's forward position against Western colonialism and "neo-imperialism"; it now suddenly appeared vulnerable to cross-border influences from the core Muslim countries. From the perspective of Islamist activists, the time had come to recover the territories once lost to the Russian and Soviet empires, and re-Islamicization became the principal tool to achieve that goal.

Mikhail Gorbachev recognized the importance of the Muslim factor too late. In 1986 he was still so mindless as to replace a veteran ethnic Kazakh with an obscure Russian apparatchik at the head of the Kazakhstani Communist Party, thereby provoking the region's first post-Stalin riots in Almaty. Barely five years later, in the final months of the Soviet state, Gorbachev was disposed to offer Kazakhstan's new locally born leader, Nursultan Nazarbaev, the premiership of a Soviet federation refurbished with a new treaty.

A renewed Soviet Union was not to be. Instead, Boris Yeltsin and his liberal advisers in the Russian Republic leadership opted for a "little Russia," thus letting go of the borderlands and giving them independence with virtually no strings attached. For Moscow's Western-oriented reformers, Central Asia bore no particular value. Even though they saw a reason to agree with Ukraine and Belarus to dismantle the Soviet Union and to create the Commonwealth of Independent States (CIS), with the stress on the middle word, initially they did not even bother to invite Central Asia to join in. The republics of the region, which had been steadily working for more autonomy, but did not strive for full independence, suddenly saw the roof of a common state blown away as if by a powerful wind. Even though the CIS was soon expanded to include them, Central Asians felt abandoned by Russia.

In terms of demographics, Russia has experienced a sea of change. When Turkestan was annexed by Russia in 1880, it had a population of just 3 million people.[8] At the time, Russia itself was experiencing a demographic boom, and that in turn led hundreds of thousands of Russian settlers to migrate to the region. The 1959 census reported 2.9 million Kazakhs and 3.7 million Russians in Kazakhstan, in addition to Ukrainians and Belorussians.[9] Since the 1970s, however, the tide has turned, with ethnic Russians returning to the Russian Republic. After the breakup of the Soviet Union, the out-migration turned into a stampede. Since the early 1990s, that population flow has also included an influx of Central Asians to the Russian Federation in search of work. As the Russian birthrate has plummeted and death rate increased, Russia faces a proportional increase of Muslims inside its own borders and the rise of populous states to the south. This demographic overhang can be illustrated by the fact that Pakistan alone (or Turkey and Iran together) now surpasses Russia in overall population numbers, and within the next few decades Uzbekistan will grow to half the population of Russia.

The initial thesis here is that, for Russia, the "time of the South" has arrived. The challenge is twofold, internal and external. As it grapples with its post-imperial condition, Russia cannot simply embark on building an ethnic Russian, Orthodox Christian nation-state. It has to factor in its growing Muslim minority and the reality of an Islamic renaissance. The principal security challenge today and in the near- and medium-term future also comes from the south—Chechen terrorists, Fergana Valley insurgents, Afghan drug lords, Iranian nuclear program, and the internal stability of a nuclear-armed Pakistan.

In the five republics of Central Asia, specifically, Russia must contend with the weakness and fragility of these newly independent states. It is a small miracle that all five have survived in their Soviet-designed borders through the turmoil unleashed by the breakup of the USSR and the instability of the post-Soviet period. These states, however, are both a buffer (barrier) and an interface (bridge) between Russia and the tumultuous world of Islam. In the early twenty-first century, Russia looks ahead to a long and painful period of post-imperial disengagement from the former provinces *and* simultaneous re-engagement with its new neighbors on a new set of principles.

This study will start by identifying Russia's main interests in the region: political, security, economic, and what I shall call "humanitarian" (a generic term that encompasses the condition of Russian minorities in the region and the role of Russian culture and the language as the means of Russia's "soft power"). At the same time, attention will also be given to the broad interests that the Central Asian countries have with regard to Russia. The analysis will then proceed to discuss Russia's overall approach to the region and its specific policies; it will seek to identify the parties that push particular policies, their perceptions, and the resultant interplay of political forces.

Russia's policies toward Central Asia have evolved since the dissolution of the USSR; it is important to analyze these various stages—from abandonment to imitated integration to economic expansion coupled with "securitization" and a roll-back of U.S. military presence. Russian public attitudes toward Central Asia will form the background of this policy discussion. The priority given by Russian policymakers to Central Asia will be compared to the attention given to other regions within and beyond the post-Soviet space. Similarly, consideration will also be given to the policies of the Central Asian states toward Russia. The final section will address the prospects for Russia's presence and influence in Central Asia. Will Russia be able to turn itself into a power center to which Central Asians, while preserving their nominal independence, will defer? Will it be able to achieve meaningful economic integration with Kazakhstan and perhaps other countries in the region? Will it be capable of assuming responsibility for the security of the volatile region? Will the Russian language and culture have a future in Central Asia over the long term, and will their new elites be educated and socialized in Russia the way their predecessors were? How will Russia relate to the outside powers that are active in the region, in particular the United States and China? Will it use China's support to roll-back American influence? Will it succeed in keeping a comfortable balance between Washington and Beijing in order to achieve its own predominance in the region? Will it succumb to China's growing influence and allow the Shanghai Cooperation Organization (SCO) to become the heart of a new Eurasia, from Brest to Hong Kong?

Briefly put, the main thesis of this chapter is that Russia's policy is in a process of post-imperial adjustment, and that process is open-ended. Tashkent, Alma-Ata, Dushanbe—that *was* the empire, that was the Soviet Union. Russia is yet to redefine itself as a modern nation in terms of twenty-first century modernity. How Russia manages Central Asia will be an important part of the answer to this seminal challenge.

Russian Interests in Central Asia

After a brief interlude immediately following the collapse of the Soviet Union and the emergence of the Russian Federation as its principal successor state, the Russian elites have regarded reestablishment of the country's great-power status as their main long-term objective. In their view, Russia can only survive and prosper in the twenty-first century if it is a free-standing great power. The Kremlin has drawn lessons from its attempts to integrate into, or with, the West in the 1990s and early part of this century, but integration on Russian terms proved impossible, while accession on Western terms was deemed unacceptable. Russia therefore had no choice but to go on its own.

No great power, however, walks alone. The Kremlin is determined to turn the Russian Federation into a power center with the countries of the post-Soviet Commonwealth of Independent States falling into its orbit. The Russian leadership and the bulk of the Russian public consider new Eastern Europe (Ukraine, Belarus, and Moldova), the South Caucasus (Azerbaijan, Georgia, and Armenia) and Central Asia's five states as a zone of Russia's vital interests. Even though the Kremlin believes Russia to be a power with a global reach, it is the CIS that has become, by the early twenty-first century, the focus of Moscow's foreign policy.

Russia openly aspires to a dominant position across the former Soviet space. But dominance that comes in a soft form does not mean physical re-integration. Moscow does not seek to restore a Eurasian super-state, or to create yet another new version of the Russian empire: Russia's main business will be Russia. Rather, Moscow wants to ensure favorable conditions for economic expansion in the former borderlands and for a high degree of Russian political influence, which guarantees loyalty. The notion of a liberal empire, first introduced in 2003,[10] set the trend. In 2005 Moscow finally lost faith in the CIS as an institution and adopted a more flexible and pragmatic approach. Instead of trying to make the unwieldy twelve-state construct work, it sought to identify specific Russian interests that would need to be promoted and protected in individual post-Soviet countries.

Moscow uses several instruments: bilateral relations; a proto-economic union called the Euro-Asian Economic Community (EAEC, also known by its Russian abbreviation EvrAzES); and a security alliance founded as the Collective Security Treaty Organization (CSTO). Moscow is realistic enough to recognize the new states' many links to the outside world. It understands foreign investment and economic competition. What Russia wants to make sure is that, when push comes to shove, its interests in the new states prevail. From the Russian perspective, this is only fair: the former republics are much more critical to Russia than to any other outside power, including China and the United States.

Post-Soviet Russia has experienced a renaissance of traditional geopolitics, which sees Central Asia as an area that should be dominated by Russia.[11] However, Moscow cannot ignore the fact that Central Asia has recently become an area of competing outside influences, which include neighboring China, distant America, rising India, and countries that are ethnically and religiously related (such as Turkey, Iran, Pakistan, and Saudi Arabia).

Moscow's overall geopolitical design would be threatened by NATO expansion that could include Ukraine and Georgia and, to a somewhat lesser extent, by the U.S. military presence in CIS countries. NATO membership is totally incompatible with Russia's soft dominance, and Moscow can be expected to pull various levers to prevent the Ukrainian accession, which indeed remains controversial in Ukraine itself. Next to security alignments, foreign military presence is traditionally regarded as a marker denoting spheres of interest.

Thus, the U.S. military intervention in Afghanistan and the introduction of American forces in Central Asia to support that operation shattered the strategic equilibrium established after the fall of the Soviet Union. Washington, not Moscow, became the principal economic donor of the new states and the region's security manager.[12]

Having grudgingly accepted this presence initially (in the hope of a fuller arrangement with the United States), Russia later changed its position. After 2004 it became increasingly evident that Moscow would seek an opportunity to evict the United States from the region. Moscow essentially claimed that a third-party military presence in CIS countries was only acceptable if it met Russian security interests, rested on Moscow's express permission, and constituted a specific mission with a reasonable time-frame for withdrawal. By 2005, an opportunity presented itself in Uzbekistan.

From the early 2000s, the center of gravity of Russian policy has been moving from west to east. The United States, while remaining central, has also become more distant. The European Union, having expanded to include much of Europe outside the CIS, is politically confused and economically stagnant. Asia, by contrast, is demonstrating dynamism. The West is not alone in its preoccupation with the rise of China and India. The Russians, too, are looking for opportunities, even as they are preparing to face the concomitant challenges.

In Russian eyes, China has greatly grown in stature in the last fifteen years, more starkly even than viewed from the West. Historically regarded as huge, but essentially inferior to Russia, China has, within a decade and a half, achieved formal equality with and informal superiority over its former hegemon and mentor. China has joined the United States and the European Union countries as one of Russia's three principal global partners.

By moving closer to China, Russia hopes to escape America's tutelage. Its strategy could be described as leaning on the east to raise its stakes in the west. At the same time, Russia wants to avoid becoming China's satellite. The calculus is that, for the foreseeable future, Beijing will focus on domestic development and assume a relatively low profile internationally. This will buy time for Moscow. By the time China becomes more assertive, Russia will have strengthened itself and consolidated its zone of vital interests.

Central Asia is a major sphere of Russian-Chinese interaction. It was with regard to that region that the SCO was founded. Originally, the SCO could well be dubbed "China in Central Asia." Over time, its purpose has expanded along with its geographical scope. The formal members of the SCO include China, Russia, and four Central Asian countries (all but Turkmenistan); India, Pakistan, Iran, and Mongolia participate as observers. At least *in potential*, some Russians believe, the SCO could become an alternative to the U.S.-led international community (North America, Western and Central Europe, Japan, Australia). Thus, for the first time since the fall of the Berlin Wall, a new global geopolitical arrangement may be emerging.

The immediate challenge to Russia's geopolitical interests, however, comes from the south. The Islamist radicals' idea that the lands once annexed by the Russian empire and subsequently included into the atheist Soviet Union should be recaptured by the world of Islam and form a new caliphate has found substantial material support in the Arab world and drawn a number of adherents in Central Asia. The Taliban regime in Afghanistan was the symbol of that new threat, but even with its demise the threat has not been abolished.

Russia is in the process of reformulating its interests in the Greater Middle East (GME). It has a major interest in Iran as a regional partner and a market, but it is concerned about Iran's nuclear program and its long-range missiles. Russia's absence from Afghanistan is more virtual than real, and in any case, temporary. Moscow keeps a watchful eye on Pakistan, an unstable nuclear power threatened by internal Islamist extremism. In addition, Russia craves to be an active member of the "Quartet" addressing the Israeli-Palestinian conflict,[13] and it is keenly following developments in the Gulf States, including Saudi Arabia, which have the potential for destabilizing the entire GME and disrupting the world energy market. It is this prospect that lets Russia present itself to the West as the indispensable energy power. Central Asia is both a gateway and, if controlled by Russia, a key forward position to execute Russia's "southern strategy."

Thus, Central Asia has become a battlefield in a new, much softer version of the Great Game—this time between Russia and the United States (overtly), and between Russia and China (covertly). In mid-2005, Washington was put on notice that its military presence in the region was conditional on China's and Russia's tolerance. By the end of 2005, Uzbekistan became the first CIS country to leave the American orbit and realign itself with Russia. However, in 2004 and 2005 Moscow reacted nervously to a highly speculative idea of a Chinese military presence in Kyrgyzstan.

Russia's overriding interest in Central Asia is in the new states' internal stability. Should they fail, and open the floodgates to chaos, the effect on Russia could be overwhelming, in view of the long open borders, the masses of potential immigrants, and the existence of a sizeable Muslim minority in Russia (even constituting a majority in several parts of the Russian Federation). In fact, only 50 kilometers or so separate one such Muslim area, Bashkortostan, from the Russia-Kazakhstan border.

The Russian leaders clearly prefer the status quo in the states of Central Asia to any attempts to overthrow these regimes or even to pressure them to introduce changes. This preference does not result from any ideological affinity or sentimental "authoritarian solidarity." In the prevailing official Russian view, the ruling authoritarians are unlikely to be succeeded by enlightened democrats; rather, they are more likely to be replaced by Islamist radicals. It is religious extremism that is defined as the clear and present danger facing the region. As to pressuring their Central Asian partners for change, Russian leaders fear such pressure would only push the region into the arms of China.

Russia is also interested in seeing that the countries of this region maintain reasonably good relations among themselves. Moscow is well aware of the arbitrary nature of virtually all the borders among the Central Asian states, which were drawn in 1924–25 to suit the needs of Sovietization and to ensure centralized control and arbitration from Moscow. The Russians are also fully cognizant of the various inequities of Central Asian economies, which were built in the twentieth century as integral part of the Soviet economy.

Russia has an overriding interest in ethnic peace in Central Asia. Although the number of ethnic Russians there has significantly decreased since the breakup of the USSR, millions still live in the region. Many would never leave. An ethnic conflict—for example, one involving local Russians in Kazakhstan—would risk a confrontation between Russia and its biggest and most important Central Asian neighbor.

Within Central Asia, Russia's interests in the five component countries vary widely, as do the countries themselves.

Kazakhstan is, for Russia, by far the most important of the Central Asian countries. It, rather than Russia (which readily claims the title for itself), is the quintessential Eurasian state.[14] Geographically, demographically, and economically, northern Kazakhstan is an extension of southern Siberia and the Urals. The Russia-Kazakhstan border, stretching for over 7,500 kilometers, is the longest in the world. This border, which did not exist as an international frontier before 1991, was only delineated in 2005. Trains running between central Russia and Siberia have to cross Kazakhstan's borders several times during their journey. The Russian-Kazakhstan border in the Caspian Sea, fixed in a 1998 bilateral agreement, cuts through a major gas field (Astrakhan-Atyrau). Policing such a border is almost a mission impossible. Protection and, if need be, defense of Russian territory require a close security and defense alliance with Kazakhstan. A vast and sparsely populated country, Kazakhstan is a useful buffer between Russia and the more fervently Muslim countries of what used to be called Middle Asia to the south. Kazakhstan also sits between Russia's more developed European and western Siberian regions and China.

Ethnic Russians make up just under one-third of Kazakhstan's population. Many of them live in the industrial centers of northern Kazakhstan. Thus, the Russia-Kazakhstan border cuts through a territory with a majority or near-majority Russian population. Moscow's interest, however, is not to divide Kazakhstan, and annex its Russophone northern portion. The Russians know that would be courting disaster, and not only did Moscow refrain from stirring trouble, but it actively assisted its neighbor in stamping out nascent Russophone irredentism. Russia's clear interest is to help Kazakhstan succeed as a viable multiethnic state. Moscow believes that the significant ethnic Russian element in Kazakhstan, though its members are now effectively barred from occupying high positions in the state, is a solid link binding the two countries together.

Kazakhstan is the largest energy-producing country in Central Asia and thus potentially a partner in Russia's drive to become an energy superpower. The Russia-Kazakhstan agreement on dividing the Caspian bolsters Moscow's position vis-à-vis the other Caspian littoral states.

The economies of the Russian and Kazakhstani border regions are closely intertwined. In the words of Kazakhstani authors, this "extreme interconnectedness" has "few, if any, parallels among other pairings in the post-

Soviet space."[15] Actually, Soviet Kazakhstan's first capital in the 1920s was located at Orenburg, in the southern Urals. Major Russian industrial centers such as Samara, Cheliabinsk, Omsk, and Novosibirsk are situated in close proximity to the Kazakhstan border. Just across the border on the Kazakhstan side, several cities—Uralsk, Aktiubinsk, Kustanau, Pavlodar, Semipalatinsk, and Ust-Kamenogorsk (which now mostly have Kazakh names—are all Russian-built and still predominantly Russian-populated industrial centers. Indeed, Kazakhstan is the only CIS country that can be economically integrated with Russia. Russian-Belarusian integration depends on Minsk fundamentally changing its economic policies; as to Russia's prospects of economic integration with other CIS countries, these are virtually nonexistent at present.

Kazakhstan's founding leader, Nursultan Nazarbaev, has long been an advocate of a "Eurasian Union," by which he means a close but equitable relationship with Russia and other CIS countries. In principle, this dovetails with Moscow's ambition of creating a cohesive power center in the CIS. However, there is much disagreement over the actual terms of engagement and the rights of the engaging parties. Nazarbaev, while an advocate of close relations with Russia, is at the same time a staunch opponent of Russia's imperialism. He would not hear of a Greater Russia incorporating its former borderlands.[16]

In a geopolitical master stroke, in 1997 Nazarbaev transferred Kazakhstan's capital from Almaty in the south to Astana, formerly Akmolinsk (Tselinograd), close to the Russian border. He thereby brought the government closer to the country's main industrial centers, reinvigorated the government bureaucracy and the political elite, and most importantly consolidated Kazakhstan's control over its Russian-populated northern regions.

Moreover, Kazakhstan is essentially engaged in a careful balancing act among its three principal partners—Russia, China, and the United States. This maneuvering is not a zero-sum game. In fact, making a clear choice in Russia's favor[17] is hardly a realistic proposition. At the other extreme, it would be utterly destabilizing to allow Kazakhstan to become a geopolitical battlefield among the great powers.

In the Central Asian context, Kazakhstan has grown self-confident. Astana aspires to the role of a "third pillar" in the Shanghai Cooperation Organization, alongside China and Russia. It seeks rotating presidency in the Organization for Security and Cooperation in Europe. At international gatherings, Kazakhstani officials have been reported to treat their fellow Central Asians with thinly veiled disdain.

Uzbekistan, the region's most populous nation, lies just outside of the Russian "integration perimeter."[18] However, it is the key element of Middle Asia. In tsarist and Soviet times, Tashkent functioned as the informal capital of the region and gateway to the Middle East and South Asia. It was also the principal center of the region's industry and culture and, following its rebuilding after the devastating 1966 earthquake, the Soviet showcase in Asia.

Ever since the breakup of the USSR, Uzbekistan has been most sensitive about its sovereign status. It is an heir to a long tradition of Central Asian statehood. All medieval khanates had their capitals in what is now Uzbek territory: Bukhara, Samarkand, Khiva, and Kokand. Much of Uzbekistan, unique among Central Asian countries, continued to be semi-independent until the early 1920s. Ancient states with long histories, Bukhara and Khiva were Russian protectorates ruled by the local emirs and khans; after the Bolshevik revolution both were, briefly, "people's republics." Bukhara was the traditional spiritual center of the region.

The rulers of these historic entities maintained difficult relations with Russia. Tamerlane, whom Islam Karimov proclaimed a national hero, is remembered in Russia as one of a succession of ruthless invaders and despots, in the same category as Genghis Khan and his grandson Batu, who subjugated Russia.

Uzbekistan's main significance for Russia now is that it is the linchpin of regional stability. As a front-line state in the battle against religious extremism, it is very vulnerable. Should Uzbekistan fall victim to Islamist radicalism, Middle Asia would also be submersed, and southern Kazakhstan seriously threatened. A strong regime in Tashkent, Moscow believes, is a bulwark against militant Islam.

Uzbekistan aspires to a hegemonic role in the region, and its relations with the other four states have been tense. Outside of Central Asia itself, it played an active role in Afghanistan until 1998, supporting the forces of an ethnic Uzbek, General Dostum.

From 1991, Tashkent adamantly demanded that Russian influence in Uzbekistan be reduced. Neither Russian troops nor border guards were allowed to operate on its territory. In 1998 President Karimov publicly denounced Russian security services, accusing them of meddling in Uzbekistan's internal affairs. Even after the 1999 terrorist attacks in Tashkent and the 1999–2000 Islamist raids (when Karimov warmed up to Moscow and hosted Putin's visits), the issue of Russian military presence was not raised. After 11 September 2001, Karimov firmly aligned Uzbekistan with the United States, signing an agreement in 2002 on the use of airbases such as Karshi-Khanabad (K2).

Karimov's decision in 2005 to realign Uzbekistan with Russia was taken in extremis. After the bloody riots in Andijon he became convinced of American involvement in attempts to dislodge him. Subsequent U.S. criticism of the use of force by the Uzbek government was tantamount to the United States "conceding Uzbekistan to Russia."[19] However, had Putin rejected the

Karimov plea, the Uzbek leader would have aligned his country with China. Uzbekistan's accession to the SCO in 2000 allowed Tashkent to handle both Beijing and Moscow better. It was to Beijing that Karimov flew in May 2005, a few days after the Andijon rebellion. The decision in favor of Russia can still be revisited either by Karimov or his successors.

Moscow's interest is not in Uzbekistan's integration into Russia, but in preventing its destabilization and radicalization. At the same time, a solid relationship with Tashkent is important for Moscow if it wants greater capacity to manage the situation in the region. Less blessed in natural resources but populous and endowed with a surviving industrial base, Uzbekistan is also a market for Russian goods and services and a partner for joint ventures.

The two small states, *Kyrgyzstan* and *Tajikistan*, are important to Russia as its forward positions in the region, historically blocking hostile entry into Central Asia from the outside. Kyrgyzstan is a country where Russian, Chinese, and American interests intersect. The United States and Russia maintain military bases there, virtually side-by-side; and China is thought to be interested in having its own base as well. Economically, northern Kyrgyzstan is an extension of Kazakhstan, also with a sizeable Russian population. By contrast, southern Kyrgyzstan, with the small portion of Fergana Valley under its control, is closely linked with Uzbekistan, Afghanistan, and Tajikistan. Moscow has been trying assiduously to reduce America's official and NGO-sponsored influence in Kyrgyzstan, which is highest in the region.[20]

Tajikistan used to be seen as Russia's checkpoint on the Afghan border. During the 1990s, it was also a supply base for the anti-Taliban Northern Alliance. With the arrival of American and NATO forces in Afghanistan and the transformation of the principal security threat to Central Asia (which now takes the form of domestic rebellions rather than cross-border attacks), the importance of Tajikistan has changed. Initially, a principal gateway to Afghanistan, it came to be seen primarily as the first station in the long route of Afghan drug trafficking, which has been expanding dramatically since the fall of the Taliban. On the positive side, Tajikistan, along with Kyrgyzstan, is key to control of the region's water resources. In the future, the importance of the water factor is likely to rise, and Russia is certainly interested in winning a commanding position for itself.

Tajikistan is the only Persian-speaking nation in Central Asia. Its long and bloody civil war (1992–97) was ended through joint efforts of Moscow and Tehran. Tajiks are a significant ethnic group in Afghanistan; their leader, Ahmad Shah Massoud, fought against the Soviet army during the Afghan war and later became the rallying figure in the anti-Taliban resistance and a Russian ally. Post 9/11, Tajikistan offered to host NATO air forces engaged in Afghanistan. Its long-time president, Emomali Rakhmonov, a nominal Russian ally, carefully maneuvers among all the players in the region, including the United States,[21] Iran, China, Pakistan, Afghanistan, and India, not to mention his powerful neighbor, Uzbekistan.

Finally, *Turkmenistan* is, above all, a major natural gas producer that Russia wants to keep tied to its gas pipeline system. This link is also an important factor contributing to Moscow's virtual monopoly on gas supply to Ukraine. With Turkmenistan's southern border mostly with Iran, Russia does not insist on a military presence there. In fact, Russia let Ashgabat quietly ease Russia's military withdrawal from a country that once hosted a major Soviet garrison.[22] However, Moscow did not mind Turkmenistan's neutrality as long as it did not offer military base facilities to the United States. Even Niiazov's decision in August 2005 to downgrade Turkmenistan's status in the CIS from a full member to an observer did not cause as much as a stir on the Russian side. Evidently, Niiazov's maverick dictatorship was a less serious problem for Moscow than either an overtly Islamist or pro-Western regime. Not to be ignored is the fact that the Turkmen used to be good warriors who sold their independence dearly, fighting valiantly against the Russian imperial army at Geok-Tepe in 1881.

Since the Afghan war, Central Asia in Russian thinking has been closely linked with Afghanistan. In the 1990s, Tajik and Uzbek enclaves in Afghanistan functioned as semiautonomous "state-lets." Tashkent, Dushanbe, and also Ashgabat pursued their own policies in Afghanistan, irrespective of Moscow's. For five years (1996–2001), the Taliban was Russia's biggest external security problem. After the defeat of the Taliban, Afghanistan has become a major regional base for the United States and NATO.

The American military presence in Central Asia exposed the region to global geopolitics. No longer simply a Russian backyard, the countries of the region now have other options. Washington's interest in Central Asia is closely linked to the war on terror, particularly in Afghanistan. The United States will probably not leave before the job is done, and that will be a long time. As a result, Moscow will no longer be able to take Central Asians for granted. America, however, is not the only major outside player whose appearance has ended Russia's near-monopoly in Central Asia.

From the early-to-mid-1990s, Russia has sensed China's increasing interest in a region that lies just across the Chinese border. Whereas a century earlier Russia was making inroads in eastern (Chinese) Turkestan, it was now Beijing's turn to move west. In 1996, upon completion of the border and security talks between China and the four adjacent former Soviet republics, a permanent mechanism was established for political and military contacts—the "Shanghai Five." In 2000, this arrangement became the Shanghai Cooperation Organization, a regional security and development pact. With its headquarters in Beijing, and its secretary general a Chinese national, the SCO marks China's comeback in Central Asia. Unlike the United States, China will not leave once the situation in Afghanistan normalizes.

In summary, from the Kremlin's point of view, Russia's principal geopolitical interest is to deny Central Asia to Islamist radicals, while finding an acceptable accommodation with the great powers, the United States and China.

Russian Security Interests in Central Asia

Today, and for the foreseeable future, security dominates Russian interests in Central Asia. This section will examine these interests, which have markedly evolved since the breakup of the Soviet Union, by placing them into two categories: "strategic" and "specific." The strategic interests are to prevent threats, deal with risks, and enhance regional security. The specific interests refer to maintaining, restoring, and developing a security infrastructure in Central Asia (through military presence, defense cooperation, arms transfers, and the like).

Strategic Interests

Russia's principal interest in Central Asia is to ensure a modicum of stability in the potentially volatile region. The main threat is the prospect of political destabilization in one or several Central Asian countries, leading to the overthrow of the existing regimes and replacement by radical Islamist rule, or sheer chaos. Since the demise of the USSR, the condition of the bulk of the population throughout the region, except in Kazakhstan, has markedly deteriorated in comparison to the 1980s.[23] Social degradation now competes successfully with feeble attempts at modernization. Absent the barrier of the former Soviet border, Central Asia freely connects with the Middle East. In the eyes of Islamist radicals, it forms a "new frontier" of the Muslim world, and it should be subjected to an intensive Islamicization that would undo the legacy of Soviet atheist rule. Hence the stability of Central Asia means, from Russia's perspective, opposing Islamist radicalism.

Keeping Domestic Stability

Militant Islamists are a major underground opposition force in Uzbekistan. They are also increasingly active in southern Kyrgyzstan, and should the regime in Turkmenistan start to unravel, they can be expected to come to the fore there as well. In Tajikistan, Islamists are a legal political force; the scars of the 1992–97 civil war run deep, and the current stability in Tajikistan (bought at a horrendous price) should not be taken for granted. Only Kazakhstan is, for the moment, largely outside of the danger zone, but it is situated uncomfortably close to it.

To thwart the challenge of militant Islam, Russia relies heavily on the authorities in Central Asian states. Initially, Moscow regarded the new, secular regimes in Central Asia (led by former Soviet-schooled, Russian-speaking ex-Communist officials) as good as it could hope for. However, the civil war in Tajikistan sent a message to Moscow that democracy and Islamism were unacceptable alternatives to secular authoritarianism. Islamism was intensely destabilizing, and threatening not only to end Russia's role in Central Asia, but to spread to Russia's own Muslim-populated regions, undermining the Russian Federation itself. As to democracy, that was not deemed a viable alternative in Central Asia: it could either pave the way for increased Western presence and pro-American policies at the expense of Russian interests, or, more likely, open the floodgates to Islamism.

Moscow has had a learning experience. The Tajik civil war arrested Russia's retreat from Central Asia and terminated the initial attitude of benign neglect toward the region. The Russian leadership had to revise the post-1991 approach to "democracy" and "communism" in the particular context of a former Soviet Central Asian republic. Instead, it adopted a hard-headed realist approach. "Democratic" Moscow took sides in a civil war; it embraced a "communist" leader as an ally; and its forces on the ground imposed a peace that brought total victory for one side and defeat and exile for its opponents. Russia later joined forces with Islamist Iran to bring about a political settlement that gave Tajik Islamists a share of power. Even though this share has decreased since the settlement was reached in 1997, Tajikistan, a nominal Russian ally, remains the only country in Central Asia where Islamists sit in parliament and in the cabinet, not in prison.

Tajikistan is a highly important, but special case. In Vladimir Putin's words, Russia does not need "a second Afghanistan in Central Asia."[24] Across the region, Russia has been trying to check the spread of militant Islam. Immediately after the breakup of the Soviet Union, the new Russian authorities were content to abandon Moscow's former protégé, Mohammed Najibullah, to his fate: he was removed from power in 1992 and brutally murdered by Taliban forces in 1996. Russia's interest in Afghanistan was revived in 1995 with the emergence of the Taliban movement. To stop the Taliban, Moscow started to arm and aid its former *mujahideen* enemies who had overthrown Najibullah.

That was a striking *volte-face*, an indicator of how far Realpolitik had penetrated Russia's foreign policy. When the Taliban captured Kabul in 1996 and continued advancing toward the former Soviet border, Russian leaders became very worried. This anxiety peaked in 1999, when a loose alliance emerged among the Chechens, the Taliban, and the Central Asian rebels. At virtually the same time that Shamil Basaev's party marched from Chechnya into Dagestan, an armed group of the Islamic Movement of Uzbekistan, numbering up to 500 men, invaded Kyrgyzstan. The Taliban-ruled Afghanistan functioned as a rear supply base and a training area. With the Islamic Movement of Uzbekistan diminished after the probable killing of its leader, Juma Namangani, in Afghanistan in 2001, Russia has proclaimed Hizb ut-Tahrir (a clandestine political group that aims to build an Islamic caliphate and that may have tens of thousands of adherents in Uzbekistan and elsewhere) a terrorist organization.

In its effort to preserve the status quo in Central Asia, Russia is taking no chances. Moscow has invariably supported the ruling regimes, keeping contacts even with their more "civilized" opponents at a very low level. The Kremlin has repeatedly rejected expert advice about switching support from seemingly eternal presidents (e.g., in Tajikistan and Kazakhstan) to their more liberal former prime ministers. Despite the often acrimonious relations with Islam Karimov in Uzbekistan and occasional spats with the late despot Saparmurad Niiazov ("Turkmenbashi"), Moscow never seriously considered undermining them from within. It is a moot question to what extent the Russians had been involved with the unfortunate former foreign minister, Boris Shikhmuradov, first exiled in Russia and then imprisoned in Turkmenistan in 2002 for plotting against Turkmenbashi. Since 2000 Russian security agencies have been seeking out Central Asian dissidents and opposition figures in Russia and turning them over to their governments.

Preventing "Colored Revolutions"

Islamists, as seen from Moscow, are potent and ruthless, but not the only threat. From 2003–4, Moscow has become concerned about the so-called colored revolutions in the former Soviet states. The example of Georgia and Ukraine, it felt, could be contagious. The Kremlin became quickly convinced that the "rose," "orange," and other revolutions were part of a U.S.-inspired plot that aimed to replace Soviet-era elites with pro-Western ones and thus forever limit Russia's influence in its neighborhood. Countering colored revolutions became a centerpiece of the Russian approach to the CIS countries.

Moscow, however, was surprised by the toppling of its ally in Kyrgyzstan, Askar Akaev, in March 2005, for his rule had seemed reasonably secure and his opposition had failed to impress the Kremlin. Once Akaev fled, however, Moscow quickly sought to establish relations with the new government and to keep Kyrgyzstan in the Russian orbit. Luckily for Russia, in the previous months, having just learned the lesson of Ukraine, Moscow had already established its first contacts with the Kyrgyz opposition—just in case a change of power were to occur. In May 2005 Russia was again surprised by the unrest in Andijon (Uzbekistan) and the massive blood-letting that ensued. After a brief period of confusion, Russia firmly backed President Islam Karimov and obliquely blamed rebellion on machinations by the United States. Across the Caspian, in late 2005 Moscow helped Azerbaijan's Ilham Aliev to purge his government of potential troublemakers and praised his government's conduct of parliamentary elections. In December 2005 Russia strongly backed Nursultan Nazarbaev's reelection as Kazakhstan's head of state. There is hardly a better illustration of Vladimir Putin's maxim that Moscow only deals with the existing authorities in the CIS.

Russian policymakers consider the promotion of democracy by the United States, not indigenous problems, as the real source of instability. Toward the end of 2005, Russia effectively modified its military doctrine to include the need to address "anti-constitutional actions" in post- Soviet states and other internal developments in the CIS countries.[25] The alliance treaty with Uzbekistan in November 2005 provides that Moscow will aid Tashkent to suppress an Andijon-type revolt in the future. Still, Russia balks at direct intervention. Nikolai Bordiuzha, the secretary-general of the Collective Security Treaty Organization, has publicly ruled out military intervention in member-states to prevent revolution. He called instead for political mediation by the heads of state and senior officials.[26]

As the current generation of Central Asian leaders grows old, the issue of succession becomes more relevant and potentially destabilizing. Closed, clan-based government systems provide rich material for intense rivalries, political killings, and palace coups. Whereas colored revolutions, which overthrow weak authoritarians, are relatively violence-free, harsh authoritarians are more likely to go down in flames. Especially worrisome is the future of Turkmenistan if the heirs of Turkmenbashi quarrel among themselves or fail to deal with the very large backlog of problems that they have inherited. In Uzbekistan at the time of Andijon, the National Security Service, led by Rustam Inoiatov, competed viciously against the Interior Ministry led by Zakir Almatov. With Almatov out in 2006, the question of who will succeed Karimov provokes new rivalries.[27] In Kazakhstan, the killing of the opposition figure Altynbek Sarsenbaev in early 2006 revealed the battle lines long drawn in Nazarbaev's entourage and his immediate family.

Containing Foreign Military Presence and Third-Party
Security Alignments

Russia's initial problem with the Taliban was not so much its radicalism as the fact that it had been created by the Pakistani special services and enjoyed some backing from the United States. Since the period preceding the ill-fated invasion of Afghanistan in 1979 (explicitly justified by the alleged recruitment of its leader by the United States and by the latter's purported plans to install Pershing II intermediate range missiles there), Moscow has been highly allergic to American military deployments and political activism in the northern part of the Middle East. Russian military doctrines of 1993 and 2000 declared foreign military presence in the former Soviet space and third-party security alignments with the new independent states a threat to Russian national security.

Ironically, it was the U.S.-led military operation in Afghanistan that eliminated the gravest external threat to Russian national security since the end of the Cold War. Putin's welcoming of American and NATO forces to Central Asia in September 2001 derived from a careful strategic calculus. First, the United States was about to do something—defeat the Taliban—that the Russians themselves wished to do, but knew they could not. Second, Moscow realized it could not prevent at least some Central Asian countries (for example, Uzbekistan) from hosting Western forces. To try to block American deployments and to fail would have been a major embarrassment, possibly leading to a collapse of the Russia-led security framework in the region. Third, whereas the Americans would come and eventually go, the Chinese, if they were to fill the vacuum, would come and stay. Some Russians see Americans in Central Asia as the placeholders for Russia until such time that Moscow would feel strong enough to dominate the region once again.

In the words of Mikhail Margelov, chair of the International Relations Committee of the upper house of the Russian legislature, "the United States entered Central Asia because we [that is, Russia] created a power vacuum there. By taking on the Taliban, the United States actually started defending our southern borders."[28] In the post-9/11 world, NATO—for decades Moscow's adversary in Central Europe—suddenly became its ally in Central Asia. In 2004 Russia reached agreement with Germany and France to allow military transit to and from Afghanistan across Russian territory. Western military presence in Afghanistan is a boon for Russian and Central Asian security. Russian analysts believe (and hope) the United States and its allies will have to stay in Afghanistan for at least fifteen years so that the country can be properly stabilized.[29]

Even as late as October 2003, Putin was praising "effective cooperation" with the United States in Central Asia and rejected any dissent on that policy. In his words, the just-inaugurated Russian air base at Kant and the U.S. base at Manas, both in Kyrgyzstan, some 30 kilometers apart, were "mutually compatible."[30] By mid-2005 that position had changed; this was the result of a major shift in Russian foreign policy and in American posture toward Russia. Russia stood by as Uzbekistan closed the American base at Karshi-Khanabad.[31] It was less successful in an attempt to evict the United States from its airbase at Manas. Moscow, however, remains more lenient toward the use of Uzbek and Tajik bases by European NATO members France and Germany.

As already pointed out, Russia reacted nervously in 2004–5 to ideas about establishing a Chinese military base, under SCO auspices, in Kyrgyzstan.[32] However, in 2005 Russia reached an agreement with India that would allow Russian and Indian troops to share the Aini air base near Dushanbe in Tajikistan. From Moscow's perspective, India is the one utterly nonproblematic major power. Introducing India to the region as a security factor would have the effect, from Russia's perspective, of limiting Chinese ambitions.

As a coleader of the SCO, Russia has resisted the securitization of the organization. While agreeing to the establishment of an SCO antiterrorist center in Tashkent, Russia sought to preserve the CSTO as the principal security arrangement in Central Asia. The two organizations have a nearly overlapping membership, with one major exception: the CSTO does not include China.

Russia has grown progressively impatient with the OSCE, whether in Central Asia or elsewhere. Moscow now sees the OSCE, once its post-Cold War favorite, as a Western tool that serves to undermine the ruling regimes across the CIS (for example, through the monitoring of elections) and to support the pro-Western opposition.

Maintaining Interstate Stability

Preventing wars among the newly independent states of Central Asia has been Russia's long-term interest. In December 1991, two weeks after the three Slavic republics met to dissolve the Soviet Union and to establish the CIS, the agreement was expanded to include the five Central Asian states. The CIS became above all a presidents' club that allowed the former metropolitan power, Russia, and the former borderlands, including the Central Asian states, to build new relations based on their formal equality and independence. The importance of that vehicle, especially in the early- and mid-1990s, cannot be over-estimated. Except for the reclusive Turkmenbashi, all Central Asian leaders regularly showed up at CIS summits. It needs to be realized that the historical role of the CIS was that of an empire-dismantlement/nation-building aid, not a reintegration mechanism.

In May 1992 members of the CIS signed a treaty in Tashkent to divide the Soviet military legacy. As a result, former Soviet army units in Central Asia were in most cases turned into national armies. This had the paramount effect of recognizing the administrative boundaries of former Soviet republics as the new state borders, even while keeping these borders relatively transparent. This was particularly important given the arbitrariness of most of the new borders that cut across territories inhabited by the same ethnic group. In the decade and a half since that decision, this arrangement has not been seriously challenged, even in the region's potential neuralgic spot of the Fergana Valley,[33] and forms the bedrock of interstate stability in Central Asia.

Russia has taken steps to finalize border arrangements with its only Central Asian neighbor, Kazakhstan. The 1998 landmark agreement on the Caspian established the principle of dividing the seabed while sharing the water and biological resources, like sturgeon (Moscow would subsequently sign a similar agreement with Baku). In 2005 Russia and Kazakhstan signed and ratified a treaty to delimit their land border as well.

In the several cases of border tensions (as between Uzbekistan and Tajikistan in 1998, Turkmenistan and Uzbekistan in 2004, Kazakhstan and Uzbekistan in 2005, and Uzbekistan and Kyrgyzstan in 2005), Moscow took no public stand but was probably trying to calm tensions behind the scenes. An open conflict between any two Central Asian states would be most embarrassing for Moscow, which prefers to avoid taking sides in a region where it believes Russia should be the ultimate arbiter. However, in the mid- and late-1990s Moscow was probably supporting Dushanbe and trying to constrain Tashkent.[34]

Meanwhile, the new borders, initially soft and transparent, have gradually "hardened." Moscow's early idea of keeping borders inside the CIS fully open, but guarding and policing the external ones (that is, those with non-CIS states) eventually fell flat. For all its outward "pragmatism," the "dual border policy" was too openly neoimperialist for the Central Asians' taste. Uzbekistan had no tolerance for the presence of Russian border guards on its territory. Kazakhstan acted in a similar fashion, but avoided confrontation. In 1999 Russia had to leave the Kyrgyz-Chinese border to the local Kyrgyz guards, and in 2004 the Tajik-Afghan border came under Dushanbe's exclusive control. The Turkmen-Russian arrangement of 1992, which called for a joint command of border guards, quietly disappeared, with Ashgabat gaining exclusive control of its borders.

On the other hand, traveling between Russia and all Central Asian states, except isolationist Turkmenistan, is still fairly easy, with no requirement for visas.

Stemming the Drug Trade

Since the early 1990s, the production of drugs in Afghanistan—first opium (just under 90 percent of global production) and later heroin—has been increasing and by 2006 production of opium had risen to 5,600 tons a year, 17 times more than second-placed Myanmar.[35] The proceeds from the narcotics trade are estimated at 30 billion dollars.[36] Russia and its Central Asian allies are transit countries (with illicit drugs being trafficked to Europe) and, increasingly, markets for narcotics trade.[37] The number of drug addicts in Russia is estimated to be around three million. Organized crime networks that operate drug trafficking rings in Russia and other CIS countries are a major threat to their domestic security. They have links to Islamist radicals, who use the proceeds from the narcotics trade to buy arms, recruit fighters, and bribe government officials. These networks also reach out to high officials in Central Asia and Russia itself, thus corrupting and criminalizing the states concerned. Tajikistan, which in September 2005 formally took over from Russia exclusive control over its border with Afghanistan, has become a producer of drugs. In Kyrgyzstan, after Akaev's ouster in 2005, politics has become overtly criminalized. There are indications that Turkmenistan has become involved in drug trafficking at the state level, and Ashgabat has refused to cooperate on antinarcotics measures with Moscow and others in the region. As elsewhere throughout the Muslim world, widespread government corruption is one of the major reasons for popular disaffection and radicalization under Islamist slogans. Moscow, however, does recognize that Iran, where thousands of trafficking gangs operate, is "waging a real war" on drug traffickers.

By contrast, Moscow is disappointed, even cynical, about the laissez-faire attitude of the United States and NATO toward Afghan drug producers.[38] Since Washington's priority is to reconstitute Afghanistan, and attacking drug production is obviously destabilizing (and thereby makes it more difficult to defeat the Taliban), Moscow believes that the United States is "soft on drugs." In Russia's view, the United States and NATO have not responded seriously to its calls for active cooperation. This situation does not make the problems the Russians face any easier.

Nuclear Nonproliferation

When the Soviet Union broke up, Moscow's overriding security concern was the fate of the Soviet nuclear legacy. With regard to Central Asia, the immediate cause for anxiety was the complex of strategic land-based intercontinental ballistic missiles (ICBMs) deployed in Kazakhstan. There were fears at the time that Kazakhstan would become the world's first "Islamic nuclear power." Russia then worked closely with the United States to place all elements of the former Soviet nuclear might under its own control and on its own territory. By 1994, when Kazakhstan, Ukraine, and Belarus signed the Lisbon Protocol, pledging to remain nonnuclear states, the problem had been resolved.

In the mid-1990s there was growing fear that nuclear weapons experts and nuclear materials from Kazakhstan and other Central Asian states might find their way to the aspiring nuclear powers of the Middle East and Asia, especially Iran, and North Korea. The Russians had few means to stop that from happening, but they were jealous of American operations, such as "Topaz," which was aimed at buying up nuclear material locally in order to prevent its leakage to the unsavory regimes. Later, there were a few minor concerns associated with the uranium mining facilities in Tajikistan.

At present, however, Russia's principal nuclear concerns are focused on the immediate periphery of Central Asia. Moscow became very agitated when Pakistan became a nuclear power in 1998. Unlike India, an unproblematic country from the perspective of Russian security interests, Pakistan has had a long history of hostile relations with Moscow. In particular, Pakistan was a founding member of the CENTO (Central Treaty Organization) alliance and a base for American spy planes that, until 1960, routinely flew over the Soviet Union. During the Afghan war in the 1980s, Pakistan was the supply and support base for the anti-Soviet *mujahideen*. Finally, in the 1990s Islamabad supported the fundamentalist Taliban regime that took power in Afghanistan and that made common cause with the Chechens and militant Islamists in Central Asia. Thus, when the military overthrew the civilian government in Pakistan in 1999, Sergei Ivanov (then-secretary of the Russian Security Council) publicly worried about a "junta with nuclear missiles." It was only after 9/11 and the subsequent warming of Russian-Pakistani relations that Moscow ceased publicly to voice concerns about Pakistan's nuclear capabilities.

Moscow's attitude toward Iran's nuclear program is more ambivalent. The Russian government is probably as convinced as anyone that Iran seeks to acquire nuclear weapons. However, it draws different conclusions from those of the United States and its European allies. Basically, Russia fears two things: a nuclear- and missile-armed Iran (which would become a major regional power, including in the Caucasus-Caspian-Central Asia region), and a preventive attack by the United States to disarm Iran. In the latter case, Moscow is particularly concerned about the war's implications for regional security, as it would likely increase militant Islamism that could sweep away the secular regimes in Central Asia.

Specific Interests

Consolidating the Moscow-Led Security Alliance

To render the inevitable changes in Central Asian leadership less disturbing to Russia's role in the region, Moscow has been seeking to upgrade the Collective

Security Treaty Organization, the regional security pact, and to enlarge it by including all the countries in Central Asia. For several years after its signing in Tashkent in 1992 (which came soon after the fall of the Najibullah regime in Afghanistan), the Collective Security Treaty (CSI) was little more than a political declaration. It linked Russia to the countries in Central Asia (except Turkmenistan).[39] In 2000 Uzbekistan opted out of the treaty, citing the treaty's inability to repel an armed invasion, and joined the rival GUAM (Georgia-Ukraine-Azerbaijan-Moldova) grouping backed by the United States.

Since 1999 Moscow has been looking for ways to turn the ineffective CST into a real, and more cohesive security alliance. The war in Iraq stimulated those efforts. In April 2003, at a summit in Dushanbe, the members established the Collective Security Treaty Organization (CSTO).[40] It has a Collective Security Council, permanent Joint Staff, and some ground forces; it is essentially a scaled-down version of the Warsaw Pact. At the 2005 CIS summit in Kazan, Russia finally moved to end military cooperation at the CIS level, concentrating instead on the CSTO. Russia's clear goal was to include Uzbekistan in the CSTO, something to which Tashkent only agreed in late 2006, a year after signing a bilateral mutual security treaty with Russia.

Progress in alliance-building, however, has been slow. The CSTO managed to form, at least on paper, an antiterrorist collective rapid reaction force, numbering some 4,000 men, with headquarters in Bishkek. Kazakhstan and Kyrgyzstan field two battalions each, while Tajikistan and Russia have three each. There has been some confusion between the CSTO force and the CIS antiterrorist center, founded in 2000 and theoretically controlling a force of 1,500 men. The center has held annual exercises since 2002.

The next task for the CSTO would be to create a regional Southern Command to which Russian, Kazakh, Kyrgyz, and Tajik forces would be subordinated. The Southern Command's stated mission is to "contain a regional conflict." Similar groupings already exist on a bilateral basis between Russia and the two non-Central Asian members of the CSTO, Belarus and Armenia. With Tashkent's policy reversal in 2005, Moscow hopes to integrate Uzbekistan into the CSTO and thereby avert an easy defection the next time around. For their part, Uzbek authorities have come up with a draft agreement on a multinational rapid reaction "anti-revolutionary force" operating under the auspices of the CSTO.

This proposal would be a hard sell. When it comes to internal security, the CSTO is still largely a political instrument. Attempts to invoke it against the Tulip Revolution in Kyrgyzstan failed. The organization happily "slept through" the regime change in one of its member states. No joint military interventions, Warsaw Pact-style, are envisaged, even at the doctrinal level. The most one can expect are joint consultations in case of an impending crisis, but even that could be problematic. Central Asian leaders and elites are mutually envious and suspicious. The joint peacekeeping force in Tajikistan, composed of Russian, Kazakh, and Kyrgyz elements, became dysfunctional soon after it was established in 1993, and the operation had to be conducted by Russia alone. The attempt by the United States in the mid-1990s to create CENTRASBAT (a joint peacekeeping battalion with Uzbek, Kazakh, and Kyrgyz participation) also foundered. For Central Asian countries, even multilateral military alignments are essentially bilateral pacts between themselves and a senior outside partner.

Nevertheless, the CSTO member states are not exclusively oriented toward Russia. The members' foreign policies are only loosely coordinated. All members, including Russia, participate in the NATO-led Partnership for Peace program. Kazakhstan has an individual partnership program with NATO and a vibrant military cooperation program with the United States. It receives American support to build a small naval force in the Caspian. A small contingent of Kazakhstani army engineers has been serving with coalition forces in Iraq. After 9/11, Kazakhstan gave the U.S. Air Force landing rights at three air bases in the country's south. In 2005 Kyrgyzstan was able to withstand Russian pressure to follow the Uzbek example and did not expel the U.S. Air Force from the Manas base that it has been using since 2001. Instead, Kyrgyzstan raised the base lease one hundred-fold (to 200 million dollars a year). Uzbekistan, which still has not joined the CSTO despite the bilateral treaty with Russia, receives Ukrainian patrol boats purchased with American funds to patrol the Oxus (Amu-Darya) River border with Afghanistan. Tajikistan, having seen off the Russian border guards, started receiving assistance from the United States and China to strengthen its borders, while Russia broke its promise to deliver two helicopters. Dushanbe also signed a memorandum of understanding with the Iranian defense ministry.

Of course, the CSTO is one of the two principal multilateral instruments that Moscow has at its disposal in Central Asia, the other one being the Euro-Asian Economic Community. Both symbolize Russia's claim to a dominant role in the region. In Moscow's view, the U.S.-led antiterrorist coalition is a temporary phenomenon, whereas geopolitical alignments are a more permanent fixture. Russian claims to regional leadership, however, are more seriously challenged by the SCO: assigning it a security role would probably render the CSTO redundant. Some, however, support "combining the capabilities of the CSTO and the SCO" in order to "strengthen multipolarity."[41] But others reject that strategy and point to "important differences"[42] between the two bodies. Confining the SCO to the economic development area, however, runs the risk of undermining the EAEC.

Moscow has been vigorously promoting the CSTO on the world arena. It managed to gain observer status for the organization at the United Nations and recognition from the OSCE, but those gestures are devoid of any practical meaning. Moscow's efforts to win U.S. recognition for its role as the principal security manager of Central Asia have failed. It has also failed to induce NATO to establish alliance-to-alliance relations with the CSTO. Russia's offer to NATO to join efforts in fighting terrorism and interdicting drugs from Afghanistan has not been taken up, with no official reason given.[43] In the words of Stephen Blank, "insinuating the CSTO between NATO and individual Central Asian states would give Moscow considerably more say over the Atlantic alliance's activities in the region, effectively forestalling the ability of regional leaders to forge independent relationships with Brussels."[44] For its part, Moscow views this failure as evidence of Washington's divide-and-rule tactics, which are aimed at preventing the reestablishment of Russian primacy in Central Asia, and as an indication that the United States has its own designs on the region.

Alongside the CSTO, Russia has been trying to create a much looser multilateral security arrangement in the Caspian. To counteract Washington's plans for a Caspian Guard, which would link Azerbaijan and Kazakhstan to the United States, Moscow has proposed a Caspian Sea Force (CASFOR), which would be modeled on the BLACKSEAFOR (with Russian participation) and which would only include the six Caspian littoral states.

In the field of nonmilitary security, Russia has been using a permanent conference of the directors of national security councils to cement relations with local security agencies and interior ministries. Cooperation in the post-9/11 environment has become more intense. Border guards regularly conduct antinarcotics trafficking exercises under a CSTO umbrella. However, war on terror has become a useful pretext for the Central Asian countries to demand, and obtain, extradition from Russia of opposition politicians. Russia's Federal Security Service (FSB) has been cooperative: Moscow did not see much to be gained from sheltering the political enemies of its allies. As a result, Central Asian dissidents began to shun Moscow and to take refuge in Europe instead.

Besides the multilateral pact, Russia has concluded bilateral agreements with all Central Asian countries (except Turkmenistan), with provision for political consultations, joint strategic assessment, joint military planning, and joint operations. It concluded such an agreement with Kyrgyzstan in October 2001 and with Kazakhstan in June 2003. Moscow signed a treaty with Uzbekistan in November 2005, preceded by a July memorandum on military and technical aid that gave Russia access to ten Uzbek airfields.[45] Under the circumstances, these bilateral arrangements may prove more effective than the multilateral ones, although the CSTO could serve as a general rubric. Infrastructure and force deployments would be key.

Immediately following the dismantling of the Soviet Union, the Russian military sought to retain key elements of the Soviet-era defense and security infrastructure—above all, the well-fortified Soviet border and the Soviet air defense system. While the "dual border" policy has failed, the joint air defense system, formed in 1995 and formally placed under the CIS, for the most part is still intact. However, Turkmenistan withdrew in 1997, and Russia's cooperation with Uzbekistan has been on a bilateral basis.[46] There are regular air defense exercises among CSTO members, and Russia plans to fold the CIS system into an integrated CSTO arrangement. However, in strictly military terms, Moscow can only rely on its own rather modest military presence in the region.

In 2004, the 201st motorized infantry division—Russia's only combat all-arms unit in Tajikistan (with headquarters in Dushanbe)[47]—acquired the status of a military base. The division, some 6,000 men strong, a surviving element of the Soviet Army, fought to impose peace in the Tajik civil conflict in the 1990s, and for years served as a deterrent to keep in check the Islamist forces in Afghanistan. It also supported the Russian-led border troops on the Tajik-Afghan border. The current status of the base allows the division to stay in Tajikistan until the mid-twenty-first century. Russia also plans to deploy an air component to the base (some twenty fixed-wing aircraft and helicopters) at Aini airfield near Dushanbe.

Air power is becoming the main thrust of the Russian military presence in Central Asia. In September 2003, Russia established a new air base at Kant, Kyrgyzstan. Acclaimed by Putin as "an air haven of the Collective Rapid-Reaction Force,"[48] it is still a very modest deployment,[49] but with symbolic significance: the Russian military is returning to the region. It is also a reflection of the new realities where air power is more important against a new enemy, Islamist fighters and drug traffickers, than traditional motorized infantry and armored troops.

In the future, Russia may expand its military presence in Uzbekistan. When and if this occurs, it is likely to be a relatively small force that would be placed under CSTO auspices. Moscow sees the value of such a presence largely in terms of deterring Islamist rebels: an attack on Uzbekistan, under the November 2005 treaty, could be regarded as an attack against Russia.

Russia also has a noncombat military presence in Kazakhstan, where it leases four test ranges, including Emba and Sary Shagan, which are used to test ABM systems. The Baikonur Space Center, which had been the principal site for Soviet space launches from 1955 to 1991, is being converted to civilian commercial use. Russia's lease on the facility runs until 2050. While its military programs have been redirected to Plesetsk (Archangel oblast in northern Russia), most Russian commercial launches, including those under the International Space Station program, are handled from Baikonur.

Due to its geographical position, Central Asia offers Russia a good opportunity not only to launch spacecraft but also to look into outer space. In Tajikistan, Moscow rents a space monitoring radar station "Okno" ("Window") at Nurek, which is capable of tracking objects in space from 200 to 40,000 kilometers. Uzbekistan hosts a satellite tracking station at Kitab (near Samarkand and formerly part of an integrated Soviet system).

While the giant nuclear test range at Semipalatinsk has been closed since the late 1980s, Kazakhstan still offers Russia important facilities for uranium enrichment.[50] In addition, in Kyrgyzstan (on Lake Issyk-Kul), Russia maintains a naval torpedo testing facility and a naval communications station.

Russia has also concluded agreements with CSTO members and Uzbekistan that would give it access to local infrastructure and facilities. It is very important, from the Russian perspective, that the Central Asian states use the same weaponry, observe virtually the same military regulations as the Russian armed forces, and largely retain the Russian and Soviet military culture. Central Asian officers still speak, and even issue commands in, Russian. Interoperability is not an issue. It is very much in the Russian interest that this continues.

Defense Industrial Cooperation and Arms Transfers

After a period of ill-advised parsimony, Russia agreed, from the early 2000s, to supply arms and equipment to CSTO members at Russian domestic prices. Russia also promised to equip the "neutral" Turkmen navy.[51] Having lost the traditional arms markets in Central and Eastern Europe, Moscow now hopes to keep the Central Asian one.

Under the 2005 agreement with Tashkent, Moscow is supplying its ally not only with military hardware, such as transport (Mi-17) and attack (Mi-24) helicopters for airborne assault brigades, but also with riot control equipment.

After 1991, when the Soviet military industrial complex disintegrated, military-technical cooperation between Russia and the Central Asian states decreased: Moscow lacked the funds to keep defense enterprises, such as those in Kyrgyzstan, afloat, while its own defense industry was starving for contracts. Later, Russia decided, wherever possible, to concentrate defense production within its own borders. It was only toward the middle of this decade that new cooperation schemes became possible, as, for example, in the Russian-Uzbekistan agreement in 2005 for the joint production of Iliushin-76 transport planes for sale in China.

To promote pro-Russian sentiment among the Central Asian military elites, Moscow has also opened its military and security academies to Central Asian students.

Enhancing Russian Military Presence in the Region

Russia has been at war along the southern periphery for the past quarter century, virtually without interruption. It has been a painful experience. The Afghan war, with approximately 14,000 Soviet soldiers killed, was a major trauma. The first Chechen campaign was an utter disaster, followed by an ignominious truce. Russia's prestige as a military power sank to an all-time low in Central Asia as well. In 2000 Moscow threatened to bomb the training camps of Chechen fighters in Afghanistan, but later had to admit that it lacked resources to carry out the threat. The same year, Russia failed to come to the assistance of its ally Kyrgyzstan when it was invaded by Islamist rebels en route to Uzbekistan.

Russia realizes that it must first improve and enhance its own assets and power-projection capabilities. The southeastern strategic axis is receiving more attention. Plans have been announced to form a 50,000-strong rapid-reaction corps with headquarters at Omsk, in southern Siberia. The strategic aviation base at Engels, Saratov oblast, is likewise starting to look toward the southeast, not just westward. The air defense test range at Ashaluk, in Astrakhan oblast, regularly hosts Central Asian forces for joint exercises. Other major Russian military assets in close vicinity of Central Asia are the Strategic Rocket Force division at Novosibirsk and the missile forces test range at Kapustin Yar, in Astrakhan oblast.

Russia has been upgrading its obsolete Caspian flotilla (headquartered in Astrakhan) and in August 2002 resumed regular naval exercises. The flotilla, with two frigates and twelve patrol boats, is being reconfigured to address new security threats such as terrorist attacks against the oil and gas infrastructure in and around the Caspian, at once to provide security for commercial vessels and to combat drug trafficking and smuggling.

Once the dual border policy failed, Russia faced the need to police the border with Kazakhstan and, in fact, to rethink its very concept of border protection. Rather than Soviet-style perimeter defenses, Moscow has had to rely on various technical means as well as close collaboration with its neighbor. And where Russia has relinquished control of the border, as in Tajikistan, it can still give advice, share intelligence, and provide training.[52]

Can Russia itself be considered a threat to Central Asian security? The short answer, in the short- to medium-term, is "no." Although Moscow wants more influence, it does not seek more territory in Central Asia. Russia's military capabilities remain limited, and it lacks the capability to dominate the security landscape of the region, especially against the wishes of its principal countries, Kazakhstan and Uzbekistan.

Economic Interests

The importance of Central Asia to Russia, long believed to be marginal, has been steadily increasing. Gone are the days when Moscow regarded Central Asians as "ballast." The Euro-Asian Economic Community is taking shape. Of its members, Kazakhstan is the one country that can be integrated with Russia economically, thus giving the idea of a Eurasian power center an element of reality. In the eyes of the Kremlin, the key to Russia's current standing in the world is its resource power, which should make Russia indispensable to the rest of the world. Central Asian countries Kazakhstan and Turkmenistan are major producers of oil and gas. To make sure that they are linked to Russia by means of joint exploration, pipelines, and common policies is the overriding Russian interest. There are also interesting opportunities for Russian business elsewhere in Central Asia.

Free Trade, Customs Union, Economic Cooperation

Throughout the 1990s, attempts to reintegrate the former Soviet economic space were total failures. The only partial exception was the Customs Union formed by Russia, Belarus, and the Central Asian states of Kazakhstan, Kyrgyzstan, and Tajikistan. The union was not an unqualified success, a fact underlined in 1998 when Kyrgyzstan became its first (and so far only) member to join the World Trade Organization (WTO). In 2000 the same five nations decided to upgrade the union to form the EAEC, which, in addition to being a customs union, would also be a free trade area and serve as a coordinating mechanism on the way to WTO membership. The union has a solid economic rationale: Russia is still a major economic partner for all of its members, while Central Asia and southern Siberia could form a regional market of some 75 million people.

Russia's trade with Kazakhstan reached 8.1 billion dollars, which puts it in third place among Russia's CIS neighbors, behind Belarus and Ukraine (15 percent of Russia's trade with all CIS countries). For Kazakhstan, Russia accounts for just under one-quarter of its foreign trade. About 70 percent of Russia-Kazakhstan trade is concentrated in two adjoining oblasts.[53] At the other extreme, Russia-Kyrgyzstan trade is a minuscule 425 million dollars (0.1 percent of Russia's total trade turnover in 2004). For Kyrgyzstan, however, this trade is very important, constituting 20 percent of the country's foreign trade.

Kazakhstan and Russia: A Single Economic Space?

Within the CIS, *matryoshka*-type arrangements have been common. Apart from the CIS itself and the Customs Union, half-hearted attempts were made in the 1990s to promote Russia-Kazakhstan bilateral economic integration. They failed: the strategy of using financial and industrial groups as vehicles failed to overcome bureaucratic obstacles.[54] Over time, however, privatization in both countries and the resolution of the thorny debt issue have laid a much healthier foundation for the bilateral economic relationship.

In 2003, Russia and Kazakhstan, together with Belarus and Ukraine, signed an agreement on a Single Economic Space (SES). The purpose was to tie Ukraine to the Russia-centered economic integration project. As such, the SES has failed: no Ukrainian government, including, ironically, the one that signed the SES agreement, was willing to advance relations with Russia beyond a free trade area. With Ukraine de facto gone from the SES, Russia can actually move faster with the other two countries, Belarus and Kazakhstan. The potential for comprehensive integration with Belarus is undeniably greater than with Kazakhstan, but meaningful integration there is hampered by the Belarus president, Aleksandr Lukashenko, who uses the slogan of a union with Russia to keep the development of economic ties under tight personal control. In Kazakhstan, by contrast, no such barrier exists, and economic integration can move ahead. When it does, it will clearly be in both Russia's and Kazakhstan's interests.

The Energy Sector: Caspian Oil

Russia has several key objectives in the energy sector: to gain something like veto power regarding oil and gas exploration and transportation rules in the Caspian basin, to dominate the region's gas business and market; and to control hydroelectric power production.[55]

Caspian oil reserves range from 15 to 29 billion barrels, which represents between 1.5 and 2.8 percent of the world total. Approximately 70 percent of that oil is produced by Western companies.[56] Of all the littoral states, Kazakhstan has the largest share of oil wealth. Its production is expected to increase to 100 million tons by 2010 and to 150 million tons by 2015. Having lost the "Battle of the Caspian" in the 1990s to Western oil companies, Russia now seeks to increase its own companies' share of Kazakhstan's oil production and to channel the maximum amount possible through pipelines that traverse Russian territory.

At present, the Russian company LUKoil has a 15-percent share in the Karachaganak and 50 percent in the Kumkol oilfields. Between 1997 and 2004, LUKoil invested approximately 1.5 billion dollars in Kazakhstan; it plans to double that amount over the next few years. Russia and Kazakhstan agreed on the joint exploration of the northern Caspian shelf. In addition to the private company LUKoil, the state-owned Rosneft is also involved in the project. Under a 2005 production-sharing agreement, 50 percent of Kazakhstan's Kurmangazy oilfield (with reserves of 1 billion tons) will be owned by Rosneft and Zarubezhneft, and the other half by KazMunaiGaz.[57] The Kazakh company is involved in another joint venture with LUKoil in the Dostyk oilfield.

Russia has sought, largely unsuccessfully, to control Kazakhstan's oil exports. Since 2001, the Caspian Pipeline Consortium (CPC), with 24 percent owned by Russia, has been pumping oil from Tengiz, Karachaganak, and Kashagan to Russia's Black Sea port of Novorossiisk. These shipments are expected to rise from 28 million tons per year to 67 million tons. Russia also hoped to modernize the Atyrau-Samara pipeline to attract even more Kazakh oil shipments.[58] However, Astana has decided to diversify its exports. In 2005, it agreed to ship up to 20 million tons via the Baku-Tbilisi-Ceyhan pipeline, which Russia had long regarded as the principal rival of the CPC. Also in 2005, Kazakhstan and China opened a pipeline to Xinjiang. Though the project was later put on hold, there are plans to expand the pipeline's capacity from the initially projected 2 million to 6–9 million tons annually. Russia's oil transit policy has given an added incentive for diversification: transit tariffs for Kazakhstani oil companies are twice as high as those for their Russian counterparts.[59]

Natural Gas

Russia's oil reserves are significant, and its production impressive, but it is to natural gas that it increasingly owes its position as a leading energy producer. However, Russia's gas production has flattened at 550 billion cubic meters a year. Production in the main gas-producing province in Western Siberia has stagnated. Exploration of new gasfields in the Arctic (Shtokman) and in Eastern Siberia is costly. Meanwhile, loss-making domestic shipments are rising, as are Gazprom's lucrative international commitments.[60] To maintain the crucial gas balance, Gazprom has decided to buy gas from other sources. Moscow sees Central Asia, explored and developed in Soviet times mostly by Russian geologists and gasmen, as a natural add-on (with proven reserves of 5 trillion cubic meters) to Russia's own reserves. In the medium term, Russia would probably need to import up to 100 billion cubic meters a year from Central Asia.[61] As Russia's dependence on Central Asian natural gas grows, Gazprom, already dominant there, will seek to expand its role even further, primarily in Turkmenistan, which has one of the world's largest reserves of natural gas.

Russia seeks to tie Turkmenistan's gas to itself, isolating the country from other potential markets. The dependency on the sole pipeline linking

Turkmenistan to Russia has put limits on Turkmenistan's production, which reached 90 billion cubic meters a year in Soviet times.[62] Gazprom seeks to win control over Turkmen gas production (63 billion cubic meters in 2005) and to become the sole purchaser of Turkmen gas (with current gas exports amounting to 45 billion cubic meters).[63] In 2003, Gazprom bought Turkmen gas production for the next twenty-five years. It is set to import 30 billion cubic meters by 2006 and 70–80 billion cubic meters by 2007–8. Ashgabat's only option is to bargain over gas prices: these have increased from 44 dollars in 2005 to 65 dollars per 1,000 cubic meters in 2006. They are expected to continue to rise. President Niiazov's demands for ever higher prices threatens to undermine the Russian-Ukrainian gas deal of 4 January 2006.

On the whole, Moscow successfully uses Turkmenistan as a tool in its policy toward Ukraine, a major consumer of Turkmen gas (up to 40 billion cubic meters in 2006). The aim is to deny Kiev an opportunity to conclude separate deals with Ashgabat and hence to leave Ukraine wholly dependent on Moscow for energy supplies. A Ukrainian analyst claimed that Gazprom's efforts aimed at turning Central Asia into Russia's "gas caliphate."[64] The Russian-Ukrainian agreement of January 2006, reached after a brief halt in gas shipments to Ukraine from the first of the year, made Turkmen, Uzbek, and Kazakh gas shipments part of the Moscow-controlled new supply scheme.

In Uzbekistan, a relatively minor but very ambitious producer (54 billion cubic meters annually),[65] Gazprom wants to become a part-owner and the sole exporter of natural gas. Production-sharing agreements on the Urga, Kuanysh, and Akchalak gas fields are under consideration. Gazprom would also become the principal developer of Ustiurt plateau gas fields. It is ready to invest up to 1.5 billion dollars. Gazprom also plans to expand its purchases of Uzbek gas, until recently 5 to 6 billion cubic meters, to 9 billion cubic meters in 2006[66] and then to 17–18 billion cubic meters a year toward the end of the decade. This would provide Gazprom a guarantee against a possible reduction of gas shipments from Turkmenistan,[67] and thus give the company a stronger position to bargain over prices. Other Russian energy companies involved in Uzbekistan are Zarubezhneftegaz and LUKoil.

Russia also plans to supply Kyrgyzstan, Tajikistan, and southern Kazakhstan with the Uzbek gas produced by Gazprom. This would reduce Tashkent's political leverage over Bishkek; it would also make Kyrgyzstan even more beholden to Russia. Gazprom also wants to prospect for natural gas in Kyrgyzstan itself,[68] and it plans to modernize and construct new gas transportation facilities in that country.

Kazakhstan's gas production, although still small (16 billion cubic meters in 2004), is rapidly rising, with the expectation that it will reach 70 billion cubic meters by 2010. Russia entered Kazakhstan's gas market in 2002, when Gazprom started a 50–50 joint venture with KazMunaiGaz. This company, KazRosGaz, has been buying Kazakhstan's natural gas (from Karachaganak and Tengiz), and selling small portions to Western European customers. Within Kazakhstan itself, Gazprom has also been providing customers in the south of the country with natural gas from Western Siberia.

Gazprom operates gas transit from Turkmenistan across Uzbekistan and Kazakhstan. It hopes to become a part-owner of gas transit companies across the region. It is with a wary eye that it views proposals to construct a 1,000 mile-long pipeline (with a projected capacity of 30 billion cubic meters per year) from Turkmenistan to fast-growing, energy-hungry Pakistan (via Afghanistan),[69] or a trans-Caspian pipeline to Azerbaijan and then on to Turkey. Moscow has successfully stymied the trans-Caspian project, but at the price of giving Niiazov a free hand in Turkmenistan. It also managed to cobble together an alliance with Iran to oppose the pipeline to Pakistan. Moscow would not mind Tehran selling its gas to India, thereby locking up Turkmenistan's production inside the CIS.

As with Kazakhstan's oil, China is emerging as Russia's leading competitor in the region's natural gas industry. In 2006 Beijing offered to buy up to 30 billion cubic meters of Turkmenistan's gas per year via a pipeline to be built across Uzbekistan.[70] But the main problem facing Russia is the need to modernize the existing gas pipeline "Central Asia-Center" (i.e., European Russia), which was built in the 1970s. The pipeline's capacity will expand from the current 42 billion cubic meters to 55 billion cubic meters a year, but this is still below the projected production.

Hydropower

Since the early 1990s, the Russian electricity company (RAO UES) has been buying electric power stations in northern Kazakhstan. After 2000 the company became interested in exploiting the hydroelectric power potential of Kyrgyzstan and Tajikistan: RAO UES now plans to invest 1.9 billion dollars to construct two hydroelectric power stations in Kyrgyzstan and another 250 million dollars to complete another one in Tajikistan. Some of the electricity produced would be then used in southern Siberia, and part of it would be offered on the European market. More important, that would put Russia in control of the water resources of Central Asia as a whole, which could be even more important than control over gas pipelines.

Russia's leading aluminum producer, Rusal, plans to use the electricity generated by the Rogun hydroelectric power state for its aluminum plants in Tajikistan. Rusal's investment commitments reach 1.3 billion dollars.[71]

Other Economic Opportunities

Until the early 2000s, Russian investment activity in Central Asia was virtually nil. As a trade partner, Russia was falling far behind the West and Central Asia's other neighbors—Turkey, Iran, and especially China. Later, however, Russian businesses began to have more of a presence, while companies from other countries were in no hurry to expand beyond the energy sector. Unlike their Western counterparts, Russian businesses are accustomed to operating in an environment of lawlessness, bureaucratic dominance, and arbitrary rule. There is, of course, a limit to how much even the hardened Russian companies will tolerate.

As elsewhere in the CIS (e.g., Armenia, Moldova, and Ukraine), Russia has been trying to convert the outstanding debts of Central Asian countries into economic assets. Thus Moscow agreed to write off 500 million dollars in Uzbek debt in exchange for control over two aircraft plants, one in Tashkent (the Chkalov plant that builds the Iliushin-76 transport planes) and another in Chirchik (which repairs aircraft). In Kyrgyzstan, Russia is seeking a gradual takeover of the entire energy sector by Gazprom and RAO UES in return for writing off the 180 million dollar Kyrgyz debt.[72] In 2004 Russia cancelled Dushanbe's sovereign debt in return for a guarantee for a long-term Russian military presence.

Outside of the energy sector, Russian companies are particularly active in ferrous and nonferrous metallurgy, the chemical industry, and machine-building. The two main telecom competitors, Vympelcom and MTS, have been acquiring local companies in Kazakhstan, Uzbekistan, Kyrgyzstan, and Tajikistan.[73] In Kyrgyzstan, this led to an open conflict between the two Russian rivals. Russian businesses have also entered the food and textile industries. Typically, Russian companies either participate in joint ventures with Central Asian partners or establish wholly owned enterprises, the latter mostly in Kazakhstan.[74]

Final Thoughts on Economic Interests

Russia's economic interests in Central Asia are considerable. Only Kazakhstan, however, can be a partner in economic integration. In the regional oil exploration and export market, Russia is a secondary player, well behind the Western oil majors. In the natural gas area, however, it almost dominates, capitalizing on the Soviet-era infrastructure and the political and terrain difficulties of building new outlets. Over time, this advantage is likely to diminish. In the trade sector, Russia is a tertiary player, except in parts of Kazakhstan. In Central Asia, China is Russia's principal economic competitor, as is evident from trade statistics, access to energy sources, and pipeline routes. In the future, China's economic power is likely to continue to rise.

Humanitarian Interests

As used here, the term "humanitarian interests" is very broad. It refers to Moscow's concern for ethnic Russian minorities who reside in Central Asia, Russia's need of labor migrants from that region, the status of Russian language and culture in Central Asia, Russia's appeal for local elites, and the inclusion of the former borderlands into Russian "information space."

Russian Minorities

Central Asia is home to several million ethnic Russians. They are a legacy of the imperial drive in the late nineteenth century and subsequent Soviet resettlement policies—the early Bolshevik need to sovietize the region and to strengthen the industrial-worker component, the massive evacuation during World War II, and Nikita Khrushchev's initiative in 1954 to exploit "virgin lands" and thus drastically expand the area of agricultural cultivation in the USSR.

The migration began to reverse itself in the 1970s. As the republics of Central Asia gradually established their own ethnic elites, politically loyal to Moscow but increasingly masters at home, many ethnic Russians saw a dismal future for themselves and especially their children. They started returning to Russia, which offered better opportunities and a more hospitable social environment. The process was further abetted by the relative liberalization of private lives of Soviet citizens under Leonid Brezhnev as compared to Nikita Khrushchev's rule, not to mention Stalin's.

Still, by the time the Soviet Union was dissolved, 7.5 million ethnic Russians were still residing in Central Asia—approximately one-third of all Russians left outside the borders of the Russian Federation when the USSR broke up. The Soviet Union in principle guaranteed that all citizens were treated equally in all union republics; its dissolution became the prime reason for the exodus of ethnic Russians to the Russian Federation, where many had never lived and had no strong family connections. Between 1992 and 1998, 1.2 million ethnic Russians left Kazakhstan alone,[75] although the outflow later slowed (with only 20,000 arriving in Russia in 2000 and another 25,000 in 2001).[76] The civil war in Tajikistan, which had already broken out in early 1991, reduced the Russian population of that country from 380,000 in 1989 to 68,000 today.

Ethnic Russians permanently residing abroad are officially considered by

Moscow to be "compatriots," a vaguely defined term. Indeed, few are citizens of the Russian Federation. Out of 600,000 ethnic Russians in Kyrgyzstan, only 15 percent hold Russian passports. Central Asian Russians are undergoing an identity crisis. Some identify themselves with the Russian Federation, but many with the USSR; still others feel themselves members of the emerging communities in the new states. Moscow's protection of ethnic Russians in Central Asia has been far less vocal than in the two Baltic States of Latvia and Estonia, which refused to confer automatic citizenship on ethnic Russian residents at the time of the Soviet Union's dissolution. The situation in Central Asian states was of course different: they considered permanent residents eligible for citizenship. However, in contrast to the Baltic case, that was precisely the point of contention with Russia. Originally, Russia sought dual citizenship agreements with its Central Asian neighbors, but only Turkmenistan (in 1993) agreed. That, however, proved a trap for about 100,000 ethnic Russians when "Turkmenbashi" suddenly abrogated the accord in 2003. Moscow barely reacted: a year before, Ashgabat had agreed to make Gazprom the sole buyer of Turkmen natural gas. Indeed, gas is thicker than blood. Overall, the Russian government has been far less concerned about the practical issues relating to the Russian minorities in Central Asian states than has the OSCE.

Astonishingly, there was no public outcry in Russia about the fate of ethnic brethren in Central Asia. The population of Russia itself was too traumatized by the rapid change in political, economic, and social conditions. Individual survival became the principal preoccupation. There was no special welcome for Russians "returning home." Many of these former urban dwellers were referred to villages in central Russia experiencing population decline. Thus, not only did Russia fail to take advantage of the intellectual and professional expertise of its new citizens, but it created social tensions that were entirely unnecessary.

The majority of Russians, hearing stories of the woes of their friends in the "mother country," chose to stay in Central Asia. By the middle of this decade, in Kazakhstan they numbered 4.5 million people (about 30 percent of the country's population). Neighboring Kyrgyzstan is home to 600,000 Russians (11 percent of the population). In the three remaining countries, the Russian share is between 4 and 5 percent; in absolute numbers, they range from 1,150,000 in Uzbekistan to 240,000 in Turkmenistan to a negligible 68,000 in Tajikistan.

Thus, Kazakhstan stands apart from the rest of Central Asia. An autonomous republic within Soviet Russia until 1936, its first capital located in Orenburg (outside of Kazakhstan's present-day borders), and ethnically dominated by Russians and their fellow Slavs (Ukrainians and Belarusians) until the post-independence exodus, Kazakhstan always had been regarded as semi-Russian, or more. In 1989, two-thirds of the population of northern Kazakhstan was ethnically Russian. After 1991, they were fated to become the "Russian Question."

The "Russian Question," in essence, was this: would Kazakhstan's size-able Russian (Slav) population agree to live in a new state where Russians, although legally full-fledged citizens, must adapt to the reality of ethnic Kazakh rule, or would they seek to secede from the "artificial" state and try to link up with the nearby Russian Federation? The answer to that question was not immediately apparent after the break up of the USSR. Fifteen years later, Russian irredentism proved to be "the dog that did not bark." Moscow did not support the few and feeble attempts by local separatists; indeed, it was tolerant of Kazakhstan's 1999 clampdown on ethnic Russian activists in Ust-Kamenogorsk who were accused of seeking autonomy for eastern Kazakhstan.

Demographic Trends: The Challenge of Immigration

Russia's population, which expanded rapidly after 1945, peaked in the late 1980s and started to decline in 1992, with demographic projections for a major population loss in coming decades. The State Committee for Statistics (*Goskomstat*) estimates that even in the best-case scenario (an increase in the birth rate, higher life expectancy, a substantial influx of immigrants), Russia's population will only be 137 million by 2026 (compared to 143 million in 2005 and 147 million in 1991). The United Nations forecast, which expects some improvement in the factors mentioned above, predicts 131 million. Should the current negative trends be simply extrapolated, Russia's population could shrink to 125 million by 2026 and to 100 million by 2050 (which, incidentally, would be equal to the population of the Russian Republic in 1950).[77]

Until now, the decline has not seriously affected the working-age popula-tion, but from 2007 that will change. After 2010 the decline in this group will be steep, averaging 1 million persons annually. In twenty years, over a quarter of the Russian workforce, which in 2005 numbered approximately 65–67 million people, would be wiped out. If productivity remains relatively low, economic growth can only be sustained if a major boost in immigration compensates for the rapid contraction of the workforce. The problems that could be ameliorated by enhanced immigration include the looming deficit of the pension fund and the gradual depopulation of the Russian Far East and Siberia.

According to Russian demographers, migration has become critical to the country's fortunes in the twenty-first century. "The demographic blanket covering Russia has become too thin, and holes in it may start appearing soon," warns Zhanna Zaionchkovskaia of the Russian Academy of Sciences. "As a resource, labor will be more scarce than energy," adds Professor Anatolii Vishnevskii.[78]

Following the breakup of the Soviet Union, the Russian Federation has become a leading target of immigrants from around the world. From 1989 to 2002, it received 11 million people; from the early 1970s, when a gradual Russian exodus from the borderlands commenced, some 24 million came to the country. However, many of the new residents have been ethnic Russians; virtually all were Russian-speaking. As former citizens of the Soviet Union, they shared in many of the features of the common culture with those who lived in Russia. Their integration has been imperfect, and accompanied by massive abuses, but so far it has not resulted in a major social crisis.

Nevertheless, tensions have been mounting. A consensus is still lacking in Russia regarding the desirability of immigration. Even those who see the need for it usually emphasize strict immigration controls over the need to attract and integrate foreign workers. After years of laissez-faire practices, in 2004 Russia adopted a new law making it much more difficult to receive Russian citizenship. The law itself, and especially its implementation, have been severely criticized by liberal economists, demographers, and entrepreneurs. They argue that Russia should not only be open to immigrants from CIS countries (which in their view is insufficient), but also tap into the demographic potential of Asia, including China, Korea, and even Southeast Asia. By contrast, mainstream political forces warn that seeking new workers beyond the CIS is socially and politically risky.[79]

Whereas East Asians are still rare in Russia (the total number of Chinese in the Russian territory at any one time is estimated at 400,000), Central Asians have already arrived. They have therefore softened the demographic blow of the early and mid-1990s. In the decade following the dissolution of the USSR, Kazakhstan lost 2.5 million people, with about 1 million (mainly ethnic Germans) going to Germany and another 1.5 million Slavs moving to Russia. Barely any ethnic Kazakhs emigrated, however. The Tajiks, by contrast, who almost never left their republic in Soviet times, are now migrating in large numbers; the number of Tajik guest workers in Russia is estimated to be between 500,000 and 800,000—a significant proportion of the 6.5 million people in Tajikistan. The proportion is at least as high in Kyrgyzstan: up to a half million people (10 percent of the population) have gone north to Russia.[80] Uzbeks are also represented in Russia (about 500,000 migrants), but that is a much smaller proportion of a nation with 25 million people. Turkmenistan's isolationism has prevented any significant migration to Russia for work.

Tajiks, Kyrgyz, and Uzbeks are usually unskilled laborers in Russia. Many in Moscow clean streets, collect garbage, help on construction sites, or sell fruits and vegetables at the city markets. In these low-paid, poorly protected niches, they meet with no competition from the locals. A majority are clearly illegal workers. They are recruited through special, often shadowy networks that deliver laborers to Russian customers. In the vast number of cases, Central Asians are subject to various abuses. Nevertheless, even the low wages and the lack of labor protection that they receive in Russia are preferable to unemployment and misery at home.[81] The remittances that Central Asian workers send home not only help to keep their families afloat: they are comparable to the official development assistance given to their home countries.[82] On the other side of the ledger, without Central Asians the City of Moscow would become dysfunctional in a number of critical areas.

Over the next several decades, the population of Central Asia will grow at a rapid pace. Only Kazakhstan, according to UN demographers, will decline in population (1.3 percent by 2015). All others will register significant increases: 16.6 percent in Tajikistan, 18.6 percent in Kyrgyzstan, 22.8 percent in Uzbekistan, and 27.9 percent in Turkmenistan.[83] Fast growth will not taper off after that. Thus Central Asia represents a major source of potential immigrant labor for the Russian Federation.

The experience of Central Asian workers in Russia has been mixed. They have been able, on the whole, to settle into an environment that is multiethnic (especially in Moscow). There have been no major ethnic or religious clashes between these immigrants and Russians; Central Asians are much "quieter" and less conspicuous than people coming from the Caucasus. Nevertheless, they are also victims of Caucasophobia, Islamophobia, and other forms of chauvinism and racism that are now spreading in Russia. According to public opinion polls, 20 percent of the Russians are "irritated" by the presence of Muslim immigrants in their cities, 21 percent hostile, and 6 percent fearful. Only 50 percent are somewhat neutral. The majority (58 percent) demand that the Russian government expel illegal workers; only 36 percent favor their legalization.[84] Individual Tajiks and Uzbeks have been subjected to racial attacks; hundreds have lost their lives.[85] In a scandalous case in St. Petersburg in 2006, a jury gave a suspended sentence to young Russians convicted of stabbing to death a Tajik girl.

Advocates of immigration in Russia are not necessarily right. In Russia's economy, an apparent labor shortage masks an actual labor surplus, based on the economy's low productivity. From that perspective, stabilizing Russia's population at the current level (just above 140 million) cannot be a goal in itself. Fears of territorial loss resulting from a decline in population are overblown. Most of Russia's territory lies in an uninhabitable zone similar to northern Canada and Greenland and should not have been permanently settled in the first place.[86] Territorial defense along the long perimeter of the country's borders is a clear anachronism. An influx of alien workers, whether as permanent immigrants or semi-permanent guest workers, carries its own hazards. A situation where one-third of the population consists of immigrants and their descendants by 2050 (and two-thirds by 2100) could be socially and politically destabilizing. More important, it is the quality, rather than quantity, of the working population, and the productivity of the economy, that should be the principal concern of Russia's elites and society. Yet this does not mean that immigration should be unreasonably restricted. It is an important input for economic growth and needs careful attention.

Should Russia choose to rely on Central Asia as a labor resource, it would need to liberalize its immigration legislation; make sure that it is properly applied by a state apparatus (that is, the immigration service, border guards, and police) that would be substantially less corrupt and more professional than it is now; and adopt and implement a policy of education and integration of the new arrivals and the subsequent naturalization of those who meet the required criteria. That would also require a different climate in Russian society itself, starting with the main cities and emphasizing ethnic and religious tolerance, respect for human rights, and so forth. All this is, of course, a tall order.

Russian Language and Culture

Once dominant, Russian is still widely spoken across Central Asia, and not only by ethnic Russians, although the degree of proficiency varies. In Kazakhstan since 1995, and in Kyrgyzstan since 2000, Russian has had status allowing official use. In Kazakhstan, 85 percent of the population, and over 92 percent of the townspeople, speak Russian. This compares with 64 percent who speak Kazakh.[87] Thus, most Kazakhs are bilingual; very few Russians are. In Kyrgyzstan 1.5 million adults can speak Russian, two-thirds of whom are Kyrgyz. In the rest of Central Asia the decline of Russian has been precipitous. Language policies throughout the region favor the indigenous tongues, which are being phased into use in the government, administration, and everyday life, although Russian still enjoys special status as a language of interethnic communication.

Until recently, Central Asian elites were thoroughly Russified. Kazakhstan's education system still keeps Russian as a language of instruction, on par with Kazakh. About half of Kazakhstan's high school pupils and two-thirds of university students opt for Russian-language education. Astana is home of the Lev Gumilev Eurasian University; it also has a branch division of the prestigious Moscow State University. A large number of Kazakh students (11,000) currently study in the Russian Federation, including 400 at Moscow State University and 30 at the Moscow State Institute for International Relations.[88] In Kyrgyzstan, however, only 25 percent of the high school pupils attend Russian schools. Bishkek has a Slavic University and several branches of Russian universities. Dushanbe hosts a Russian-Tajik Slavic University, and 800 Tajik university students study in Russia.[89]

Of late, Moscow has openly affirmed that its interests across the former Soviet space demand that the education and socialization of local elites in the Russian Federation and in the Russian language at home be on a large scale. That would have the effect of keeping the region culturally within the Russian sphere of influence. Russophone Central Asian rulers are seen as a guarantee of the continuing secular nature of the local regimes and hence a barrier to Islamism. At the same time, such cultural affinity would give Moscow an edge over its great-power competitors, America and China.

A Common Information Space?

Since the demise of the Soviet Union, the reach of Moscow-based media has sharply decreased in Central Asia. Television broadcasting now reaches only part of Kazakhstan. Similarly, radio broadcasting in the medium wave band has virtually disappeared. Most Moscow newspapers have minuscule print runs and are not readily available even in Russia's provincial centers, not to speak of the neighboring countries.

Still, the Russian media are not completely gone. Even in Turkmenistan, Moscow TV channels are available by cable or satellite. Popular Moscow papers—are printed in Central Asian capitals. Several major publications (*Kommersant Daily* and *Ekspert* weekly) have local editions in Kazakhstan. Even more striking, local Russian-language media dominate the market in Kazakhstan and Kyrgyzstan, where they account for roughly 70 percent of the print runs and broadcast time.

Clearly, the common information space that existed in Soviet times is a thing of the past. However, the Russian electronic and print media relatively closely follow developments in Central Asia, have a network of correspondents in the region, and write with relative freedom (in comparison to the local TV and press). Russian media reports, in turn, are closely followed by the local governments and publics and can have a considerable impact. Immediately following the Andijon riots in May 2005, President Islam Karimov of Uzbekistan publicly railed against the Russian media reporting on the government's use of force. Improbably, he called the Russian coverage more hostile to his government than Western reporting. This outburst could be explained by the fact that the Russian media have a vastly larger audience than Western broadcasts and that for older generations Moscow's views still carry some authority.

In sum, Russia's humanitarian interests in Central Asia are wide-ranging and genuine. Russia faces extraordinary and virtually unprecedented challenges related to building a post-imperial nation. How is it to relate to "compatriots," who share its culture and the language, but are citizens of independent states? How is it to tap into the migrant labor resource without creating instability in Russian cities? How is it to preserve a modicum of Russian language proficiency among the region's elites even as Russia is losing out in the global information marketplace?

Policies, Policymakers, and Actors

The Russian government is routinely accused of having no policy toward Central Asia. Similar accusations, however, are leveled against Moscow's foreign policy in other parts of the world. It is true, of course, that amidst the upheaval that followed the collapse of the Soviet Union, one could hardly talk of a consistent policy or institutionalized policymaking. Nevertheless, if policy is seen as the outcome of an interplay of competing interests (not the implementation of some carefully designed blueprint), Russia could be said to have had several successive identifiable policies.

Another frequent criticism relates to the regional versus country-specific approach: namely, the Russian government is said to have no region-wide concept of Central Asia. Its approaches to Kazakhstan, Uzbekistan, Turkmenistan, Tajikistan, and Kyrgyzstan are poorly coordinated. In principle, this is true. However, as noted earlier, the degree to which Central Asia constitutes a region is debatable. From any Russian perspective, Kazakhstan stands out as being of qualitatively greater importance than the rest of Central Asia. Moreover, the countries in the region tend to emphasize bilateral links with outside players rather than cooperate in a common regional approach.

An overview of the principal trends in Russian policymaking and implementation shows that outcomes generally have not been the result of conscious and well-conceived policies toward Central Asia. The main goal of this section is to address the question of who makes Moscow's Central Asian policy—that is, who are the principal actors in the policymaking process and in implementing the outcome of those deliberations.

A Succession of Policies: "Leave and Forget," "Outposts as Placeholders," "Reconquista"

Since 1991, Moscow's policies toward Central Asia have gone through several evolutionary phases. The first policy was that of abandonment and voluntary withdrawal. The Russian democrats who came to power in August 1991 were not interested in reviving Gorbachev's plan of a Soviet confederacy. All republics other than Russia were considered a burden, and Central Asia's five, the greatest onus of all. Central Asian states were invited to join the CIS only as an afterthought. The end of the ruble zone in 1993 was the final act of Russia's liberation from its former borderlands. Concurrently, Moscow cut off support for the Najibullah regime in Kabul, which had been able to hold out against the *mujahideen* after the Soviet army withdrew in March 1989. The "Afghan syndrome" (which could be summed up as "cut and run") was a major reason for Moscow's decision to leave Central Asia to its own devices.

The "leave and forget" phase was short-lived, succeeded by what could be described as the creation of outposts to serve as placeholders for Moscow's eventual return. Russia's retreat to the north continued, but slowed. Dangerous developments in Central Asia made Russia pay more attention to the region. Reluctantly, Moscow had to take sides in Tajikistan's civil war,[90] as it decided to maintain a limited combat military presence in the war-torn country. Realizing that the demise of the USSR left it with totally unprotected borders, Russia sought to keep control of the Tajik and Kyrgyz land borders and to revive the former Soviet air defense system.

The "outposts as placeholders" policy, lasting from 1992 until 1999, was not a success by its own standards. Despite Yeltsin's pronouncements favoring CIS integration,[91] Russia continued its retreat from Central Asia, enabling outsiders to move in. The initial scare over Ankara building a community of Turkic-speaking countries from Azerbaijan to Central Asia quickly subsided, as did fears that Iran would export Islamic revolution to the region. However, Russia looked on passively as Western companies began to develop Caspian oil reserves. Moscow also suffered a major political defeat when the United States backed plans to build pipelines from the Caspian to the world market that did not go through Russia, thereby undercutting Russia's monopoly on Caspian oil transit. The idea of an East-West transit route from China to Central Asia across the Caspian to the Caucasus and on to Europe, popularized as a "New Silk Road" and discussed within the TRASECA project,[92] appeared to Russia as a deliberate slight: Russia, which traditionally saw itself as the East-West mediator, was de facto left out. At the same time, the new states of Central Asia were busy reestablishing links to their immediate neighbors, from China to Iran. In October 1996, the *mujahideen*, Russia's enemies-turned-allies in Afghanistan, were driven from Kabul by the Taliban, who seemed to pose a credible threat to stability in Central Asia and even to Muslim areas within the Russian Federation itself. All Moscow could do was to dispatch Prime Minister Viktor Chernomyrdin to a regional summit in Almaty. Finally, and most importantly, Russia suffered a major defeat in the war in Chechnya. The 1996 Khasaviurt peace agreement and the 1997 treaty between Moscow and

Groznyi reverberated across the southern region of the former Soviet Union, sending Russia's prestige to an all-time low.

The third phase of Russia's policy started in 2000. Moscow, at last, re-awakened to the gravity of the problems coming from south of its border. The second war campaign in Chechnya, resulting in the separatists' military defeat, heralded Russia's reassertion of initiative in the North Caucasus. Putin, the new president, re-energized Russia's engagement in Central Asia. Political dialogue between the Russian leader and his Central Asian counterparts became much more active and substantive. Russia sought to build a broad-based international anti-Taliban coalition that would include the United States, Iran, and India.[93] Moscow leveled direct military threats against the Taliban to force it to cease giving assistance and support to the Chechen separatists.[94]

But Russia still lacked sufficient resources for such an expanded engagement. The war in Chechnya, despite the seizure of Groznyi, dragged on; Moscow never delivered the promised strikes against the Taliban. On the contrary, in 1999 and again in 2000 Russia failed to prevent incursions by armed Islamists into Kyrgyzstan and Uzbekistan. Unable to come to their assistance, Moscow left Bishkek and Tashkent to deal with the crises themselves. In Afghanistan the Northern Alliance, which had Moscow's support, continued to lose the war. The Collective Security Treaty, prolonged in 1999 (but this time without Uzbekistan, and Turkmenistan had never joined), was proving an ineffective security instrument.

The events of 11 September 2001 and its aftermath led to a fundamental change in the regional situation. Suddenly, Central Asia appeared on Washington's radar screen as the United States began to plan a military operation in Afghanistan. In Martha Brill Olcott's words, the arrival of the American bases "marked the end of the Russian and Soviet empires."[95] In reality, the United States was filling a void created by Russia's withdrawal. Putin's famous "strategic decision" to align Russia with the United States in the war on terror in effect represented Moscow's acceptance of a U.S. military presence in Central Asia.[96] The decision was essentially a pragmatic move, designed to use the opportunity as a way to forge a new U.S.-Russia relationship. Putin must have suspected that some Central Asian states (for example, Uzbekistan and Kyrgyzstan) would in any case ignore a Russian protest against military deployments by the United States, which would be a shattering blow to Russia's position in the region. On the positive side, the Kremlin hoped that the new relationship with Washington would be based on a general understanding that Russia would become a major American ally in exchange for recognition of Russia's predominant position in the CIS.

Putin's approach was a clear case of political leadership. Most of his colleagues reluctantly agreed to follow. Senior Russian officials insisted that the

American presence in Central Asia could only be temporary, strictly tied to the situation in Afghanistan, and conditional upon Moscow's good will. The United States generally perceived Russia to be a weak player, trying to keep up the pretence of being a great power, but hardly a serious competitor.[97] As hopes for a wide-ranging strategic agreement between Russia and the United States faded and ultimately dissipated, Moscow's policies hardened. Namely, it endeavored to establish closer ties with individual Central Asian states; to upgrade the multilateral organizations that Russia led (such as the Euro-Asian Economic Community and the Collective Security Treaty Organization), and to work together with China as de facto coleaders within the now institutionalized Shanghai Cooperation Organization.

Thus, from late 2003, Russia embarked on something that might be termed a *reconquista* policy, aimed at regaining positions temporarily forfeited to the United States, at restoring the "natural borders of Russian influence,"[98] and at reconstituting Russia as a regional power center for the entire post-Soviet space. In Central Asia, Moscow focused on Uzbekistan, where the first stirrings of a succession struggle were becoming evident. The policy bore fruit: already in June 2004, a year before Andijon, when Russia and Uzbekistan upgraded their relations to that of "strategic partnership."

A corollary to that policy has been "revolution-prevention." The Rose Revolution in Georgia (November and December 2003) and the Orange Revolution in Ukraine (exactly one year later) sent shock waves across the CIS. Moscow saw these revolutions, and the one that preceded it in Belgrade in 2000, which toppled Slobodan Milošević, as Washington-inspired ploys to tear the newly independent states away from Russia and to draw them into the Western sphere of influence. The fallout from the 2004 Ukrainian presidential election, where the Kremlin and Putin personally suffered a humiliating fiasco, was particularly intense.

Within less than a year, however, Moscow rebounded. Although it appeared almost desperate in early 2005, it regained confidence later in the year. Russia did not expect the toppling of Kyrgyzstan's President Askar Akaev in March 2005, but unlike its actions during the Orange Revolution in Ukraine, it did not make serious blunders. Rather, having learned its lessons from Ukraine, it reached out to opposition leaders ahead of the parliamentary election and did not denounce them when Moscow's preferred leader in Bishkek was chased out of office and the opposition formed a new government. Although Russia did give refuge to Akaev and his family, it actively helped broker a deal between the two new strongmen, Kurmanbek Bakiev and Feliks Kulov, as they prepared to run for the Kyrgyz presidency in July 2005. Russia also saw to it that people deemed too close to the United States, such as the new foreign minister Roza Otunbaeva, were excluded from the new administration.

The challenges that Moscow-backed regimes in Tajikistan and Kazakh-stan faced in the parliamentary and presidential elections held in 2005 were relatively minor. Moscow made clear that it supported the local rulers against the "orange plague." Russian political technologists, some with close links to the Kremlin, worked under contract for the governments of Kazakhstan.[99] To many observers, it seemed natural that the Kremlin "tsar" would support the "sultans." In the view of Central Asia's liberal politicians, this ran the danger of making Russia a "gendarme" of the region, risking its treasure and political capital to support the current regimes.[100] In reality, Moscow was so obsessed with stability that it grasped for a remedy that would banish the disease for a time rather than treat it, at the risk of making the next attack far worse.

Russia's true triumph in Central Asia, however, was in Uzbekistan—the one country that had defied Moscow's influence through most of the post-Soviet period. Ironically, Moscow owed this singular success to its rival, Washing-ton. While American attitudes toward the authoritarian regime in Tashkent were becoming more ambivalent in 2003 and 2004, President Islam Karimov was pursuing a policy of reinsurance by strengthening links to Moscow and Beijing. Karimov, however, did not contemplate a full break with the United States. The initiative was not his.

Karimov's change of heart resulted from a shift in American attitudes. Those in Washington who saw Uzbekistan as a valuable ally and a useful platform in the war on terror in Afghanistan were eventually overruled by those who argued that the authoritarian regime of Karimov and the brutalities of its security services were a liability and a time bomb waiting to go off. In late 2004 and early 2005 Realpolitik finally gave way to a policy seeking to promote liberty and democracy. That approach had the effect of driving Uzbekistan into the arms of Russia.

The Russians were watching this closely. After the suppression of the Andijon revolt (12–13 May 2005), Moscow threw its support behind Kari-mov, even as first the European Union and then the United States, after a brief pause, condemned the use of force by Uzbek authorities and demanded an international inquiry. In response, Karimov publicly accused the West of being behind the plot to overthrow his government and to bring pro-Western liberal reformers to power. Putin was on record stating that the Russian se-curity services had apprised their Uzbek counterparts of the rebels' activities and their movements in the region. Informally, Russian officials blamed the United States for the attempt to destabilize Uzbekistan.

Tellingly, however, Karimov's first foreign trip after Andijon was to China, not Russia. After consultations in Beijing, he then issued his demand that the United States withdraw its air force planes and personnel from Uzbekistan. Hence Russia did not lead, but *joined* Uzbekistan and China in demanding that the United States leave its military bases in Central Asia. When the issue was put on the agenda of the SCO summit in June 2005, Russia cosponsored the resolution. However, it was clear to serious Russian observers that, while the use of the Soviet-built airfield in Central Asia was emotionally and psychologically unpalatable to Russia, the American presence in the region was a real security problem for China, which had a policy of treating both Central Asia and Russia as its strategic rear.

The removal of American air power from Uzbekistan encouraged those Russians who saw this as the beginning of a counteroffensive that could help reclaim territories lost to Western political influence in the 1990s. Thus Russia was able to capitalize on the disappointment the Central Asian governments felt over their relations with the United States.[101] Interestingly and tellingly, however, the SCO decision was not enforced. Moscow tried hard to persuade Kyrgyzstan to follow suit and expel the U.S. forces from the Manas base. The effort failed: the Kyrgyz explained to Moscow that the American financial contribution was essential for the small republic's budget. Russia, of course, was unwilling to compensate for the loss of U.S. funding, but applied no pressure. As noted earlier, Bishkek later cited Russian pressure and managed to raise the lease of the airbase 100 times, to $200 million.[102]

Even though the United States could still redeploy its planes from Uzbekistan's K2 to Afghanistan's Bagram and Kyrgyzstan's Manas airfields, Moscow celebrated a major victory. Uzbekistan was moving quickly into the Russian orbit. In November 2005 it signed a treaty of alliance with Russia, and in January 2006 it joined the EAEC. Moscow had thus acquired a "second pillar" in Central Asia. Russia has "regained" Uzbekistan, the most populous nation and, after Kazakhstan, the largest country.[103] Russia's next objective is to integrate Uzbekistan into the CSTO.

In 2005, Russia displayed the widest array of military activity in Asia: naval maneuvers in the Caspian, air defense exercises at the Ashuluk test range near Astrakhan, and the first-ever bilateral exercises in Uzbekistan,[104] India, and China. In 2006 Russia held joint maneuvers with Kyrgyzstan. But much of this is geopolitical symbolism, with little relevance to the situation on the ground. Russian resources in this critical region are definitely subcritical. With both Kazakhstan and Uzbekistan, the region's two biggest states, having become Russian allies, Moscow's policy in Central Asia must become more balanced and sophisticated.

In recent years Russia has been rediscovering Central Asia as an object of economic expansion. In 2005 the Moscow-led EAEC absorbed the Central Asian Cooperation Organization, which Russia only joined in October 2004.

In March 2002 Russia signed a declaration with Kazakhstan, Turkmenistan, and Uzbekistan on energy cooperation and protection of the interests of gas producers—described in the press as a "gas OPEC.")[105] Then Gazprom concluded long-term agreements with Turkmenistan and Uzbekistan, thereby establishing its dominant position in the region. Russia has been seeking to buy Central Asian gas from its producers rather than grant them access to Gazprom's export pipelines to Europe. The link to Ashgabat allowed Moscow to deny Kiev an option of buying Turkmen gas directly and thereby achieving energy independence from Russia.

Major Russian energy companies (for example, Gazprom, Rosneft, LUKoil, and RAO UES) and metal producers (such as Rusal) have announced investment projects in all five states.

In the humanitarian field, Moscow has also begun to act. In his annual report to the Federal Assembly in April 2005, Putin highlighted "the civilizing mission of the Russian nation on the Eurasian continent." Albeit on a modest scale, Russia has begun to donate books to Russian-language schools and universities.

Very importantly, in 2006 Russia liberalized its migration legislation, making it easier for millions of illegal workers, including many from Central Asia, to come out of the shadows, register and, if they wish, become permanent residents or citizens of the Russian Federation.

Recognizing the extremely negative image generated by a quarter-century of continuous wars against various Muslim adversaries, Moscow has been endeavoring to reach out to the Muslim world. In 2004 it joined the Organization of the Islamic Conference as an observer, with Putin personally addressing its annual summit. In 2005, during a stopover in Groznyi, Putin proclaimed Russia the defender of Islam.

Policymakers and Other Actors

The standard critique on Russian foreign policy (in general, and in particular with respect to Central Asia) emphasizes its lack of coordination.[106] This is largely true, but of course not unique to Central Asia.

Foreign policy matters in Russia generally can be categorized in one of two ways. The smaller category, which could be called "the Kremlin file," concerns issues of exceptional geopolitical, economic, or strategic importance, especially those that affect the interests of the Kremlin leadership directly, or even personally. These are resolved by the president, on advice from his administration, using mainly information and analysis furnished by the Russian security services. These "presidential issues" are normally handled by the Kremlin apparatus. It is the presidential administration in Moscow that speaks directly with its counterparts in Central Asian capitals. Summit diplomacy is the principal tool for resolving critical issues. Whereas Yeltsin favored CIS-wide gatherings, Putin has dramatically increased the number of direct meetings with his Central Asian counterparts. In 2005 he established a special office within the Kremlin administration to oversee inter-elite contacts with the newly independent states.

All other business falls into the far larger category, which is handled by a plethora of government ministries, agencies, and committees. Since the abolition of the short-lived Ministry for CIS Affairs, the principal agent in dealing with Central Asia is the Russian Ministry of Foreign Affairs (MFA). The MFA's Third Department of CIS countries conducts day-to-day business with the governments of Central Asia. Russian ambassadors in the region's capitals are mostly career diplomats and normally keep a low profile. Only a few have become known outside the MFA—for example, Dmitrii Riurikov (Yeltsin's former foreign policy adviser, who served as ambassador in Tashkent) and Ramazan Abdulatipov (former cabinet minister and former Duma deputy serving in Dushanbe). No Russian ambassador today has privileged access to the host country's leadership. Occasionally, Russian diplomats are accused of having been "bought off" by Central Asian regimes and turned into the agents of the local rulers rather than defenders of Russian national interests.[107]

The role of the Ministry of Defense (MOD) has declined since the early 1990s—a time when the army was the only Russian government presence on the ground in Central Asia. The MOD is particularly active where Russian forces are deployed (that is, Tajikistan and Kyrgyzstan). It also participates in military and security assistance programs with Uzbekistan. This ministry's main objective is to continue the institutionalization of CSTO and to raise its effectiveness. To make membership more attractive, Russia decided to provide nominal allies with weapons at subsidized prices and to open its military training and education programs to military personnel from Central Asia.[108]

The Russian security services have become an increasingly important player. Their most important function is to provide strategic and operational planning for the Kremlin and to oversee the implementation of policies. These services also maintain close contacts with their counterparts and often former colleagues in Central Asia. In principle, this may enable them to participate in "king-making" when the present leaders leave the scene.

Trade and economic issues fall into the province of the cabinet and the prime minister. Other important players in this field include the Ministries of Industry and Energy; Finance; and Trade and Economic Development.

Major Russian companies are partly owned by the state. In the energy sector, the government has assumed, under Putin, a dominant role. Gazprom and Rosneft are the two flagships of the state in the energy sector. In return, the government's slogan has been: "What's good for Gazprom is good for the country." It is the goal of Gazprom to become the world's largest company (now only ninth in capitalization).

Even the companies that used to be independent are now toeing the new line. LUKoil, which during the 1990s famously dissented from the government's view on the Caspian, openly declares: "We are simply a patriotic company and if the guidance from above is clear, we take it and act upon it."[109]

Anatoly Chubais, architect of Russian privatization in the 1990s, presently heads the leading electricity company (RAO UES), and is the country's most powerful behind-the-scenes liberal politician. In 2003 he advanced the idea of Russia as a new-look great power. In fact, he proposed[110] enhancement and consolidation of Russia's leading role in the post-Soviet space, powered by an expansion of Russian capitalism. In Chubais's vision, over the next half-century Russia's mission should be to build what he called a "liberal empire." His vision of a new empire, however, has elicited a generally negative reaction in Central Asia.

Russian regions, from Ekaterinburg to Novosibirsk, have a vested interest in expanding trade and economic ties with neighboring Kazakhstan, but they are concerned about illegal immigration, drug trafficking, and the potential impact of Islamist radicalism on their own Muslim populations.

Prospects

From the Russian perspective, the "time of the South"—ushered in by the cataclysmic developments of the late twentieth century—continues. Never has the South been as important to Russia as it is now. Central Asia, the biggest part of the former Soviet South, will be increasingly important to Russia, both for good (energy shipments, labor immigration, business opportunities) and for bad (instability).

In Central Asia, Russia is not an outside power, but the metropolis of a former empire. While dealing with the countries of the region, it enjoys great intimacy, but also bears a heavy legacy—for example, ecological disasters like the desiccation and destruction of the Aral Sea and the contamination at the Semipalatinsk nuclear test site.

In the medium term, Russia's main political problem is its relationship to authoritarian regimes in the region. At present, Moscow's position in Central Asia amounts to an unconditional embrace of authoritarians. Indeed, Moscow even prides itself on not placing any conditions on this cooperation, refusing to deal with the opposition and to nudge the local regimes to change. To persist in giving unqualified support would not only put Russia on the wrong side of history, but damage Russia's interests and generate, not prevent, instability.

Moscow, which has embraced Tashkent, will now bear a moral responsibility for what happens in Uzbekistan.

Moscow, however, has no idea how it should deal with the ever-more-likely sociopolitical crises in Uzbekistan, Turkmenistan, and Kyrgyzstan—which can fuel an upsurge of Islamist radicalism. With its focus on "fighting terrorism" and building up "antiterrorist centers," Moscow may be surprised by mass unrest that no antidote can counteract.

As shown in Kyrgyzstan, Moscow has scant knowledge (even less understanding) and limited capacity to deal with succession crises. The impending succession in Kazakhstan, Uzbekistan, and Turkmenistan will be of critical importance. It will hardly suffice merely to work at the level of the presidential palace or security service headquarters.

Russia's fundamental handicap lies in a host of factors: the nature of its own political regime; the quality of governance; the archaic geopolitics-dominated "software" of its foreign policy; the slow, uneven, and highly reluctant adjustment of security and defense policies to post-Cold War realities (in stark contrast to enlightened economic and financial policies). Russia's role in Central Asia would be greatly reduced, in contrast to the nineteenth and twentieth centuries, if it were permanently to cease being a force for modernization and instead to become a reactionary, conservative agent.

Thus far, Russia's policies have been lacking in both dynamism and vision. A region-wide strategic approach is wanting. Guidance and coordination among the various agencies involved in foreign policymaking is minimal and insufficient. The near-monopolization of foreign policy planning by the security services leads to its de-intellectualization. As a result, creative conceptualizing is replaced by simple stereotypes, policymaking is reduced to special operations planning and the use of "political technologies."[111]

Russia usually does not set the agenda, but reacts to events in its relations with the Central Asian countries. Even in the principal vehicles of Moscow's regional policy, CSTO and EAEC, Russia has not been actively promoting policy coordination among its allies. Now that Kazakhstan and Uzbekistan are in that category together, the task has become even more difficult.

Russia has not been able to find the right balance between the alliances where it is the leading member (CSTO and EAEC) and the wider grouping to which it belongs (SCO). Unsure of itself, it vacillates between attempts at regional leadership and occasional "bandwagoning" on China. Should these trends continue, Russia would steadily lose its influence vis-à-vis both China and the United States. In the event that Washington loses interest in Central Asia, Beijing would naturally be the prime beneficiary.

Russia has not been able to engage the United States for productive collaboration in Central Asia and Afghanistan. Russians overestimate the effect of American support for freedom and democracy in Central Asia, which they regard as a major destabilizing factor. This approach leads Moscow to offer even more unconditional support to the authoritarian and often repressive governments in the region, which leads to further deterioration of the political situation in Central Asia.

At the same time, the parallel unwillingness of the United States to engage Russia as a principal regional partner in Central Asia is tantamount to missing a major opportunity to stabilize an important region. The danger of desta-bilization of Uzbekistan, which has now shifted from American to Russian hands, should be sobering. Dealing with the narcotics problem in Afghanistan, likewise, requires a joint effort.

On the economic front, Russian government support for Russian business activity in Central Asia, outside of the major energy companies, is slight or nonexistent, energy sector is generally low.

Russia has been shy in its use of soft power. Moscow idly watches as the Russian language and culture are steadily vanishing in the region (except in Kazakhstan). Leaders like Kyrgyzstan's first president, Askar Akaev, who had spent seventeen years in Leningrad before returning to his native land to assume a position of prominence, are now unthinkable. Unless Russia dra-matically expands its program for Central Asian students, the former intimacy between the elites will be lost forever.

A key problem affecting Moscow's foreign policy in Central Asia derives from the fact that Russian officials are often rather arrogant and paternalistic in dealing with the former borderlands. This is especially damaging in rela-tions with the region's principal countries, Uzbekistan and Kazakhstan, but it affects others as well. Moscow must learn to treat these new countries with due respect.

Most important of all, Russia's appeal to Central Asians is limited.[112] That can only be changed if Russia acts to modernize the economy as well as the political and social systems in this region.

Conclusions and Policy Recommendations

Russia needs an integrated "southern strategy" to deal with the challenges of the Muslim world. The following could be the principles and building blocks for such a strategy:

• *Jettison the notion of the post-Soviet space; it is gone forever.*[113] Learn to deal with the Central Asian countries as independent states—as nations with a long history predating Russian rule. Renounce the traditional arrogance and condescending attitudes toward "under-states." Study the new states, their economies, policies, cultures, and languages.

• *Closely monitor potential trouble spots, starting with the Fergana Valley.*
• *Actively help the new states to grow stronger.* Focus on aiding modernization, while breaking it down into feasible components. Help improve state governance and administration by expanding the support base of the local regimes. Push the Central Asian regimes toward more openness and professionalism—and away from reliance on clan-based nomenklatura behavior patterns.

• *Reach out to rising elites.* Help them by offering education, socialization, internationalization, and opportunities in Russia. Emphasize education as the solid basis and vehicle of modernization. Create a large number of stipends for Central Asian students who want to study at Russian universities. Increase assistance to Russian-language programs at Central Asian schools and universities. Create a network of centers for Russian culture, science, and technology in Central Asia.

• *Reach out to Central Asian societies, not just governments.* Maintain working contacts with opposition figures and thus help to institutionalize civilized opposition. Reach out to mainstream Muslim clergy and moderate Islamists. Turn them into effective allies against Islamist radicals.

• *Improve the process for making foreign policy.* Develop a region-wide approach to Central Asia, along with country-specific strategies. Define the overall goals and particular policy objectives. Avoid utopian formulas like "zones of influence," "closed military blocs," and so forth. Be realistic: Russia can be a major outside player in the region, but it will no longer hold a monopoly on regional domination. When arbitrating between the states in the region, be an honest broker.

• *Promote economic integration with Kazakhstan.* Aiming for a common market on the basis of four freedoms (namely, free flow of goods, services, capital, and labor).

• *Focus on Uzbekistan as the key country south of Kazakhstan's border.* Help it improve governance and political and socioeconomic stability.

• *Develop the twin instruments of Russian policy, the CSTO and the EAEC.* Continue building the CSTO as a modern alliance (not as a clone of the defunct Warsaw Pact), focusing on antiterrorism and regional stability rather than old-fashioned defense. Adapt the Russian military and security services to the realities of the twenty-first century. Use Central Asia, the Caucasus, and the Greater Middle East context as the relevant external security environment that should shape the Russian armed forces and security agencies in the twenty-first century.

• *Treat allies and alliance commitments seriously.* Expand military assistance programs with Central Asian militaries, thereby enhancing their potential contribution to joint efforts. Focus on joint efforts to combat drug trafficking.

Cooperate in improving border security. However, do not let Russia's commitments go beyond its capabilities and a safe level of engagement. Avoid becoming embroiled in internal conflicts. Over-involvement, such as using military force to support an isolated governing clique against a mass rebellion, could lead to a disaster. Moscow should also make sure that the resources it is prepared to spend in the region will yield a commensurate payoff.

• *Regard the EAEC as an economic project first, not a geopolitical construct.* Do not attempt to reestablish Russia's former monopoly on economic relations with Central Asia.

• *Allow Central Asian workers to immigrate to and settle in Russia.* Also promote their integration into Russian society. Do not treat immigration as a quick-fix solution. Be prudent when seeking foreign labor. Focus on improving labor productivity, which is a safer and much more effective means to solve Russia's economic problems.

• *Do not attempt to become the sole security guarantor of Central Asia; that is beyond Russia's capacity.*

• *Learn to cooperate with other players for the common good.*

• *Recognize that, in Central Asia, the fundamental interests of Russia and the United States coincide.* Cease regarding the American presence in the region as inherently anti-Russian.

• *Cooperate with the United States, not just compete with it.* Engage the United States in a dialogue on regional security and development. Join efforts to strengthen the weak states through modernization programs. Develop a common approach to Islamist radicalism. Engage in serious information exchange and a joint strategic assessment for Central Asia and Afghanistan. Institutionalize these contacts. Create permanent structures, under the NATO-Russia Council, for diplomatic, security, and intelligence exchange and joint policy planning. Continue developing interoperability with U.S./NATO forces with an eye to Central Asia, Afghanistan, and the Greater Middle East. Promote an international initiative to interdict drug trafficking from Afghanistan. Offer the United States observer status within the SCO.

• *Strike a new balance in relations with the increasingly powerful China.* Recognize China's natural and legitimate interests in the region and its role as a major player in Central Asia. Avoid unnecessary overlap and confusion between the CSTO/EAEC, on the one hand, and the SCO, on the other.

• *Work toward a great-power concert in matters pertaining to Central Asian stability and security* (Russia, the United States, China, and India), the goal being to reduce conflict potential among the leading outside players and to emphasize cooperation over competition.

• *Conduct a major policy review of Russia's policies regarding the Greater Middle East.* Formulate new goals and objectives that transcend great-power competition. Future developments in Iran, Afghanistan, Pakistan, Iraq, the Persian Gulf, and between Israel and the Palestinians can profoundly affect the situation in Central Asia and Russian interests there. These issues and developments require close cooperation among the major powers.

Notes

1. Interestingly, this is also the distinction that the Moscow-based think tank, Council on Foreign and Defense Policy, makes in its 2006 annual paper.

2. This notion was first adduced by Prince Aleksandr Gorchakov, foreign minister of Russia in the second half of the nineteenth century.

3. As Irina Zviagel'skaia points out, Kazakhstan and northern Kyrgyzstan are part of the Eurasian steppe, traditionally populated by nomads, whereas Middle Asia with its desert oases and mountains has been an area of sedentary settlement. Being more mobile, and able to blend easily into the landscape, also in the cultural sense, they have little difficulty accepting external influence and adapting it to their own way of life. Cf. Irina Zviagel'skaia, "Russia and Central Asia: Problems of Security," in *Central Asia at the End of Transition*, ed. Boris Rumer (Armonk, NY: M.E. Sharpe, 2005), 71–72.

4. There was a parallel and concurrent renaming of "Mitteleuropa" ("Sredniaia Evropa," in Russian) as Central Europe. Reportedly, Uzbekistan's Islam Karimov felt one could extend the scope of Middle Asia to include Kazakhstan, but Nursultan Nazarbaev insisted on Central Asia as the common description of the region. Cf. Gennadii Evstafev, "Nekotorye razmyshleniia ob evoliutsii podkhodov SShA k problemam regional'noi bezopasnosti v Tsentral'noi Azii," in Azii. PIR-Center, *Arms Control and Security Letters*, no. 1 (164), February 2006.

5. Robert Legvold, ed., *Thinking Strategically: The Major Powers, Kazakhstan, and the Central Asian Nexus* (Cambridge MA: MIT Press, 2003).

6. S.B. Ippo, *Moskva i London. Istoricheskie, obshchestvennye i ekonomicheskie ocherki i issledovaniia* (Moskva: Universitetskaia tipografiia, 1888), 5–15.

7. *Istoriia vneshnei politiki Rossii. Vtoraia polovina XIX veka* (Moskva: Mezhdunarodnye otnosheniia, 1997), 88, 95.

8. Ibid., 115.

9. Entry for Kazakh SSR in *Sovetskaia istoricheskaia entsiklopediia*, 6 (Moskva: Sovetskaia entsiklopediia, 1965), 787–815.

10. *Nezavisimaia gazeta*, 25 September 2003.

11. Cf. Evgenii Vertlib, "Geostrategicheskie vyzovy bezopasnosti i stabil'nosti stranam Tsentral'noaziatskogo regiona" (http://www.regnum.ru), dated 24 January 2006.

12. Boris Rumer, "Central Asia. An Overview," in *Central Asia at the End of the Transition*, ed. B. Rumer 40.

13. Putin's controversial decision to invite Hamas leaders to Moscow in March 2006 was motivated primarily by the perceived need to raise Russia's profile among the Quartet members. The Hamas electoral victory was an opportunity to be exploited.

14. The leadership of Kazakhstan looks forward to assuming, in 2009, chairmanship of the Organization for Security and Cooperation in Europe.

15. Sultanov and Muzaparova, "Great Power Policies and Interests in Kazakhstan," in *Thinking Strategically*, ed. R. Legvold, 195–96.

16. Nursultan Nazarbaev's press conference in Moscow, 18 January 2005.

17. Cf., for example, statements by Andrei Grozin in an interview with Rosbalt News Agency on 20 November 2005. See www.rosbalt.ru/2005/11/20.

18. This is recognized even by the supporters of a "Russian union." Cf. Vitalii Tret'iakov, "Uzbekskii faktor," *Komsomol'skaia pravda*, 1 September 2005.

19. Sergei Karaganov, "Tsentral'naia Aziia: vozvrashchenie Rossii," *Rossiiskaia gazeta*, 9 December 2005.

20. After the 2005 popular revolt Moscow was rumored to have worked successfully behind the scenes to block parliamentary confirmation of Roza Otunbaeva, deemed to be "too pro-American," as Kyrgyzstan's foreign minister.

21. Especially after Rakhmonov's first visit there in December 2002.

22. Its 60,000 troops, plus border guards, were first placed under a joint command, and eventually formed the basis of Turkmenistan's armed forces.

23. For a thorough analysis of the situation in Central Asia, see Boris Rumer, ed., *Central Asia at the End of the Transition*.

24. President Putin's press conference of 31 January 2006 (http://www.president.kremlin.ru).

25. Sergei Ivanov, "Russia Must Be Strong," *Wall Street Journal*, 11 January 2006.

26. Nikolai Bordiuzha's interview is in *Nezavisimoe voennoe obozrenie*, 2006, no. 1 (13–19 January 2006), 2.

27. Mikhail Zygar and Dmitrii Butrin, "Goriuchii storonnik Islama Karimova," *Kommersant*, 19 January 2006.

28. Mikhail Margelov, "Evoliutsiia dlia Rossii," *Rossiiskaia gazeta*, 19 August 2005.

29. V. Naumkin, "Ekonomika—kliuch k bezopasnosti," *Strategiia Rossii*, 2005, no. 12 (December), 18.

30. Putin's statement at Kant, 23 October 2003 (http://www.president.kremlin.ru).

31. Some Russian analysts had predicted the United States would stay in Uzbekistan for up to 25 years. Cf. Dina Malysheva, "Tsentral'naia Aziia i iuzhnyi Kavkaz v 'postirakskom' geopoliticheskom kontektse," in *Tsentral'naia Aziia i Kavkaz. Nasuchchnye problemy*, ed. Boris Rumer (Almaty: East Point, 2003), 27–28.

32. Cf. Stephen Blank, "China Joins the Great Central Asian Base Race" (http://www.eurasianet.org), posted 16 November 2005.

33. All this despite the fact that Uzbekistan proceeded to mine its borders with Kyrgyzstan.

34. Following the Kudoiberdev raid into northern Tajikistan, Rakhmonov allowed opponents of Karimov in the Islamic Movement of Uzbekistan to use Tajik territory to mount operations in Uzbekistan. This could not have escaped Moscow's attention, but Russia apparently did not object to it: yet another case of Realpolitik. Cf. Sultan Akimbekov, "Rossiiskaia politika v Tsentral'noi Azii," *Pro et Contra* 5:3 (summer 2000), 75–88.

35. www.AsiaNews.it, December 4, 2006.

36. Sergei Ivanov's remarks at the meeting with NATO defense ministers in Berlin, 13–14 September 2005.

37. Cf. Sergei Luzianin, "Mezhdu politicheskim islamom i 'oranzhevoy demokratiei,'" *Nezavisimaia gazeta*, 24 January 2005.

38. Bordiuzha interview in *Nezavisimoe voennoe obozrenie*, 1–2.

39. Within the CIS, the only other countries that did not join were Ukraine and Moldova.

40. With Russia, Kazakhstan, Kyrgyzstan, and Tajikistan, as well as Armenia and Belarus, as members.

41. Sergei Permiakov, "Sblizhatsia s ODKB ne khotiat," *Voenno-promyshlennyi kur'er*, 2006, no. 2 (18/24 January 2006), 3.

42. Bordiuzha interview with *Nezavisimoe voennoe obozrenie*, 2.

43. Permiakov, "Sblizhatsia," 1.

44. Stephen Blank, "Russia Looks to Build a New Security System in Central Asia" posted (4 January 2006 on http://www.eurasianet.org).

45. This includes Fergana, Andijon, Kogayty, Chirchik, Karshi-Khanabad. Cf. Vladimir Mukhin, "Karimov razzhilsia vertoletami i vodometami," *Nezavisimaia gazeta*, 5 July 2005.

46. The Joint Air Defense System comprises some 20 command posts and 80 units of air defense systems, fighter aviation, and radar. Cf. Marcin Kaczmarski, "Russia Creates a New Security System to Replace the CIS" (posted 11 January 2006 on http://www.eurasianet.org).

47. The division's two regiments are located in Kuliab and Kurgan-Tybe.

48. Putin's statement at the Kant air base, 23 October 2003 (see http://www.president.kremlin.ru).

49. It is said to have five Su-25 ground attack aircraft, and four L-39 trainers, along with 350 to 500 servicemen. Plans call for additional deployment of seven Su-27 fighter bombers and two Mi-8 helicopters. The number of servicemen would double. See Oleg Sidorov, "Rossiiskaia politika v Tsentral'noi Azii," *Nezavisimyi obozrevatel'Stran Sodruzhestva*, 14 March 2005.

50. Naumkin, 41–42.

51. Mikhail Zygar and Natalia Grib, "Turkmenbashi vzyali v torg," *Kommersant*, 23 January 2006.

52. "S ukhodom rossiiskikh pogranichnikov vliianie Moskvy na Dushanbe oslablo," *Voenno-promyshlennyi kur'er*, 2005, 38 (105) (12/18 October 2005), 3.

53. "Torgovo-ekonomicheskie otnosheniia mezhdu RF i Respublikoi Kazakstan" (official brief by the Third CIS Department, Russian Foreign Ministry, 1 March 2005). See http://www.mid.ru.

54. Naumkin, 84.

55. Martha Brill Olcott, *Central Asia's Second Chance* (Washington: Carnegie Endowment for International Peace, 2005), p. 193.

56. Vladimir Sviridov, "Pritiazhenie Kaspiia," *Krasnaia zvezda*, 25 June 2005, 5.

57. Sergei Blagov, "Russia Seeks To Restore Its Role in the Caspian Region" (posted 19 July 2004 on http://www.eurasianet.org). In a parallel move, KazMunaiGaz bought 50 percent of the shares of Russia's Orenburg gas processing plant.

58. Sultan Akimbekov, "Rossiiskaia politika v Tsentral'noi Azii (sostoianie i perspektivy)," *Pro et Contra*, 5:3 (summer 2000), 75–88 (here p. 78).

59. Oleg Sidorov, "Aziatskoe napravlenie," *Perspektivy Moskvy* (posted 2 February 2006 on http://www.gazeta.kz).

60. Domestic shipments totaled 258 billion cubic meters in 2004 and 325 billion cubic meters in 2005; exports to the West are planned at 151 billion cubic meters in 2006 and are expected to rise to 163 billion cubic meters by 2008. See Daniel Kimmage, "Eurasia: Central Asian Gas Powers Regional Aspirations" (posted 25 January 2006 on http://www.eurasianet.org).

61. Jonathan Stern, *The Future of Russian Gas and Gazprom* (Oxford: Oxford University Press, 2005), as quoted in Kimmage, "Eurasia."

62. Olcott, *Russian*, 76.

63. RFE/RL Newsline, 12 January 2006.

64. V. Saprykin, "Rossiiskii 'Gazprom' v stranakh Tsentral′noi Azii" (posted 1 May 2004 on http://www.uceps.org).

65. Thus, Uzbekistan ranked sixteenth in proven reserves and tenth among the world's producers. By 2020 Tashkent expects to expand gas production by 275 percent over the 2003 baseline.

66. RFE/RL Newsline, 23 January 2006.

67. Zygar and Butrin, "Goriuchii," 9.

68. Arkadii Dubnov, "Kulov privedet v Kirgiziiu 'Gazprom,'" *Vremia novostei*, 27 December 2005, 5.

69. Scott Baldauf, "Afghan Gas Pipeline Nears Reality," *Christian Science Monitor*, 15 February 2006, 4.

70. RFE/RL Newsline, 18 January 2006.

71. Interview with Grigorii Rapota, secretary general of the EAEC, in *Tribuna*, 23 March 2005.

72. *Kommersant*, 5 September 2005.

73. Valerii Kodachigov, "Abonent po tsene avtomobilia," *Kommersant*, 19 January 2006, 5.

74. Sidorov, "Aziatskoe napravlenie."

75. Sultanov and Muzaparova, "Great Power Policies," 195.

76. As quoted by then-Russian foreign ministry spokesman Aleksandr Iakovenko, in an interview with "Maiak" radio station, 1261–19–06–2002.

77. Zhanna Zaionchkovskaia, "Rossiia pered litsom migratsii" (unpublished manuscript, 2006), 1.

78. Both statements made at the inaugural session of the UK-Russia Roundtable, at Ditchley Park, England, on 24 February 2006.

79. Thus a 2005 report on the demographic situation in Russia commissioned by the United Russia Party supports ethnically Russian immigration from the former Soviet republics.

80. *Tribuna*, 23 March 2005.

81. In Kyrgyzstan, at the time of President Akaev's ouster in 2005, official unemployment stood at 80,000, but unofficial estimates put the figure as high as 200,000.

82. Kyrgyzstan, for example, receives somewhere between 120 million and 200 million dollars from its migrant workers in Russia. See the interview with then-Prime Minister Nikolai Tanaev, in *Rossiiskaia gazeta*, 1 February 2005; and Grigorii Rapota, secretary-general of the Eurasian Economic Community, in *Tribuna*, 23 March 2005.

83. All figures are compared to 2000 levels. See http://www.un.org/pop.

84. *Obschestvennoe mnenie* (Moscow: Yuri Levada Analytical Center, 2005), table 19.17.

85. According to Grigori Rapota, about 600 Tajiks died in Russia in a single year; two-thirds of these fatalities were violent deaths. See *Tribuna*, 23 March 2005.

86. This argument is eloquently advanced by Fiona Hill and Clifford Gaddy in *The Siberian Curse* (Washington, DC: Brookings Institution Press, 2003).

87. Report of the Russian minister of foreign affairs on "The Russian Language in the World" in 2003. See http://www.mid.ru.

88. Ibid.

89. Interview with Ramazan Abdulatipov, Russia's ambassador to Tajikistan (posted 27 February 2006 on http://www.regnum.ru).

90. For an excellent analysis of Russia's policies in Tajikistan, see Lena Johnson, "The Tajik Civil War," London, RIIA, Paper 74 (1998), and also "Russia's Policy in Central Asia: Tajikistan Case-Study," in *Central Asia and the Caucasus* 1997, no. 8.

91. For example, see the presidential decree of 14 February 1995 or the decision of the Security Council of the Russian Federation for 15 December 1999.

92. The TRASECA conference was held in Baku in 1998, with very low-level Russian participation.

93. The first meeting of the U.S.-Russian working group on Afghanistan took place in Washington in August 2000.

94. Sergei Ivanov, then-secretary of the Russia's Security Council, warned that Russia would strike to eliminate Chechen training camps in Afghanistan.

95. Olcott, *Central Asia's Second Chance*, 18.

96. Cf. Robert Legvold, "All the Way. Crafting a U.S.-Russian Alliance. *"The National Interest"* (Winter 2002, and Dmitri Trenin, U.S. Anti-Terrorist Operation and Russia's Policy. A Carnegie Moscow Center Briefing (September 2001).

97. Olga Oliker and Thomas Szayna, "Faultlines of Conflict in Central Asia and South Caucasus" (Rand Corp., 2003), 195, 197.

98. Vitalii Tretiakov, "Uzbekskii faktor," *Komsomol'skaia pravda*, 1 September 2005, 8.

99. These included Gleb Pavlovskii (Effective Policy Foundation), Igor Bunin (Center for Political Technologies), Igor Muntusov (Nikkolo-M), and Sitnikov (Image-Contact). See Vasilii Kharlamov, "Vsuchila poliottekhnologii Nazarbaevu," *Nezavisimaia gazeta*, 22 July 2005.

100. For example, compare Akezhan Kazhegeldin (prime minister of Kazakhstan, 1994–97), "Stavka bol'she, chem neft'," *Vremia MN*, 18 October 1999; Zainidin Kumanov of Kyrgyzstan in an interview with Regnum News Agency, 2 February 2006.

101. See Dina Malysheva, "Voenno-polevoi roman Rossii" (posted 4 October 2005 on http://www.novopol.ru).

102. Besides the lease, the Kyrgyz government assessed charges on the United States for each kind of activity at the base; the take-off of each plane, for example, costs 7,000 dollars. Altogether, in 2002 Kyrgyzstan earned 250 million dollars.

103. See V. Nikolaev, "Islam Karimov: vozvrat k istoricheskomu soiuzniku," *Rossiiskie vesti*, 1/8 February 2006.

104. The Russo-Uzbek exercise was held in September 2005 near the Tajik border where the IDU kept its camps in 1998–1999. Cf. Dina Malysheva, "Voenno-polevoi roman Rossii."

105. Neil Buckley, "NATO Fears Russian Plans for 'Gas OPEC,'" *Financial Times*, November 14, 2006.

106 Cf. the Council on Foreign and Defense Policy's 2006 report on the broader Middle East and Central Asia.

107. Cf. Andrei Grozin, interview with Rosbalt News Agency, 20 November 2005.

108. Thus, in 2005 Russia agreed to grant military technical assistance to Kyrgyzstan worth five million dollars, a puny sum compared with U.S. payment for the Manas base.

109. Leonid Fedun, vice president of LUKoil, in an interview with *Ekspert*, 46 (5/11 December 2005), 33.

110. Originally in a speech to students in St. Petersburg in September 2003, later published by *Nezavisimaia Gazeta*, 1 October 2003.

111. Cf. "Rossiia i 'rasshirennyi Blizhnii Vostok," a background paper by the Council for Foreign and Defense Policy (March 2006).

112. Cf. L. R. Skakovskii, "Geopoliticheskaia rol' Rossii v sovremennoi Tsentral'noi Azii. Materialy tret'ei ezhegodnoi Almatinskoi konferentsii po voprosam bezopasnosti i regional'nogo sotrudnichestva," Almaty, 21 June 2005.

113. I set out this argument more broadly in my article "Rossiia i konets Evrazii," in *Pro et Contra*, 2005, no. 1.

3

Central Asia in China's Diplomacy

Huasheng Zhao

China's understanding of Central Asia, its interests in Central Asia, and its policy and strategy toward Central Asia have changed in the past decade and are still in a process of evolution. Changes in the international situation and in Central Asia, together with the Chinese concerns about domestic security and its economic interests, have had an impact on its strategy and policy toward Central Asia.

At this juncture, one cannot say that China has definitively formulated a Central Asian strategy. On the contrary, one might even say that China does not really have a clear-cut strategy toward this region. Although China does have macro-conceptions and specific goals and tactics, they do not constitute a formal strategy.

It is not easy to broach this question: even Chinese scholars find it difficult to conduct research on their country's policy toward Central Asia. In particular, one must contend with a dearth of materials: the accessible complex of official and public materials and information about relations with Central Asia are incomplete and unsystematic. The sources that researchers can consult and cite are very limited. This makes it very difficult to conduct research on China's relations with Central Asia.

It bears emphasizing that I do not represent China's official position. Although the focus in this chapter is Chinese foreign policy toward this region, in no sense should this analysis be seen as a statement of official views or policy.

The Evolution of China's Basic Interests in Central Asia

Most Chinese and foreign researchers hold broadly similar views about China's strategic interests in Central Asia: security, economic relations, and energy.

These can be broken down into six key elements: (1) border security; (2) combating the "East Turkestan" movement; (3) energy; (4) economic interests; (5) geopolitics; and (6) the Shanghai Cooperation Organization (SCO). This conception therefore goes beyond the general consensus to include three additional components—border security, geopolitical interests, and the SCO.

China's interests in this region are fairly obvious, but there are some unanswered questions that will be addressed in this chapter: How did they take shape? How important are they to China? How do they rank in terms of priority? What are the preconditions and potential for China to realize them?

The six elements of Chinese interest in Central Asia did not emerge simultaneously, but arose sequentially. The priorities of Chinese diplomacy are not immutable, but rather change, as we have already seen in the Central Asian context. Ever since the breakup of the USSR and the formation of independent states in Central Asia in 1991, China has been continually rethinking its interests and policy in that region.

This dynamic reformulation of interests derives from a series of subjective and objective factors. First, the newly independent states of Central Asia were subject to rapid change; they faced a complex external environment, acute internal problems, domestic political volatility, a fragile economic base, weak regional integration, and little capacity to coordinate regional development. The region was, moreover, highly susceptible to diverging external influences. Once the Central Asian countries became independent, their relations with China included both historical and newly emerging concerns, both short- and long-term issues. The resolution of some issues diminished their importance, but enhanced the urgency of others. The result changed the structure of China's interests in Central Asia. At the same time, over the past decade or so China's view of the region has undergone changes. Domestic policies, along with political, security, and economic demands, have also affected this evolution of the Chinese perspective. No doubt all this has had a major impact on China's conception of its interests. Finally, changes in the international situation, especially the development of relations between the great powers after 11 September 2001 have compelled China to revise the definition of its vital national interests in Central Asia.

During the first years of independence for the Central Asian states, China's main goal was border security and stability. Until 1997, China had no other strong strategic interests.

That focus in the early 1990s coincided with the rise of the "East Turkestan" terrorist movement in the Xinjiang Autonomous Region. China's relations with the Central Asian countries were still in gestation; there was no basis for mutual political trust; historical border issues had not been resolved; and the independence of the Central Asian countries had generated new questions.

Under these circumstances, China fought terrorism mainly on its own; it had yet to create a framework of cooperation with Central Asia or to identify this issue as its principal interest in the region. Economically, China had just established ties with the Central Asian countries; although border trade became more active (with large quantities of cheap Chinese goods entering Central Asian markets), this was not a primary interest in Beijing. To put this in quantitative terms, in 1996 and 1997 the annual trade volume between China and five Central Asian countries was less than one billion U.S. dollars. In the energy sector, China had just become a net oil importer; given the weak demand for oil and low prices, China had no strong incentive to tap Central Asian energy. Geopolitically, the United States was not yet involved deeply and was not a cause of serious concern in Beijing.

Borders were another issue. When the USSR dissolved, Sino-Soviet border talks were half completed. To be sure, issues regarding the eastern section of their common border had been resolved, and in 1989 China and the Soviet Union initialed the Sino-Soviet Agreement on the Eastern Section of the Border. However, the two parties had not yet reached an agreement on the western section of the border. There is only 45 kilometers borderline between China and Russia in the western section. Far more extensive are the borders between China and the newly independent states of Central Asia: these are more than 1,700 kilometers with Kazakhstan, about 1,000 kilometers with Kyrgyzstan, and about 450 kilometers with Tajikistan. The involved countries decided to hold further negotiations, with China as one party and the other four countries (Russia, Kazakhstan, Kyrgyzstan, and Tajikistan) as the other. In September 1994 the parties reached an agreement on the western section of the Sino-Russian border, where, after Sino-Soviet armed border clashes in 1969, both sides had deployed troops and equipment on a huge scale. With the improvement in bilateral relations, the parties significantly reduced military forces deployed in the border regions, but still required an institutional mechanism to guarantee border security. To meet this need, on 26 April 1996 China, Russia, Kazakhstan, Kyrgyzstan, and Tajikistan signed the Treaty on Deepening Military Trust in Border Regions, which contained the following provisions:

- military forces deployed in border regions will not attack each other;
- no side will conduct military exercises that are targeted against the other;
- the scale, range and number of military exercises are to be limited;
- each side will inform the other of important military activities scheduled to be conducted within 100 kilometers of the border;
- each side will invite the other to observe military exercises that involve the use of live ammunition;

- dangerous military activities are to be avoided; and
- friendly communications between military forces and frontier guards in border regions should be promoted.

On the basis of this treaty, in 1997 the parties agreed to a reduction of military forces in the border regions:

- military forces deployed in border regions were to be reduced to a level compatible with the good-neighbor relations and defensive in nature;
- no side would use, or threaten to use, force against the other or unilaterally seek military superiority;
- the military forces deployed in border regions would not attack the other side;
- all sides would reduce the number of military personnel including army, air force, air defense forces, and frontier guards, and also reduce the quantity of the main categories of weaponry deployed within 100 kilometers of the border;
- the upper limit after reduction, as well as the method and time limit for implementation, would be specified at a later date;
- the parties would exchange pertinent information on military forces in the border regions; and
- implementation of the treaty was to be supervised.

The treaty also stipulates that the total number of army, air force, and air defense forces after reduction would be no more than 130,400 within 100 kilometers on each side of the border having a length in excess of 7,000 kilometers. These two agreements (the Treaty on Deepening Military Trust in Border Regions and the Treaty on Reduction of Military Forces in Border Regions) are of fundamental significance for the border security of China, Russia, and the Central Asian states. The documents signify an institutional resolution and guarantee for security along a border running more than 7,300 kilometers.

Border security and stability have always been the central focus of China's diplomacy in Central Asia. Resolution of border issues and border security are a prerequisite for China's goal of a favorable environment. The 3,000-kilometer border in China's northwest is weaker and historically the site of significant events. Obviously, security here is vital to China's interests and its relations with Central Asia. It is wrong to ignore border security and stability, as some have done, when assessing China's interests in Central Asia.

Since 1997, however, border security has dropped in China's priority and now ranks below the task of combating terrorism. The 1998 Almaty Joint

Statement of the "Shanghai Five" proclaimed, for the first time, that the member states (Russia, China, Kyrgyzstan, Kazakhstan, and Uzbekistan) would unite to combat terrorism and that none would allow its own territory to be used for activities that harm the sovereignty, security, and social order of another member state.[1] These countries established the SCO in June 2001 and adopted the Shanghai "Convention on Combating Terrorism, Separatism, and Extremism." This meant not only a redefinition of SCO activities but also a reconsideration of China's interests in Central Asia. The main motive for this change was the resolution of border issues and creation of an institutional guarantee of border security. Resolution of border and security issues also resulted in a qualitative change in the relations between China and the Central Asian countries and made more extensive cooperation possible. Moreover, the issue of terrorism in Central Asia has become more urgent. Thus, while border security remains a major Chinese interest, it is no longer the dominant issue; rather, the fight against terrorism has become the main focus of relations with Central Asia.

The primary goal of China's antiterrorist policy in Central Asia is to counteract the "East Turkestan" movement in Xinjiang—that is, maintain stability in northwestern China and oppose a separatist division of the country. This issue is not really new to China. The northwest is a vast territory, far from China's industrial centers, with a harsh climate, diverse population, and difficult environment. This region has always been a problem for China's central government: since the Han Dynasty, China has fought secessionist, rebellious forces there. These secessionist forces have differed during the rule of each dynasty, but generally have had the same objective—to establish an independent kingdom with a status equal to that of the central government.

The main secessionist movement in China's northwest in the twentieth century has endeavored to establish an "East Turkestan"—a geographical, linguistic, and cultural concept. The Tujue (Göktürks) were a nomadic tribe active in the Altai Mountain areas; in the sixth century they appeared in northern China and conquered a vast territory stretching from the Menggu Grasslands in the east to the Caspian Sea region in the west (thus including what is now Central Asia and China's Xinjiang). After the Tujue Khanate split into western and eastern parts, the West Tujue Khanate laid claim to Xinjiang and Central Asia. This Tujue Khanate was destroyed by Tang Dynasty in the seventh century and disappeared approximately in the tenth century, but left a deep social and cultural imprint. Because of the protracted interaction and linkages between the Tujue and indigenous peoples, the Tujue have had an impact on the language, culture, society, and customs of local ethnic groups. That process left linguistic and cultural ties with the Tujue as the historical link; it has had an impact on all the relevant ethnic groups and regions, including Xinjiang. China has seven ethnic "Turkic" groups; five are in Xinjiang (Uighur, Kazakh, Kyrgyz, Uzbek, and Tatar), two others in Gansu and Qinghai (the Yugur and Salar, respectively).[2] This is the historical and cultural origin of "East Turkestan" in China's Xinjiang.

However, "East Turkestan" in modern Xinjiang has nothing to do historically with West Tujue or East Tujue. The term "East Turkestan" was first used by Russian scholars in the eighteenth century to describe the Central Asian areas belonging to China (mainly the South part of Xinjiang region). The Central Asian region proper was called West Turkestan—the area of Central Asia that later belonged to Russia. Such is the origin of the modern concept of "East Turkestan." It is a geographical term used by Russians and Westerners to distinguish China's Xinjiang from Central Asia. Thus "East Turkestan" refers neither to an ethnic group nor to a country; hence it has no ethnic or national historical foundation. The modern "East Turkestan" movement in China's Xinjiang first appeared in the early twentieth century. In 1933, secessionist forces in Xinjiang, with the support of foreign forces, rebelled and proclaimed the "East Turkestan" Republic in Kashi (southern Xinjiang), but the new "state" collapsed after a few months. In 1944, an armed uprising against the Kuomintang government led to the creation of the "East Turkestan Republic" in Xinjiang. Such were the earliest emanations of the modern "East Turkestan" movement.

The principal political objective of the "East Turkestan" movement is the independence of Xinjiang and the formation of an "East Turkestan" state. To achieve that goal, the movement resorts to violence and terrorist means. Since the founding of the People's Republic of China in 1949, secessionist forces have not ceased operations in Xinjiang; from the early 1950s to the late 1980s the Xinjiang region witnessed more than twenty large-scale rebellions and disturbances.[3]

The security situation in Xinjiang deteriorated in the 1990s. One contributing factor was the independence of the Central Asian countries, which inspired aspirations for an independent "East Turkestan" in China. Moreover, the new Central Asian countries had limited capacity with respect to politics, economy, security, and ideology; that had the effect of turning Central Asia into a huge vacuum. International terrorists and religious extremists poured into the region; the internal terrorism and extremism of Central Asia spread as a result of domestic pressures and the external environment. All this enabled international terrorist and extremist forces to advance toward the Chinese frontier of Xinjiang and to erode its security.

Such was the background for a new upsurge of "East Turkestan" terrorist activities in Xinjiang. From 1990 to 2001, "East Turkestan" terrorist forces perpetrated more than 200 terrorist incidents in Xinjiang, killing 162 and injuring another 440.[4] The "East Turkestan" threat was quickly becoming a major concern for China. However, before 9/11, China did not report the terrorist activities of the "East Turkestan" movement; given the sensitivity of the issue, there was no public discussion of the problem. To combat the "East Turkestan" movement, China sealed off the region and refused the assistance of other countries. This reflected traditional attitudes, the main objective being to maintain the image of domestic stability. Only after the 9/11 attacks did China publicly discuss "East Turkestan" and terrorism.[5]

The reason China changed its policy was a shift in its thinking: it now concluded that framing "East Turkestan" as part of the international struggle against terrorism would be more effective. That is because the internationalization of terrorism had created a "united front" and made a regional solution ineffectual. The changes in Central Asia in the 1990s obviously increased this region's role in the development of the "East Turkestan" movement in China: after all, this lengthy border is a main link between Xinjiang and West Asia, South Asia, and the Middle East. For historical, ethnic, cultural, linguistic, and religious reasons, Xinjiang has countless ties with Central Asia. Moreover, during the Cold War tensions between China and the Soviet Union, Central Asia had already become the base camp for the "East Turkestan" movement, which used Soviet support to become active in Central Asia and made Xinjiang its target. In 1962, at the instigation of the Soviet Union, more than 50,000 ethnic minority residents from Xinjiang fled to Central Asia.

To judge from the present situation, Central Asia provides a link between the "East Turkestan" movement in China and international terrorist and extremist forces, enabling the latter to penetrate China and direct terrorist activities there. Central Asia, in short, is an important base for many "East Turkestan" organizations and a refuge for its activists who have fled from China.[6] Realistically speaking, "East Turkestan" cannot become a dominant movement in China without external support and assistance. Hence China must confront the "East Turkestan" issue in an open internal and external environment. Attempts to seal off the internal and external environment, as was done earlier, will not suffice. China simply cannot isolate Xinjiang: as China expands its economy and cooperates in border trade, the contacts with Central Asia will surely grow. This raises new questions about how China is to control "East Turkestan" as it expands relations with the states of Central Asia. Under these circumstances, if Central Asia provides a base for "East Turkestan" militants, it will become increasingly difficult for China to contain the movement. On the other hand, if Central Asia severs the barrage between "East Turkestan" and the external world, which will significantly help China to stifle the movement. That is the crux of China's antiterrorism interest in Central Asia. On its own China has the capacity to control "East Turkestan." To judge from historical and current conditions, so long as there is no large-scale internal disorder in China and so long as the central government is functional, "East Turkestan" will not achieve its goal of independence.

It is, however, very difficult to resolve completely the issue of "East Turkestan." China can effectively limit the movement, but not easily eradicate it altogether. The fundamental aim of these secessionist forces is the establishment of an independent "East Turkestan" Islamic state. Its philosophical basis is not only material but also spiritual; hence any material approach (e.g., economic development and improvement in the living standards of local residents) may ameliorate the problem, but cannot eliminate the philosophical basis of "East Turkestan" and altogether resolve this issue. Indeed, economic development can even stimulate the growth of ethnic awareness and further aggravate the problem. In short, China may not completely resolve the "East Turkestan" issue in the foreseeable future. The primary objective should be to keep it dormant.

A second major Chinese interest in Central Asia is energy, and since 2001 this has become a central focus of Beijing's strategy and diplomacy in the region. Energy had certainly been on China's diplomatic agenda earlier, but was not a top priority. Only after 2001 did energy become an important strategic interest, and there are two reasons for this: (1) the growth in China's domestic energy demand; and (2) the change in the international situation after the events of 11 September 2001.

In 1993 China became a net oil importing country, but before 1997 the annual volume of oil imports was less than 15 million tons (less than 10 percent of the country's annual oil demand). Thus at that point oil imports did not yet constitute a serious problem. In 1997, the volume of oil imports jumped to more than 35 million tons and remained at this level until 1999. Although oil imports obviously increased, they could be bought on a very stable international oil market. The oil supply was ample and the price was cheap (falling to less than 10 U.S. dollars a barrel at one point). Under these circumstances, China sought to buy oil on international markets rather than invest heavily to acquire its own sources of oil. This was the most economically rational strategy. Later China did invest in foreign oil concerns, but the aim was mainly commercial—to earn profits, not provide a secure oil supply. In other words, China regarded energy imports primarily as an economic issue and did not consider the issue from political-economic and strategic perspectives. In 2000, China's oil imports increased sharply, rising to 70 million tons annually (over 30 percent of domestic oil demand), and it is estimated that imports will continue to rise rapidly. That has caused China to reconsider the energy issue and, by 2001, to develop a new strategy. It eventually formulated an "energy strategy for the twenty-first century" that sought to diversify energy imports and to "go global" in these operations. In short, China came to treat the energy issue from a strategic perspective and to follow new policies and tactics for developing foreign energy sources.

In addition, the events of 11 September 2001 have brought changes in the international situation. In terms of the international energy situation, the greatest impact of 9/11 was to intensify global competition and to exacerbate tensions regarding energy supplies. This event also imparted to the world a strong psychological suggestion that the Middle East is vulnerable to long-term turbulence and instability—critical problems for a region that is the world's primary source of energy.

As a result, the international energy situation underwent a sudden transformation and entered a new phase of rapid change: the fierce scramble for energy led to constant, sharp increases in international oil prices. China was the first country to be deeply affected by this shock wave. One impact was on the oil pipeline running from Angarsk to Daqing: China and Russia had negotiated this deal for many years, but Japan suddenly intervened and became China's strong rival. India, another late-developing country with large energy demands, also became engaged in world's energy competition and sought to secure energy resources at all costs. Another impact was geopolitical: American military forces established bases in Central Asia, occupied Iraq, and put pressure on Iran in an apparent attempt to assert control over global energy supplies.

Meanwhile, China's demand for energy and its dependence on global supplies were steadily increasing. China imported 74.2 million tons of oil in 2001, 69.4 million tons in 2002, 92 million tons in 2003, and 102 million tons in 2004. The sharp surge in energy prices added to the energy pressure on China. In 2004, China paid nearly 60 U.S. dollars more per ton of imported oil than in the previous year, because of the price increases, the total extra cost exceeds 7 billion U.S. dollars. These radical changes in the international energy situation forced China to pay more attention to energy policy.

These factors have had a major impact on China's energy strategy and on the perception of its crucial energy interests in Central Asia. In 1997 China became involved in the Central Asian energy field on a large scale. Two symbolic events can be cited here: one was the decision by the China National Petroleum Corporation (CNPC) to invest in Central Asian oilfields and to participate in the region's development; the other was Beijing's readiness to construct an oil pipeline from Kazakhstan to supply its oil needs. As noted above, however, China did not make energy its principal interest in Central Asia; investment in Central Asian energy resources essentially represented the commercial behavior of an oil company. Nor was the venture large-scale; to some extent it was still a kind of experiment. Although the China-Kazakhstan oil pipeline is an important cooperative energy project and has strategic significance for the two countries, it bears stressing that Kazakhstan initiated the project and was far more enthusiastic than China. However, because of doubts that the supply of oil can ensure the minimum economic rationality of the project, construction did not begin as scheduled and the project had to be put on hold. This shows that China attached growing importance to its interests in Central Asia, but did not assign them top priority. Only after 2001, when China's energy strategic thinking began to change sharply, did Beijing assign utmost importance to its energy interests in Central Asia. Resumption of construction on the China-Kazakhstan oil pipeline in 2003 was a direct result of this change. China's energy interests in Central Asia are not limited to Kazakhstan, but also include Turkmenistan (which has rich natural gas reserves) and Uzbekistan (which holds moderate quantities of oil and gas resources).

The energy resources of Central Asia are important to China in several respects. First, Central Asia can satisfy an important portion of China's oil imports. These imports now exceed 100 million tons per annum, but only about 2 million tons come from Central Asia and hence are not of strategic significance. After the pipeline is put into operation, it is expected that China will import at least 10 million tons of oil per year from Central Asia and hopes to increase such imports to 20 million tons and more. Thus Central Asia will account for more than 8 percent of China's oil imports. That is a very substantial share and shows the importance of Central Asia for China. Second, as Central Asia provides a new supply source, it will improve the structure of China's energy imports and help diversify its energy sources. Supply diversification is one of the key objectives of China's energy strategy. At present, about 50 percent of the country's oil comes from the Middle East and about 22 percent from Africa; China therefore depends on these two regions for more than 70 percent of its oil imports.[7] Given the current and potential instability of the Middle East and Africa and given the security issue of long-distance transport by sea, this dependence is obviously excessive and fraught with risk. The solution is to diversify the sources of energy, and Central Asia represents one of the regions that can help China achieve this diversification. To be sure, the Middle East will remain the primary source of China's oil and gas; neither Central Asia nor any other region can possibly replace the Middle East. Nevertheless, these new regions can effectively reduce the dependence on the Middle East. In addition, the China-Kazakhstan pipeline can also deliver oil from Russia's Siberian oil fields; that will raise the utilization ratio and economic efficiency of the pipeline and also enhance Sino-Russian energy cooperation.[8]

China has other economic interests in Central Asia besides energy. In economic terms, Central Asia has not had a great overall impact on the Chinese

Table 3.1

Trade Volume Between Xinjiang and the Five Central Asian States, 1992–2005 (in billions of U.S. dollars)

Year	Trade Volume
1993	0.5
1994	0.48
1995	0.67
1996	0.75
1997	0.76
1998	0.83
1999	1.07
2000	1.37
2001	1.02
2002	1.55
2003	2.56
2004	4.5
2005	6

Source: Hu Hongping, "Vigorously Marching Towards Central Asian Market and Extending Economic and Trade Cooperation," *Russian, Central Asian and East European Markets*, September 2005, 29. The figures for 2004–5 are estimated by the author.

economy, for its share of China's total trade volume is small. Thus, in 2005, when total trade reached more than 1,400 billion U.S. dollars, trade with Central Asia totaled just slightly more than 8.7 billion U.S. dollars. Whether in absolute or relative terms, Central Asia thus represents a small portion of China's foreign trade (about 0.6 percent). On the other hand, China accounts for about 10 percent of Central Asian foreign trade volume. From Beijing's perspective, Central Asia is of economic importance primarily with respect to the development of the country's Northwest, especially Xinjiang, the main beneficiary of trade with Central Asia.[9]

Development of China's Northwest and the prosperity of border areas are a part of the country's development strategy. The Northwest is distant from China's developed eastern coastal regions, lags far behind the economic level of the latter, cannot compete economically, and finds it difficult to integrate into eastern China's economy. The Northwest, particularly Xinjiang, is close to Central Asia, has a common border extending more than 3,000 kilometers, has natural advantages of exchange and transportation, and shares cultural traditions. All this makes economic cooperation with Central Asia a convenient channel for the economic development of the Northwest and especially of Xinjiang. This can also help China promote economic growth in the border areas. Moreover, Central Asia is of great importance to China's links to the outside

Table 3.2

Trade Volume Between China and the Five Central Asian States,
1992–2006 (in billions of U.S. dollars)

Year	Total Trade Volume
1992	4.59
1993	6.06
1994	5.78
1995	7.81
1996	7.74
1997	8.70
1998	9.56
1999	13.30
2000	18.12
2001	n.a.
2002	23.80
2003	41.02
2004	58.44
2005	87.3
2006*	95.3

Source: Author's calculations according to the statistics of the Chinese General Administration of Customs and the Ministry of Commerce of PRC.
   * January–October 2006.

world: it is a transportation hub linking China with western Asia and Europe. The same is true of the transport links to Europe: the route through Central Asia is more than 1,000 kilometers shorter than that through Siberia.

Third, Central Asia has rich mineral resources that are especially needed for China's accelerated economic development. China can make ample use of the mineral resources that Central Asia is capable of supplying.

Finally, the Central Asian market is not yet fully developed. However, the region is closely related to China (politically, economically, and geographically), the Chinese economy itself is moving toward regionalization, and China promotes this process in surrounding countries. Beijing also hopes to build an economic framework for regionalization in Central Asia. This is an integral part of a strategy aimed at enhancing Chinese economic influence in contiguous areas.

China also has a geopolitical strategic interest in Central Asia and judges this region's position in terms of its overall foreign policy. The assessment of these geopolitical interests, moreover, has evolved, but the fundamental concept is that Central Asia constitutes the country's "strategic rear." Now and for a considerable time to come, southeast direction is the principal focus of Chinese strategy and the main source of countervailing strategic pressure. Specifically, the most critical, difficult objective of Chinese foreign policy is to prevent Taiwanese independence and to thwart secessionist challenges from Taiwan. The greatest strategic pressure will come from a potential Chinese-American confrontation over Washington's support for Taiwanese independence as well as tensions sparked by American attempts to contain China's rise. In strategic terms, China therefore needs stability on other fronts so that it can concentrate resources on Southeast Asia. Although China has conceptually defined its strategic front and rear, the distinction between "front" and "rear" is now less clear than it once was. Nonetheless, Central Asia occupies a relatively independent strategic region on the Chinese periphery and constitutes an integral part of China's strategic rear.

This ascription of Central Asia to the strategic rear predetermines China's desire to maintain stability and avert geopolitical challenges in this region. Prior to 11 September 2001, China was not seriously concerned about the geopolitical security of Central Asia. To be sure, it could not ignore the fact that NATO had extended its Partnership for Peace program to Central Asia and that, since 1997, the United States has conducted Central Asian Battalion military exercises with Central Asian countries. But these were not a cause of excessive concern in Beijing: although the United States and NATO penetrated militarily into Central Asia, that did not constitute a geopolitical threat.

After 9/11, however, the geopolitical situation changed dramatically: the United States intervened directly and established military bases in the region. To be sure, these bases were to support antiterrorist operations in Afghanistan. The United States has also explicitly characterized this military presence as "temporary." Nevertheless, China regards the American military bases here as an important geopolitical issue. The Manas air base in Bishkek, Kyrgyzstan, is in fact quite close to the Chinese border. No matter what the military functions of the U.S. bases might be, they are fraught with significant implications for China and require that it reassess its geopolitical security in Central Asia. Nor has the United States set a precise terminus for its military presence in the region. In response, the SCO summit in Astana in July 2005 demanded that the United States fix a final date for the withdrawal of its military forces from Central Asia.[10] That resolution, however, did not receive positive response from Washington and, to the contrary, elicited expressions of dissatisfaction. This response indicates that the United States has no intention of ending its military presence in Central Asia in the immediate future. After Uzbekistan demanded that the United States remove its military base, Washington persuaded Kyrgyzstan to permit the American U.S. military base in Manas to remain.

Views in China differ regarding the impact of these geopolitical changes on China's strategic security: some regard the American military presence in Central Asia as a major geopolitical threat, while others deny this to be the case. Whatever the view, 9/11 has clearly raised China's interest in the geopolitics of Central Asia.

In my analysis (which is not shared by all), the SCO is important for China's interests in Central Asia. This multilateral organization (embracing China, Russia, and all of the Central Asian states except Turkmenistan) gives China an instrument to pursue its own interests in the region. That, unquestionably, is the main thrust of Chinese diplomacy with regard to the SCO. Given China's active participation in the organization, its special role in the establishment and development of the SCO, and its close relations with the organization, China has a special relationship to this organization; and the SCO has undergone some changes with respect to its functions and its significance for China. Accordingly, it is widely thought that the development of the SCO corresponds to the growth of China's ties to Central Asia, and a weakening with a corresponding decline in China's influence. Hence the SCO and its development have become an important dimension of Chinese diplomacy in Central Asia. Although this interest is not substantial and arose spontaneously, not through deliberate Chinese policy, the SCO has established China's presence and image in Central Asia and is important for that very reason.

As the foregoing suggests, prior to 1998 China's top priorities in Central Asia were to resolve boundary issues and ensure border security. After 1998 concerns about terrorism have emerged as the main focus of Chinese interests in the region. Since 2001 energy has become increasingly important and now constitutes one of China's most salient interests; at the same time, changes in the geopolitical situation and the importance of geopolitical interests have obviously been enhanced. Moreover, as the functions of the SCO have evolved, that organization has become critical to Chinese interests in Central Asia. In sum, over the past decade China's interests in Central Asia have undergone significant development and change, and this process is still underway. While China's interests there may yet undergo some evolution, its rough outline and structure are not likely to change substantially if no sharp change happens in international, regional, or China's domestic situation.

In terms of structure, China's interests in Central Asia have become increasingly complex, encompassing political, economic, security, and geostrategic spheres. These interests are closely interrelated and consist of three levels, in order of priority: (1) terrorism and energy; (2) economy and the SCO; and (3) geopolitics and border security.

This prioritization is based on that combating the rise of a separatist "East Turkestan" movement and supplying energy have the most prominent impact on China's interests in Central Asia. Although economic interests are also strategic, China's economic involvement in Central Asia is to some extent local; the SCO, while very important to China, has mainly instrumental character and is perceived as a kind of China's interest only in some sense and therefore ranks as a secondary priority. Geopolitical interests are strategic, but—in the absence of radical changes in the international situation—the Central Asian geopolitical threat to China remains latent. Border security is of vital importance to China, but in Central Asia the border disputes have been resolved and that is not a critical problem; hence geopolitics and border security issues are of tertiary importance there. However, the rank order of Chinese interests in Central Asia is not immutable; drastic shifts in the international or regional situation, or in China's domestic situation, may reorder these priorities.

Basic Features of China's Policy Toward Central Asia

Central Asia is a special region. From the perspective of Chinese diplomacy, this region not only shares common features with other regions but also has its own special characteristics. This region is located inland and has an underdeveloped economy; the countries are small and weak. The peoples of Central Asia are Muslim, and they face serious threats of terrorism and extremism. Although China's neighbors, these countries have but a superficial knowledge of China. Bilateral relations are not fully developed. As former republics of the Soviet Union, the countries of Central Asia retain special, close relations with Russia. All these factors have made China's diplomacy toward Central Asia different from that toward other regions.

Central Asia's Place in Chinese Diplomacy

Central Asia is important to China and hence constitutes one of key dimensions of its foreign policy. What, however, is the relative position of this region in China's overall diplomacy? It is essential to answer that question in order to provide a clear assessment of the region's relative importance in Chinese foreign policy. China has not issued an official document specifically outlining its diplomatic strategy and giving a systematic explanation of its objectives, priorities, and methods. Hence this estimate of Central Asia's ranking in the diplomatic priorities of China is somewhat hypothetical.

Chinese diplomacy does have its own special mode of analysis. It divides relations with the outside world into three basic categories: great powers, neighboring countries, and developing countries. Relations with great powers mainly seek to resolve issues pertaining to the international structure and strategic balance. Links with surrounding countries concentrate mainly on issues pertinent to China's immediate environs. Relations with developing countries primarily concern the issues of China's posture toward the south-north contradictions and its relations with the vast number of small- and medium-size countries. Such is the ordinate (vertical axis) of Chinese foreign policy. There is also an abscissa—primary foreign strategic objectives and issues to be resolved. The main strategic objectives include security, economic interests, and the special issue of Taiwan. Maintaining international recognition of one China and creation of international conditions to resolve the Taiwan issue are a central strategic goal of China's diplomacy. In addition, given the growing importance of energy for economic security and development, energy may well become a strategic objective on its own. In short, security, economic interests, Taiwan, and energy constitute the basic objectives of China's diplomacy. The strategic objectives in the ordinate of Chinese diplomacy are consistent with those of its abscissa, but are developed from different perspectives. These fundamental axes of China's diplomacy constitute the primary frame of reference for judging the relative importance of any given country.

As for the general layout of China's diplomacy, there are several main spheres—Northeast Asia, Southeast Asia, South Asia, Russia, and Central Asia. Of these, Northeast and Southeast Asia are the most important strategic areas. Hence the eastern and southern directions constitute the main strategic fronts, with the western and northern directions comprising a strategic rear. The principal factors for this ranking lie in China's political and economic focus on the eastern and southern regions as the most important and developed. China derives its greatest economic output from these regions. The eastern and southern regions are also China's main political and economic cooperative partners. These regions provide China's main contacts with the United States, Japan, the Republic of Korea, Southeast Asian countries, (partially) Russia, and Europe. At the same time, the east and south are sources of the primary challenges to China's strategic interests. These two regions also border on the oceans, the main link with the outside world. The development of aviation cannot diminish the enormous role of sea routes in international transportation.

In the ordinate of Chinese diplomacy, the countries of Central Asia are small or medium-size, and hence do not belong to the category of major powers. Central Asia's ranking corresponds to the Chinese conception of "periphery diplomacy," one of the principal concepts in its foreign strategy. This concept has three connotations. First, it refers to the neighboring countries that share borders with China. Second, it not only refers to contiguous states but also those that are very close, such as Japan and South Korea. This second meaning expands the components of the diplomatic conception but is still based on a geographic delimitation. Third, as China's diplomacy developed, it has extended the concept of periphery still further. This notion refers to peripheral areas that are important for China's security, economic, and political interests. It is based on diplomatic logic, not geography. The concept of a larger periphery has some ambiguity in practice; it can be expanded without limit and include the Middle East and even farther territories. The concept of the larger periphery is employed mainly at the theoretical level and rarely used in diplomatic practice. There is no corresponding larger periphery policy.

The goal of China's peripheral strategy is to promote friendly relations with all the contiguous or proximate countries that form a stable belt around the country. The significance of the peripheral strategy lies in the fact that it can help construct a good security environment, improve China's strategic position, augment its diplomatic resources, and expand its international influence. The peripheral strategy derives from the fact that China has borders with fourteen countries and run more than 20,000 kilometers on land. Hence China's periphery is quite complicated. The surrounding countries differ greatly and their relations with China vary considerably. The territorial issues bequeathed by history affect all parts of the border. Therefore relations with these surrounding countries have a great influence on China's foreign policy and security, and that in turn has increased the importance of the concept of "periphery" in China's diplomacy.

Of the five Central Asian countries, three (Kazakhstan, Kyrgyzstan, and Tajikistan) border directly on China, and Uzbekistan and Turkmenistan are proximate neighbors. Hence Central Asia is integral to China's peripheral policy and its attempt to construct a good peripheral environment. This underlies the importance of Central Asia in China's diplomacy. The position that Central Asia occupies as a surrounding region enables it to have a substantial impact on China's environment and its policy toward the periphery. If China does not successfully handle its relations with the Central Asian countries, it can cause substantial harm to its peripheral policies and its goal of building a favorable regional environment.

As for the abscissa of Chinese foreign policy, Central Asia is important in some aspects but less so in others. With respect to security, Central Asia itself does not pose a threat. Although the military presence of other great powers in this region could turn into a strategic threat, that may be primarily diversionary and not the source of an attack. Rather, the principal menace that Central Asia poses for China's security comes from terrorist, separatist, and extremist forces; hence it is essential for China to counteract the "East Turkestan" movement. Fundamentally, however, the problem of "East Turkestan" emanates from China itself; the primary agent for containing the secessionist forces of "East Turkestan" must be China itself, with Central Asia playing only a secondary role. In any event, the "East Turkestan" menace is limited; Xinjiang, the main locus of its activities, is far removed from the heart of China. Therefore the insecurity of this area may inflict considerable harm to China's security, but cannot undermine the national stability of the country as a whole (unless, of course, it were to trigger chain reactions elsewhere in China).

As noted earlier, in terms of economic interests (excluding energy), Central Asia is of limited significance. Although future trade between China and Central Asia may increase substantially (given the prospect of increased activity in the energy sector), this trade will still comprise only a small percent of China's foreign trade structure. In short, Central Asia is important from the absolute perspective, especially for China's northwest region, but in terms of China's overall economic development and foreign trade, this neighboring region cannot significantly affect China's macroeconomic development.

With respect to China's main foreign policy objectives (including resolution of the Taiwan issue), Central Asia is of importance. China's strategic conception envisions a single, interrelated whole; each of these components has an impact on the others. Maintaining stability in the strategic rear is of vital importance if China is to resolve the issues in the main strategic areas. If a crisis were to occur in the Taiwan Straits simultaneously with a major problem in Central Asia, that would strategically divert China from concentrating its energy and resources on Taiwan and would force it to respond on two or more fronts. China will do its utmost to avoid this situation. Although the configuration is complicated, Central Asia's role is important, but not crucial and decisive in the Taiwan issue.

Energy, by contrast, is a salient factor in China's interest in Central Asia. Compared with other factors, energy from Central Asia holds a relatively significant place in China's energy imports. Given that Central Asia has rich oil reserves and has common borders with China, imports from this region are a highly attractive option. Predictions about oil imports from Central Asia are high; energy from this region could constitute a significant proportion of China's total imports and play a substantial role in satisfying domestic energy demand. As noted above, the Middle East supplies more than 50 percent of China's oil, with more than 22 percent coming from Africa, the second largest supplier. The third main source of oil is the Asia-Pacific region, which accounts for over 15 percent of China's petroleum imports. By contrast, Central Asia supplied only about 2 million tons of oil in 2005. After the completion of China-Kazakhstan oil pipeline, it is expected that Kazakhstan will initially deliver 10 million tons of oil to China each year, with plans to increase the flow to 20 million tons. Hence, in coming years China could import 10 to 20 million tons of oil from Central Asia annually. To put this in perspective, it bears noting that China imported about 130 million tons of oil in 2005; that volume is expected to increase to about 170 million tons by 2010. In short, the proportion of Central Asian oil could become a significant share of total imports in the next few years.

If calculated by country, the potential of Central Asian countries is still more striking. Among all countries, including those in the Middle East, the number of countries that can export more than 10 million tons of oil per annum to China is not large. Significantly, Kazakhstan can export an estimated 10 million tons of oil to China and can substantially increase that volume in the near future. If cooperation in the energy sector develops normally, Kazakhstan will doubtless be among China's largest suppliers.

Central Asia, therefore, is manifestly important for Chinese interests, especially with respect to security and energy. At the same time, compared with countries and regions like the United States, Europe, Northeast Asia, and Southeast Asia, it has a relatively small impact on China's political and economic development.

However, priority in foreign policy is only a static description of relative significance in the overall diplomatic framework. It does not reflect absolute importance or unimportance, but only relative status. Absolute and relative importance are different conceptions; relations are dynamic and mutable under certain conditions. Therefore Central Asia's status in the priorities of China foreign policy can vary as circumstances warrant.

In the past fifteen years, the place of Central Asia in Chinese diplomacy has undergone a gradual evolution. The basic pattern has been toward a gradual enhancement and toward greater independence of the Central Asian factor. Initially, China regarded Central Asia within a single Russian and Central Asian framework. It did so for two reasons. First, Russia and the Central Asian republics formed a single party in border talks with China. Second, for years after the Central Asian states became independent, the region did not bear much weight and hence was not assigned separate importance. That situation still more or less obtains. For example, international studies in China often assign Central Asia to Russian area programs rather than treat it as a separate field. That essentially reflects the traditional diplomatic attitude toward Central Asia.

The evolution of Central Asia's place in Chinese diplomacy is partly due to the changes in the region itself and partly to changes in China's needs. As Beijing's interests in Central Asia increased, the status of Central Asia in Chinese foreign policy has risen correspondingly.

To judge from recent developments, that rise in status and role will continue. There are several reasons why this is the case.

1. There are increasing indications that Central Asia will be one of the most important regions where the great powers interact, cooperate, and compete. It is a site where global and regional powers have concentrated—a phenomenon that is rare in other parts of the world. Namely, Russia, China, the United States, Europe and NATO, India, Japan, Iran, and Turkey are all vigorously expanding their influence and assigning greater importance to Central Asia. This region has become a large stage for interaction between the great powers and other countries.

2. The establishment of American air bases in Central Asia raises the pos-sibility of a long-term military presence in the region. That may mean a change in the status of Central Asia as China's strategic rear. In the event of a serious conflict or confrontation between China and the United States (over Taiwan or other issues), Central Asia could turn from a strategic rear into a strategic front. That would compel China to make an adjustment and to deploy forces to strengthen its position in the northwest.

3. Central Asia is an emerging new focus of Chinese diplomacy. It is lo-cated between China and Russia, borders on Mongolia in the east, abuts Iran in the west, and looks toward India and Pakistan in the south. Central Asia is therefore the axis linking Northeast Asia, West Asia, South Asia, China, and Russia. If China successfully promotes its relations with Central Asian region, this region could become an important fulcrum in China's rise as a global power. Meanwhile, Central Asia is also a suitable region for China to apply its new diplomatic thinking. With the expansion of China's interests and demands, with its growing dependence on the international market, China will—consciously or not—revise its traditional diplomatic thinking, which has been conservative and mediocre, and shift to a more transparent, active, and forward-oriented foreign policy. This will be embodied in Central Asia.

4. Most important, the role of Central Asian energy in the Chinese economy will grow substantially. Once the oil pipeline from Kazakhstan to Xinjiang is complete, oil imports from Central Asia will increase significantly. This will be the first transnational oil pipeline coming into China, which has made huge investments in exploration and producing of oil, pipeline construction and refining infrastructures. Furthermore, additional energy projects between China and Central Asia are expected. Over time, Central Asia's importance to the Chinese economy and economic security will obviously increase, thereby enhancing its strategic significance to China.

Once Central Asia becomes a major energy supplier, the significance of Central Asia will pertain not only to the issue of "East Turkestan" secessionism, but will extend to investments, energy, and economic relations. As China and Central Asia expand commercial ties, the transformation of the Central Asian states—politically, economically, and diplomatically—will have a greater impact on China and cause Beijing to pay more attention to this region. At the same time, as China expands its strategic interests there, the relations with the other great powers will become more direct and more complicated, with a corresponding increase in competition and cooperation.

In conclusion, as Central Asia's strategic significance for China grows, this will inevitably lead to a reassessment of that region's place in Chinese foreign policy. In general, the significance of this region will shift from the task of combating terrorism to broader security issues. Economically, Central Asia will be transformed from a lesser to an important trade partner. Strategically, Central Asia will cease to be regarded as a peaceful strategic rear and instead become a strategically active region.

China's Central Asian Policy: Fundamental Ideas and Objectives

China's policy toward Central Asia is of course a part of Beijing's overall strategy; diplomacy toward this region and global policy are inextricably intertwined. That global policy sets basic principles and shapes regional policy. At the same time, China's specific interests predetermine concrete policies toward Central Asia; these policies are regionally specific and independent of interests in other regions. These two dynamics, in essence, determine the specific features of policy toward Central Asia.

Based on the overall strategic conceptions, China's primary objective is to satisfy domestic demands, especially economic ones, not to expand the country's power and influence. In other words, China seeks to meet domestic needs, not establish sphere of its influence. This diplomacy is introverted, not extroverted. And Chinese policy toward Central Asia bears the same character. Its primary goal is to satisfy China's domestic demands, particularly with regard to its security and energy needs. China has not demonstrated any other objective except to satisfy these domestic requirements. Some, however, contend that China is seeking to establish its own sphere of influence or even control over Central Asia. That view, however, misrepresents China's strategic intentions and capabilities, at least under present circumstances. If one examines China's current role in Central Asia, there is no indication that Beijing seeks to carve out its own sphere of influence. Nor, indeed, does China have any real capacity or the requisite conditions to do so. Were China to attempt to transform Central Asia into its own sphere of influence or to assert control over the region, that would mean the exclusion of the other great powers—and hence a confrontation with them. That is obviously not what China is seeking, and it would be irrational to pursue such a policy.

China is very pragmatic and prudent in its policy toward Central Asia; it wants to avoid giving the impression that it is challenging any great power; it makes every effort to dispel the idea that it seeks to eject and replace any foreign power in the region. The fear that Beijing seeks to carve out its own sphere of influence in Central Asia is primarily due to anxiety about China's rapid rise and reflects a fundamental ignorance of Chinese realities and policies toward the region. The present author, when exchanging views with foreign scholars (including specialists from Russia and Central Asia), has observed a recurring pattern of thought: in response to a policy or proposal by China, however well-intentioned and reasonable, some scholars always attribute an ulterior motive and interpret Chinese motives from this incredulous, distrustful perspective. That reflects an inflexible approach toward China and its Central Asian policy; it shows an insensitivity to the complex background and changes in Chinese foreign policy. This kind of analysis presupposes that China has expansionist ambitions and constitutes a threat to other countries. Given these assumptions, such analyses of Chinese policy toward Central Asia are invariably negative and misleading.

In 2003 China formulated a new conception of foreign policy that assigned first priority to building an amicable, tranquil, and prosperous neighborhood. This concept reflects China's new awareness and approach toward surrounding countries. The background for this policy statement was the accelerated growth of the Chinese economy and the increase in its national strength—a process that naturally affects the expectations and concerns of its neighbors, most of whom are weaker than China. The critical task was to redefine relations under the new conditions.

The key element in the new conception holds that China should not only develop relations with surrounding countries on the basis of its own concerns and interests, but should also take into account the concerns and interests of its neighbors. This premise is fundamental and crucial. It represents a breakthrough in Chinese diplomatic strategy and shows an awareness of the need for policies that accommodate the new situation and that can improve China's relations with surrounding countries. This idea has become a basic component of China's peripheral diplomacy, especially with regard to weaker, smaller neighbors. Some contend that this approach may induce other countries to conclude China has assumed a position of supremacy. The fact remains, however, that there is an objective gap between the power of China and most of its neighbors. Under these circumstances, the goal of building an amicable, tranquil, and prosperous neighborhood is both pragmatic and positive.

The meaning of an "amicable neighborhood" is very clear: it gives priority to developing friendly relations with all the surrounding countries. The phrase "tranquil neighborhood" implies the need for China to make its neighbors, especially small and weaker ones, feel safe and secure in neighboring with China. Given that China has a much larger population, area, and power, the neighboring countries cannot but feel weak and vulnerable. Moreover, the dissemination of the "China threat theory" provokes anxiety about its growing power. All this undermines mutual trust between China and its neighbors. China hopes to eliminate such concerns by making nearby countries feel secure. Only then will they react favorably to China's development. The phrase "prosperous neighborhood" refers to economic policy; it requires Beijing to provide more aid to its neighbors and enable them to benefit from China's own growth. The term also connotes greater bilateral economic cooperation, with the mandate that China give greater consideration to the interests of surrounding countries. Given the scale and rate of Chinese economic development, the small and medium-size neighboring countries find it extremely difficult to compete. The policy of promoting a "prosperous neighborhood" seeks to ameliorate that problem.

This principle of promoting an amicable, tranquil, and prosperous neighborhood is also fundamental to Chinese policy in Central Asia. The specific circumstances in this region require adaptation. It bears noting that, before China formulated this concept, its Central Asian policy had already incorporated some of these elements. For example, China has showed a desire for an amicable, tranquil neighborhood as it developed bilateral relations with countries in this region and negotiated a resolution of border and security issues. The notion of a "prosperous neighborhood" is comparatively new in relations with Central Asia, but it has become an important guiding principle.

China's interests in Central Asia determine its specific policies and objectives in the region. Beijing has several basic objectives:

- *Ensure border security.* This is a long-term, constant objective. Despite the establishment of the bilateral relations between China and Central Asian countries and the creation of corresponding mechanisms for implementation, border security nonetheless remains a central issue and source of concern. To guarantee implementation of the Treaty on Deepening Military Trust in Border Regions in 1996 and the Treaty on Reduction of Military Forces in Border Regions in 1997, the signatories (China, Kazakhstan, Kyrgyzstan, Tajikistan, and Russia) established a joint inspection group to meet regularly and oversee implementation.

- *Combat terrorism, separatism, and extremism.* The goal in this effort is to fight "East Turkestan" secessionists, avert secession, and ensure stability in Xinjiang. In all likelihood, the "East Turkestan" movement in Xinjiang and international terrorism will exist for some time to come. In the immediate future, China will find it difficult to eradicate "East Turkestan" sentiment; Central Asia will also have to struggle to contain terrorism. Therefore an active campaign against terrorism, separatism, and extremism will remain China's long-term objective in Central Asia.

- *Guarantee that Central Asia is a stable strategic rear.* Given this objective of strategic security, China must prevent the formation of any real and potential strategic threat, ensure that the region not be controlled by any country or state group hostile to China, oppose militarization of the region and the competition of external military forces, and thwart the formation of any political and military group directed against China.

- *Ensure that the energy resources of Central Asia are accessible for China.* Energy is a principal interest of China and other countries vying for influence in Central Asia. To realize its energy interests, China must first ensure access to the region's energy resources. While Beijing does not seek to control these resources, it does oppose any attempt by another external country to monopolize and control the development and export of energy resources. China's goal is to participate in the development of Central Asian energy through normal competition and to cooperate with other countries.

- *Establish friendly ties with the countries of Central Asia.* Good bilateral relations with these states are a precondition for realizing China's interests and objectives in the region. To achieve this goal, China must amicably resolve border and security issues, and it has already done so. In addition, China must exhibit an attitude of amicability and fairness toward Central Asian countries. It must also concentrate on interests that are acceptable to the states in this region. These conditions are essential to any attempt by China to establish good relations with these countries. And it must do so on the basis of common state interests, not ideology and choice of regime. Only that approach can guarantee stable, amicable relations over the long term.

- *Maintain Regional Stability.* China values regional stability very highly. From China's perspective, stability serves as the precondition for developing normal and predictive political and economic relations with the region. Any instability in the region contains risk of chaos and harms China's interests in the region.

- *Preventing Central Asia from becoming a battlefield of the great powers.* Confrontation of the great powers in Central Asia is not desirable for China. It makes the region, directly close to China, a source of strategic intension. Such competition could destabilize the region, which is contrary to Chinese interests. Although China does recognize the presence and interests of other great powers in the region, it does not like that any great power control it.

Chinese Foreign Policy in Central Asia: Principal Methods and Instruments

China conducts its Central Asian policy through multilateral and bilateral channels. The main multilateral instrument is the SCO, which provides a good venue for developing positive relations with countries in the region. It provides an institutional framework for contact with Central Asian countries; enables China to become part of the Central Asian political, economic, and security process; facilitates a merging of Chinese and regional interests; and provides favorable conditions for carrying out foreign policy. The bilateral relations with individual Central Asian countries are as important as multilateral relations, but have more fundamental significance. That is because bilateral relations, in contrast to the multilateral framework, can address and resolve the full gamut of issues. It is essential that, in dealing with Central Asia, China balance the development of bilateral and multilateral relations. Each has its specific functions and features; the best approach is to complement the bilateral and multilateral channels. Reliance on the SCO and bilateral relations has enabled China to establish itself firmly in Central Asia.

Geopolitically, China is not only a neighbor of the Central Asian states but also a major power in the region. This geopolitical advantage enables China to become an important, lasting factor in Central Asian affairs. The Chinese presence is natural, not arbitrary; no matter what happens, China cannot withdraw from the region. Its influence is permanent and can only change in response to specific stimuli. Geographically, China shares long boundaries with Central Asian countries and has convenient transportation links (road, railway, and air transport) facilitating the exchange of people and goods.

China is an irreplaceable partner of Central Asian countries in establishing secure borders and providing regional security. The security of its 3,000-kilometer border with three Central Asian states is of vital importance to all. Only China, given this common boundary, can collaborate in maintaining security. Through bilateral agreements and the SCO, China also provides Central Asia with a security guarantee.

As a great power, China is a crucial factor in the foreign policy of Central Asian states. It is regarded as being capable of playing a positive role as a counterweight to other great powers and has a beneficent influence by helping Central Asian countries to maintain a balance and pursue a multidirectional diplomacy. Moreover, Chinese diplomatic culture has great affinity for the Central Asian countries. It does not seek to establish hegemony or control; it does not bully small countries, but treats them as equals; it does not meddle in their internal affairs; and it is willing to resolve all issues through negotiations and in a just manner. This has helped China to foster a positive image, which in turn is a valuable resource of its diplomacy.

China's principal diplomatic and political resource related to Central Asia is its economy, which appeals strongly to the countries of the region. China has a huge economy that is expected to continue its rapid pace of development. The growth of the Chinese economy will of course increase its influence and importance for its neighbors in Central Asia. China will thus be an important trade partner, investor, donor country, export market, and transportation link. It is fair to conclude that Chinese influence in Central Asia will increase because of the economic factor.

China has some disadvantages in its relations with Central Asia. These result primarily from the protracted separation and estrangement, from the relatively cursory period of post-Soviet ties, the weak basis of bilateral relations, and popular misunderstandings (especially deep-rooted stereotypes that encourage distrust and suspicion of China). China's economic capability is increasing and represents its greatest diplomatic resource; investment, however, has been limited relative to its economic power. In addition, the younger generation in Central Asia does not find China's political and social culture very appealing. And contradictions and disputes may easily occur along the lengthy borders.

In general, China's diplomatic resources bring both advantages and disadvantages. The advantages are long-term, but are slow to yield returns. The disadvantages are short-term, but will gradually weaken over time. From the long-term perspective, China's resources will steadily increase in their impact.

In addition to its basic foreign policy principles—noninterference in internal affairs, treatment of other countries as equals, respect for their autonomous political choice, and avoidance of indiscreet remarks and criticisms—Chinese diplomatic culture traditionally emphasizes the golden mean, eschews the drastic and extreme, and allows for the unforeseen. Peace and harmony hold the highest value. This diplomatic tradition enables China to handle diplomatic relations, avoid abrupt changes (which can significantly affect bilateral relations), and maintain normal relations with other countries.

China's Growing Role in Central Asia

The expansion of China's involvement in Central Asia has been smooth and peaceful. It gained strength from favorable conditions and overcame some unfavorable ones. In the past decade, China's progress in the region has been considerable and, to judge from current trends, is likely to remain so in the foreseeable future.

The Scale of Chinese Involvement in Central Asia

Shortly after the Soviet Union was dismantled and the countries of Central Asia proclaimed their independence, China became involved in the region. That was a natural process, driven by a number of factors.

Geographical contiguity was a factor that naturally predisposed Beijing to become active in Central Asia. In addition to its 3,000-kilometer border, no country borders on more Central Asian countries than China and no country is closer to Central Asia than China. Russia has a very long boundary line with Central Asia, but it only borders on Kazakhstan and faces the other four Central Asian countries across the vast Kazakh grasslands, far away from the Central Asian hinterland. Moreover, northern Kazakhstan, which borders on Russia, historically was not regarded as part of Central Asia. Iran and Afghanistan are the main neighbors of Central Asia, but both are much smaller countries than China and have less influence. Contiguity is a unique factor in creating close relations. Under normal circumstances, contiguity generates demands for mutual understanding and communication and leads to large-scale and frequent nongovernmental contacts. It may also raise issues that do not exist for noncontiguous countries.

Xinjiang has countless ties with Central Asia—ethnicity, religion, culture, history, and habitude. This is another unique factor in China's relations with Central Asia. Xinjiang has some of the same ethnic groups that reside in Central Asia: Kazakhs (1.3 million), Kyrgyz (more than 160,000), and some Tajiks and Uzbeks as well. Contrariwise, approximately 300,000 Uighurs reside in Central Asia. In short, Xinjiang and Central Asia have natural ethnic ties. Over the past century, these ethnic groups have lived within the Chinese and Russian states; they have therefore experienced different historical and cultural influences. Despite the resulting differences, they speak the same or similar languages, are Muslim, share common cultural origins, and have similar traditions and customs. This factor has naturally drawn China closer to Central Asia. The interaction between the residents of Xinjiang and Central Asian countries constitutes part of the process of China's relationship with that region.

China and Central Asia have deep historic roots that shape their mutual relationship. Their close ties commenced in 60 B.C. under the Han Dynasty, when this region was known in China as the "Western Regions." That term can be used in a broad or narrow sense. In the narrow sense, it refers to the area west of Yumenguan and Yangguan, Dunhuang, Gansu Province, and the region east of the Pamirs. In the broader sense, it denotes the area west of the Pamirs.[11] Since then China has had constant contact (political, economic, cultural, and historical) with Central Asia for two millennia. That experience has become an integral part of China's historical memory and entered into its history and culture. In modern times, after annexation by tsarist Russia, Central Asia ceased to exist as an independent political, cultural, and geographic unit and as a geographic hub. The loss of independent political status disrupted the traditional historical links with China. However, the deep historical ties were not totally effaced; these quickly reappeared as Central Asia regained independence and rejuvenated its historical memory of ties to China. Historical memory has also had a deep influence on China's attitudes and conceptions of Central Asia; it has been a unique factor in propelling China's reengagement with Central Asia.

In short, geographic proximity and cultural propinquity (ethnic, religious, linguistic) are critical factors in China's relationship to Central Asia. These do not predetermine policy, yet do have some impact. Compared with the other great powers, China has these extraordinary dimensions to its interaction with Central Asia.

Concretely, China's reengagement with Central Asia began with border issues. As noted earlier, negotiations to delineate boundaries were underway when the Soviet Union was still in existence. After the USSR was dismantled, most of the western section of the Sino-Soviet border became the boundary between China and three of the newly independent countries of Central Asia. These three states (Kazakhstan, Kyrgyzstan, and Tajikistan) decided to join Russia and to continue the border talks with China. The talks lasted for seven years. Resolution of the border issue was an important condition for China's new relations with Central Asia; it represented a project of cooperation between the two parties. Moreover, border security served to engender close ties. The successful cooperation in resolving border issues led directly to the formation of the "Shanghai Five," which would subsequently evolve into the SCO.

The Shanghai Five and later the SCO have created an important instrument for China to establish its presence and influence in the region. The Shanghai Five grew from an ad hoc meeting into a regional organization, and its agenda developed from border talks to a comprehensive dialogue and cooperation in politics, security, economy, and other spheres. The development and expanding role of the Shanghai Five, accompanied by the growing cooperation between China and Central Asian countries, brought a steady increase in China's presence and influence. In 2001 the Shanghai Five was reconstituted as a regional cooperation organization, the SCO. Establishment of the SCO represented a major shift in foreign policy and a strategic decision to become engaged in Central Asia. China's basic goal was to ensure security and stability in the northwest front and to advance Chinese interests in the region. From China's perspective, the SCO provides a security guarantee, an institutional channel enabling China to participate in Central Asian affairs, and a general platform for cooperation between China and this region. The SCO also signaled a strategic compromise between China and Russia: the two countries agreed to a strategic balance, recognized each other's interests, and embarked on strategic cooperation. It bears noting that a lot of Western observers ascribe an entirely different motivation behind the SCO: namely, they see it as merely a Sino-Russian joint effort to prevent the United States and NATO from gaining access to Central Asia.

Of the factors stimulating Chinese interest in Central Asia, trade has played a salient role. From the early 1990s, large quantities of cheap Chinese consumer goods poured into Central Asian countries and quickly came to dominate the markets for medium- and low-quality goods. For a while, cheap products from China saturated these markets; individual vendors from China and Central Asia played the key role. The central and local governments of China approved and supported this private trade. However, individual businesses and profit-seekers, not the government, were the main impetus for the influx of Chinese goods. Under the circumstances that then obtained, the individual vendors with flexible operating methods could adapt, while state commercial enterprises found it impossible to compete and survive.

Several additional factors promoted the development of consumer trade between China and Central Asia. After the dissolution of the Soviet Union and the independence of Central Asian countries, private contacts became much easier, as both sides adopted a system of mutual visa exemption, enabling residents to travel freely between the two sides. That, of course, opened the door to private border trade. In the first half of the 1990s, the rapid expansion of border trade between China and Central Asian countries was closely linked to the visa exemption. Later, however, the visa system became increasingly rigid, as countries required visas for private and later public affairs. Nevertheless, ordinary businesspeople could easily acquire visas through normal channels from Kazakhstan, Kyrgyzstan, and Tajikistan; the only exceptions were Uzbekistan and Turkmenistan.

Nevertheless, even after the change in visa regulations, trade between China and Central Asia did not decrease and merely shifted to other markets in the region. The economic depression triggered by the breakup of the USSR left many in this region impoverished, with low purchasing power, and huge quantities of cheap Chinese goods became the staple for everyday consumption. Chinese goods came in such large volume and at such low prices that other countries found it impossible to compete. China's dominance on the consumer markets of Central Asia had unexpected political effects; this became the dominant sign of China's presence in the region. The ubiquitous China goods left a deep impression on local residents and became part of local social life. Their political and social impact was so great that Maulen Ashimbaev, the former head of the presidential Institute for Strategic Studies in Kazakhstan, declared that prior to 11 September 2001, this commodity trade was the basis for China's foothold in the region and underpinned its attempt to create a tripartite balance with the United States and Russia.[12]

Energy is another focus of China's engagement in Central Asia, with Kazakhstan as the main partner. This cooperation takes two forms. One is the participation of Chinese oil companies in the exploration, development, and construction of infrastructure in Kazakhstan. The other is the Kazakhstan-China oil pipeline to deliver oil from Kazakhstan and Russia. This energy cooperation between China and Kazakhstan began in the second half of the 1990s. In June 1997 the Chinese National Petroleum Corporation (CNPC) placed bids on the privatization of Kazakh Aktiubinsk Oil and Gas and won the tender, obtaining 60 percent of the company stock. After this turning point, the PetroChina became active on the Kazakhstan energy market on a large scale, and bilateral energy cooperation between the two countries gradually increased. Subsequently, it expanded its share of the oil market of Kazakh. In May 2003 the Committee on State Assets and Privatization of the Ministry of Finance of the Republic of Kazakhstan sold its 25.12 percent of stock in the CNPC International Aktobe Munaigaz; CNPC purchased those shares through competitive bidding. Thus, the CNPC came to possess 85.42 percent of the stock in Aktobe Munaigaz. In 2003 output of the oilfield reached 4.65 million tons. In 2003, PetroChina Company Limited purchased 35 percent of the stock of a joint venture from Saudi Arabia's Nimir Petroleum and the remaining 65 percent from the Chevron Texaco, acquiring full rights to develop the North Buzachi Oilfield (in western Kazakhstan). In 2002, its output was 320,000 tons. PetroChina Company Limited plans to increase annual output to one million tons in the coming years.

In August 2005 CNPC invested 4.18 billion U.S. dollars to purchase Petro-Kazakhstan. This international oil company is registered in Canada, but all of its oil and gas fields and its refineries are located in Kazakhstan. Its annual crude oil capacity exceeds 7 million tons.[13] In October 2005 a PetroKazakhstan Stockholders Meeting approved the purchase of the company by the China National Petroleum Corporation International (CNPCI) under the CNPC. At the same time, CNPCI and the Kazakhstan National Oil and Gas Company signed a Memorandum of Understanding for the Kazakhstan National Oil and Gas Company to receive part of the stock of PetroKazakhstan so as to preserve national strategic control of mineral resource development and the right to manage a refinery jointly under PetroKazakhstan, as well as to share finished oil products on equal terms.[14] In October 2005 the purchase was approved by a local court in Canada. CNPC proclaimed the purchase a success; it represented one of China's key steps in the Central Asian energy field and its largest overseas energy investment.

Another sphere of China-Kazakhstan cooperation is the construction of an oil pipeline. This important cooperation has attracted considerable attention. In September 1997 CNPC signed the agreement for the project, which had been initially proposed by Kazakhstan. Between 1997 and 1999, the two sides completed a feasibility research report. According to the design, the pipeline will start from the Caspian Sea port Atyrau in Kazakhstan, run westward through the Aktiubinsk oilfields (including Kenkijak), which has been purchased by CNPC, and then cross through Kazakhstan to the Ala Tau Pass on the Chinese-Kazakh border. The length of the pipeline is more than 3,000 kilometers, of which about 2,818 kilometers are in Kazakhstan and about 270 kilometers in China. The total cost is estimated at 3 billion U.S. dollars. According to the initial plans, the whole pipeline were to be completed and go into operation in 2005. But according to the estimate of the PetroChina, the pipeline must deliver at least 20 million tons of oil per year to become cost-effective. In 1998, however, Kazakhstan's total petroleum output totaled just 25.9 million tons. When domestic consumption is deducted, the balance obviously cannot meet the demands of many pipelines and the minimum requirement of 20 million tons for the China-Kazakhstan pipeline. As a result, the two sides decided to realize the project by stages.

The China-Kazakhstan oil pipeline was put in three parts. The first section of the pipeline runs from Kenkijak to the Caspian Sea port city of Atyrau. It is 448 kilometers long, all in Kazakhstan. The pipeline can link the Kenkijak Oilfield purchased by the CNPC in Kazakhstan with Russian pipelines, enabling CNPC to ship crude oil westward to the Russian city of Novorossiisk on the Black Sea. This section does not have the problem with insufficiency of oil supply and was arranged as the first stage of the construction. In 2002 CNPC and KazMunaiGaz jointly financed construction of this part of the project. In March 2003, the pipeline was linked up and commenced operation. Its initial annual capacity was 6 million tons, but will eventually increase to 15 million tons.

The second section begins in the small city Atasu in the center of Kazakhstan and runs to the Ala Tau Pass in Xinjiang, with a length of 988 kilometers and an estimated cost of 850 million U.S. dollars.

During a visit by Chinese President Hu Jintao to Kazakhstan in June 2003, the two countries signed a declaration on the strategic significance of China-Kazakhstan energy cooperation. The parties agreed to strengthen cooperation in the oil and gas sector and to adopt measures to ensure the smooth implementation of existing projects. They also agreed to continue research on the China-Kazakhstan oil pipeline project, on relevant oilfield development projects, and on the possibility of constructing a natural gas pipeline from Kazakhstan to China. Kazakhstan supports China's participation in the exploration and development of its oilfields on the continental shelf of the Caspian Sea.[15] This means that the Chinese and Kazakhstani governments are determined to restart the project to build the China-Kazakhstan oil pipeline. During this same visit, CNPC signed an agreement with KazMunaiGaz and the Kazakh Ministry of Finance—An Agreement on Joint Investment Evaluation on Section-by-Section Construction of a Crude Oil Pipeline Between China and Kazakhstan. In May 2004, CNPC and KazMunaiGaz signed a further Agreement on the Basic Principles of Crude Oil Pipeline Construction from Atasu in Kazakhstan to the Ala Tau Pass in the People's Republic of China. In June 2004 China and Kazakhstan reached an agreement to establish a joint oil company, called the Sino-Kazakh Pipeline, with each party holding 50 percent of its stock.

Construction of the second section of the China-Kazakhstan oil pipeline began in September 2004 and was completed, on schedule, in December 2005. Its initial annual capacity was 10 million tons. In July 2006, the first flow of crude oil reached Dushanzi refinery in Xinjiang, through China-Kazakhstan oil pipeline. It signals that the pipeline was put into operation. This pipeline can also deliver Russian oil to China by tapping a pipeline that runs from Omsk in Siberia, via Kazakhstan and Uzbekistan, to Charjeu in Turkmenistan, passing through Atasu. Construction of that pipeline began in the Soviet era; it commenced operation in 2004. With completion of the pipeline from Atasu to Ala Tau Pass, it will be possible to deliver Russian oil from Atasu to Xinjiang.

The third section of the pipeline runs from Atasu to Kenkijak and links the above pipelines. The plan is to complete this section (which is about 1,340 kilometers long) in 2011. Once that is operative, the pipeline network will stretch from Atyrau on the Caspian Sea to Xinjiang in China. Its annual oil capacity can increase to 20 million tons, and that will mark a significant advance in China-Kazakhstan energy cooperation.

China has also been active in the energy sectors of Uzbekistan and Turkmenistan. In May 2005 CNPC and Uzbekneftegaz signed a cooperation agreement whereby CNPC would invest 600 million U.S. dollars in twenty-three oilfields in Uzbekistan. In July 2005, during the visit of Chinese Vice Premier Wu Yi to Uzbekistan, the Sinopec and Uzbekneftegaz signed an agreement providing that Sinopec would invest 100 million U.S. dollars in Uzbekistan over the next five years, with one half for oil exploration and the other half for the redevelopment of existing oilfields. A Sinopec subsidiary will set up a joint venture with Uzbekneftegaz.

Another important sphere of Chinese economic activity in the region is transportation. China has a natural interest in this infrastructure; transportation is essential for its ties to Central Asia and for the growth of bilateral trade. In addition, the transportation route to Europe through Central Asia is nearly 1,000 kilometers shorter than through Siberia, with corresponding savings in time and cost. In addition, given that the Central Asian countries are landlocked, transportation networks to the outside world are what they need most. All this has fueled China's strong interest in the construction of roads and railways in Central Asia.

There are now five road and railway routes linking China and Central Asia. These are the Ala Tau Pass and Huoerguosi frontier port (to Kazakhstan), the Torugart and Yearkeshtam frontier ports (to Kyrgyzstan), and the Kalasu frontier port which opened in December 2003 (to Tajikistan). Of these five, Ala Tau Pass is a railway line; the rest are roads. The Eurasian Railway linking China and Central Asia has already been put into operation. In addition, China has opened more than fifty international truck transport lines to Central Asia. Kazakhstan accounts for the bulk of goods shipped between China and Central Asia.

The construction of the transportation infrastructure will remain a key facet of China-Central Asia cooperation. Some large projects are already moving forward. As for railways, a second railway trunk line from China to Central Asia (linking China, Kyrgyzstan, and Uzbekistan) is under preparation. It will enter Central Asia from Kashgar in Xinjiang via Torugart. China and Kazakhstan are also preparing to build a new Eurasian railway trunk line; it will use the international standard 1,435mm gauge, which will greatly increase its efficiency. The original railway lines in Kazakhstan use Russian broad gauge and therefore cannot directly link with the railway lines in China and European countries, thereby reducing their efficiency. As for roadways, China is developing plans for a China-Kyrgyzstan-Uzbekistan road (the Kashi-Yearkeshtam-Sarytash-Osh-Andijon-Tashkent highway); this includes more than 230 kilometers in China, about 280 kilometers in Kyrgyzstan, and about 450 kilometers in Uzbekistan. This line is of great political and economic significance. In addition, China has moved ahead with a tentative plan to reestablish the old Eurasian Silk Road, which made Central Asia an integral part of the Asian transport network. In April 2004 in Shanghai, representatives of twenty-three Asian countries signed the Governmental Agreement on the Asian Road Network. This network will link the capitals, industrial centers, important ports, tourist sites, and commercial places of strategic importance of Asian countries, covering almost the whole Asia except its western part.[16]

Investment and aid are also important to the development of relations with Central Asian countries. China's assistance does not come through a single channel but rather comes through many departments and programs (and hence are not necessarily coordinated). Official data on Chinese aid to Central Asia is not accessible. But information about investment is available: in 2004 Chinese investment in the region was more than one billion U.S. dollars.[17] If one adds its investment in the energy sector, the overall scale is considerable. In the next five to ten years, investment will be one of the chief demands of Central Asia. Although China is not a major investment country, its capacity and interest are obviously increasing. In 2004 China announced plans to provide

900 million U.S. dollars in loans on favorable terms to member states of the
SCO. China has also provided assistance to Central Asian countries through
other channels and in different forms. As the economic environment in this
region improves, China's investment and economic assistance will continue
to increase.

China also has some military engagement in the region. In October 2002
China and Kyrgyzstan held joint military exercises—the first time that Chinese
forces had participated in military exercises abroad. In August 2003 China joined
in the military exercises conducted within the framework of the SCO. The first
phase of the exercises was in Kazakhstan, and the second in Xinjiang (at Yili).
In September 2006, China and Tajikistan jointly conducted antiterrorist military
exercises in Kuriab, Tajikistan. Thus, China has held joint military exercises with
all three neighboring Central Asian states. Although China has only participated
in these three military exercises in Central Asia, their political significance is
greater than their military one, for they demonstrated China's readiness to join
military actions to combat terrorism in the region.

Bilateral Relations Between China and Central Asian Countries

The basic principles in China's bilateral relations with each of the states in
Central Asia are identical: good neighbor and friendship, development, and
cooperation. Politically, China treats them equally and does not favor any
particular state. However, because these countries do differ (having, in particular, different economic potentials and geographic positions), their interest
for China does vary, with corresponding differences in bilateral relations.

Kazakhstan

In the next five to ten years, relations with Kazakhstan will be especially prominent, given its special geographic condition, natural resources, and economic
potential. Kazakhstan is the largest country in the region, its border with China
running more than 1,700 kilometers—over half of the entire Chinese-Central
Asian border. That makes Kazakhstan particularly important in terms of border
security. Moreover, in combating the "East Turkestan" movement, Kazakhstan
is central: it is the site of illegal activities and a conduit for interaction between
international terrorist forces and "East Turkestan" forces in China. During the
Soviet period, with the tensions between Moscow and Beijing, Kazakhstan
served as the base for many of the secessionist organizations. Since the fall of
the USSR in 1991, Kazakhstan has remained a center for underground "East
Turkestan" organizations. Thus China clearly needs Kazakhstan to cooperate
in its attempt to combat the "East Turkestan" forces.

Table 3.3

Trade Between China and Kazakhstan, 1992–2006
(in hundreds of millions of U.S. dollars)

Year	Total Trade Volume	China's Exports to Kazakhstan	China's Imports from Kazakhstan
1992	3.691	2.2793	1.4117
1993	4.3473	1.7169	2.6304
1994	3.35	1.38	1.96
1995	3.91	0.75447	3.16
1996	4.59	0.95306	3.64
1997	5.274	0.9460	4.3278
1998	6.36	2.05	4.31
1999	11.38	4.94	6.44
2000	15.57	4.94	6.44
2001	n.a.	n.a.	n.a.
2002	19.5	13.5	6
2003	32.9	15.7	17.2
2004	45	22.1	22.9
2005	68	39	29
2006*	67.09	37.69	29.4

Source: Chinese General Administration of Customs. http://www.mfa.gov.cn/chn/wjb/zzjg/dozys/gjlb/1716/default.htm.

The figures of 2005–6 are according to the statistics of the Ministry of Commerce of PRC. http://ozs.mofcom.gov.cn/aarticle/date/200601/20060101402644.html, http://ozs.mofcom.gov.cn/aarticle/date/200611/20061103821313.html.

* January–October 2006.

In addition, Xinjiang has more than 1.3 million Kazakh residents, most of whom reside in areas bordering on Kazakhstan. They have ethnic, historical, linguistic, and cultural ties with the Kazakhs on the other side of the border. Over the past century, the Kazakhs in Kazakhstan and Xinjiang have been influenced by Russian and Chinese politics, cultures, and languages, thus giving rise to significant differences. Nevertheless, the ethnic, historical, linguistic, and cultural roots remain important. Although some other ethnic groups of Central Asia do reside in Xinjiang, they are small and do not compare with the large Kazakh population—an important factor in shaping China's special relationship with Kazakhstan.

In economic and trade matters, Kazakhstan is by far China's largest partner in Central Asia. Thus, of the 8.7 billion U.S. dollars in total trade between China and Central Asia in 2005, approximately 7 billion was with Kazakhstan. Most of Xinjiang's frontier ports face Kazakhstan, which of course makes this the most active trade border. Imports from Kazakhstan include steel, nonferrous metals, metal ores, and petroleum and oil products. Chinese exports to Kazakhstan include basic consumer goods, such as textiles, garments, headwear, and shoes. By 2005 Chinese investment in Kazakhstan exceeded 1.4 billion U.S. dollars,[18] concentrated mainly in the oil sector, food processing, leather-making factories, catering, and trade. More than 2,000 joint enterprises with Chinese investment were registered in Kazakhstan.

China's energy interests in Central Asia are concentrated mainly in Kazakhstan, which has the main reserves and ranks as the largest producer in the region. The two countries have cooperated on energy for many years; the oil pipeline is a prime example of their cooperation. In the future, Kazakhstan will become one of China's most important sources of energy, and cooperation in this sector will substantially increase their political and economic cooperation.

China and Kazakhstan have not only laid a solid foundation for bilateral relations but have also collaborated to develop a high-level political, economic, and strategic framework. In February 1995 the Chinese government issued a public declaration of its willingness to provide a security guarantee for the Kazakhstani government. By 1998 the two countries had fully resolved border issues. In 2002 they signed the "Good Neighbor Treaty of Friendship and Cooperation," "Agreement on Cooperation Against Terrorism, Separatism, and Extremism," and "Agreement Between the Chinese Government and the Kazakhstani Government on Preventing Dangerous Military Activities." In 2003 the two countries worked out a cooperation program for the period between 2003 and 2008. In 2004 they agreed to create the China-Kazakhstan Cooperation Commission, with the vice-premier of each country serving as the co-chairs. The commission has ten subcommittees (e.g., economy and trade, communications, frontier port and customs, and science and technology). In the fields of energy, communications, trade, culture, and education, the two countries have adopted intergovernmental development plans. In July 2005 they also established a strategic partnership; Kazakhstan is the first Central Asian state to form a strategic partnership with China—and one of a select few in this category. The strategic partnership shows the great importance that China attaches to Kazakhstan and serves to strengthen mutual trust, to deepen security cooperation, to bolster security and stability, to promote economic cooperation, to stimulate common development and prosperity, to expand humanistic cooperation and nongovernmental contacts, and to enhance traditional friendship between the peoples of the two countries.[19] In sum, this strategic partnership mainly aims at promoting bilateral relations.

To be sure, there are some problems in the bilateral relations between China and Kazakhstan. Politically, the "China threat theory" to some extent exists in Kazakhstan and is more prominent here than in other states of Central Asia. Historical and modern reasons lay behind this concern. Thus, in the nineteenth century, the boundaries of these two states were drawn in a treaty between the

Qing dynasty in China and the Romanov dynasty in Imperial Russia. Although from a Chinese historical view the boundary was based on the unequal treaties imposed by Russia, China recognized their legal effect. The border issue did not subside when both dynasties fell, and during the period of Sino-Soviet confrontation, the border precipitated military clashes and tensions, including the Zhenbaodao incident in 1969 that remains entrenched in the memory of Kazakhstan. Decades of Soviet propaganda have instilled in Kazakh people a negative image of China as an unfriendly and aggressive power that is far stronger and predominant. Such is the origin of the menacing image of China in Kazakhstan. Over the last decade, the development of bilateral relations and exchanges has helped to show that this Sinophobia is groundless and subjective. As a matter of fact, border issues between China and Kazakhstan have totally been resolved and China has no territorial claim to Kazakhstan. While military fears keep diminishing, however, there is also a negative image of China's economic power—namely, fear that China will turn Kazakhstan into an appendage that supplies raw materials. This idea inspires fear and calls for vigilance toward China. However, the "China threat theory," whether in military or economic terms, is neither mainstream nor official view in Kazakhstan. Intelligent strategists in Kazakhstan's elite, in particular, recognize that China represents an opportunity, not a menace, to Kazakhstan.

Another point of discord is the sharing of water resources. At issue are the two main rivers—the Ertix (Irtysh) and Yili (Ili), both originating in the Tian Shan Mountains. The Ertix flows from China to the Arctic Ocean through eastern Kazakhstan and Russia; the Yili flows from China to Lake Balkhash in Kazakhstan. The upper estuaries are in China; the middle and lower reaches pass through Kazakhstan. In general, Kazakhstan (like other countries in Central Asia) has insufficient water and claims that China's over-utilization has aggravated its own shortages. This issue defies easy resolution: water resources are limited and cannot satisfy all the demands of both countries. Disputes about water are therefore bound to persist. The water issue between China and Kazakhstan itself is not a serious problem and the two sides have been negotiating to find a rational solution. The problem is that some people in Kazakhstan are inclined to make it a political problem in China-Kazakhstan relations.

If the above factors are taken into consideration, over the next ten to fifteen years Kazakhstan will most certainly loom ever larger in Chinese foreign policy. Their annual trade volume will exceed 10 billion U.S. dollars; Kazakhstan will become one of China's primary suppliers of energy; and both will intensify their economic and energy cooperation. Kazakhstan's main concerns with respect to China pertain to territorial integrity and security. In fact, however, China will not provoke a conflict over these issues, and the psychosis of fear in Kazakhstan will abate. The expansion of economic cooperation and extra-governmental contacts will gradually build mutual political trust. Nonetheless, some issues will remain and cause some difficulties in bilateral relations.

Uzbekistan

Uzbekistan, a large country, lies at the center of the region and borders all the other countries of Central Asia. It accounts for half of the total population in the region and has a high level of industrialization. During the Soviet era, Uzbekistan was the core of the traditional Central Asia. China recognizes the importance of Uzbekistan and seeks to develop good relations with this country. From the Chinese perspective, however, Uzbekistan is different from Kazakhstan. For one thing, China and Uzbekistan do not share a common border, and that diminishes the potential for disputes about boundary lines, water resources, and environmental pollution. Nor is the "China threat theory" widespread. Since the two countries are not contiguous, Uzbekistan has little reason to fear pressure from a powerful neighbor. At the same time, the lack of a common boundary also reduces the opportunity for direct contact, transportation links, border trade, and nongovernmental interaction. Uzbekistan also shunned participation in the Shanghai Five; and only in 2001 officially joined this instrument for regional cooperation. That belated engagement was mainly because Uzbekistan has no common boundary with China and because it saw no need to become involved in a regional organization for cooperation. However, this nonparticipation in the Shanghai Five during its first five years deprived the two countries of the opportunity to develop mutual understanding and cooperation.

Nevertheless, the two countries have no serious political differences and have raised their relations to the level of good partnership. At the same time, there are some limitations to their bilateral relations. Economic ties between China and Uzbekistan are limited, and the trade volume is small, although developing quickly. In 2005 the two countries reached a record level of trade turnover, but even so it was only about 900 million U.S. dollars—about one-eighth of the trade turnover between Kazakhstan and China. This level is disproportionately low for a country with a population of 25 million and a relatively developed industrial sector.

China seeks to develop political relations and to expand economic ties with Uzbekistan. Given the steady growth of China-Kazakhstan ties, the scale of China's relations with Uzbekistan could become even more marginal—which is something that Beijing would not like to see. The key to closer bilateral relations is clearly economics. At present, the two countries seek to improve

Table 3.4

Trade Between China and Uzbekistan, 1992–2006
(in hundreds of millions of U.S. dollars)

Year	Total Trade Volume	China's Exports to Uzbekistan	China's Imports from Uzbekistan
1993	0.5426	0.4280	0.1146
1994	1.24	0.5145	0.7720
1995	1.19	0.4756	0.7098
1996	1.87	0.3815	1.49
1997	2.02	0.6153	1.41
1998	0.9026	0.5788	0.3236
1999	0.4033	0.2738	0.1294
2000	0.5147	0.3943	0.1203
2001	n.a.	n.a.	n.a.
2002	1.3	1.04	0.2740
2003	3.47	1.47	2
2004	5.75	1.72	4.03
2005	6.8	2.3	4.5
2006*	8.4	3.28	5.11

Source: Chinese General Administration of Customs. Quoted in http://www.fmprc.gov
.cn/chn/wjb/zzjg/dozys/gjlb/1791/default.htm.
   The figures of 2005–6 are according to the statistics of the Ministry of Commerce of
PRC. http://ozs.mofcom.gov.cn/aarticle/date/200601/20060101402644, html http://ozs.
mofcom.gov.cn/aarticle/date/200611/20061103821313.html.
   * January–October 2006.

transportation links. Shipping between the two countries goes primarily through Kazakhstan and entails high transit costs. It is estimated that bilateral trade could double if the transportation issue could be resolved. Uzbekistan does have oil and natural gas reserves, which are obviously of interest to China. The latter has, accordingly, begun to prepare for long-term, large-scale cooperation and to make investments in the energy sector of Uzbekistan. Energy thus could make a significant contribution to bilateral relations and raise Uzbekistan's position in Chinese foreign policy.

Kyrgyzstan and Tajikistan

Kyrgyzstan and Tajikistan are small Central Asian countries that border on China, and both have good relations with Beijing.

   China and Kyrgyzstan have a long boundary running more than 1,000 kilometers. The convenient transportation links and two roadway frontier ports help to promote a flourishing border trade. Although Kyrgyzstan has a compact territory and small population, it has a relatively large trade volume

Table 3.5

Trade Between China and Kyrgyzstan, 1992–2006
(in hundreds of millions of U.S. dollars)

Year	Total Trade Volume	China's Exports to Kyrgyzstan	China's Imports from Kyrgyzstan
1992	0.3584	n.a.	n.a.
1993	1.0224	0.3655	0.6587
1994	1.05	0.2992	0.7545
1995	2.31	1.07	1.24
1996	1.05	0.68	0.37
1997	1.06	0.6153	0.3602
1998	1.98	1.72	0.2569
1999	1.35	1.03	0.32
2000	1.7761	1.1017	0.6744
2001	n.a.	n.a.	n.a.
2002	2.01	1.46	0.55
2003	3.14	2.45	0.69
2004	6.02	4.927	1.095
2005	9.72	8.67	1.05
2006*	16.44	15.49	0.949

Source: Chinese General Administration of Customs. Quoted in http://www.fmprc.gov
.cn/chn/wjb/zzjg/dozys/gjlb/1721/default.htm.
    The figures of 2005–6 are according to the statistics of the Ministry of Commerce of
PRC. http://ozs.mofcom.gov.cn/aarticle/date/200601/20060101402644.html, http://ozs
.mofcom.gov.cn/aarticle/date/200611/20061103821313.html.
    * January–October 2006.

with China (compared with the other countries of Central Asia). Thus in 2005 the trade volume between the two countries exceeded that between China and the much larger Uzbekistan; the Kyrgyz-Chinese trade volume was second only to that of Kazakhstan and China. To a significant degree, this is due to the convenient direct transportation links. The two countries are also making preparations to build a new transnational roadway and railway. The railway in China will lead to Kashgar, only 200 kilometers from the China-Kyrgyzstan border, then will link with the China's national railway network. It is only a matter of time before the new road and railway are opened. The two states have no significant political issues. They have resolved border issues, but this has provoked some opposition and protests from some political forces in Kyrgyzstan. The border issue cannot be resolved without compromises from both sides, and China has also made great compromises and concessions. The resolution of the issue conforms to the fundamental interests of the two countries and is beneficial to the long-term stability and development of bilateral relations. Nevertheless, some do propound the "China threat theory," but these are a minority and do not pose a serious problem for bilateral relations.

Table 3.6

Trade Between China and Tajikistan, 1992–2006
(in tens of thousands of dollars)

Year	Total Trade Volume	China's Exports to Tajikistan	China's Imports from Tajikistan
1992	275	195	28
1993	1236	648	588
1994	318	68	250
1995	2385	1461	924
1996	1171	764	407
1997	2023	1105	918
1998	1923	1104	819
1999	804	229	574
2000	1717	679	1038
2001	1076	545	531
2002	1239	650	589
2003	3881	2081	1801
2004	6893	5356	1537
2005	15794	14374	1420
2006*	23481	21843	1638

Source: Chinese General Administration of Customs. Quoted in http://www.fmprc.gov
.cn/chn/wjb/zzjg/dozys/gjlb/1776/default.htm.
    The figures of 2005–6 are according to the statistics of the Ministry of Commerce of
PRC. http://ozs.mofcom.gov.cn/aarticle/date/200601/20060101402644.html, http://ozs
.mofcom.gov.cn/aarticle/date/200611/20061103821313.html.
    * January–October 2006.

Security and terrorism are serious issues, however. Southern Kyrgyzstan
is part of the Fergana Valley, an important transit from Central Asia to China.
Fergana is also a site of Central Asian terrorist and extremist forces and a
major source of instability in the region. Kyrgyzstan is also the area where
the "East Turkestan" movement is active and projects a direct influence on
security in Xinjiang. Kyrgyzstan has actively fought against terrorism and
the "East Turkestan" movement, and that policy is of great importance to
China. It was no accident that the joint military exercises between China and
Central Asian countries were first conducted with Kyrgyzstan: it was not only
because they have good political relations, but also because fighting terrorism
and "East Turkestan" is a major concern in bilateral relations.

    Tajikistan has good relations with China, with no major conflicts in their
bilateral relations. The two countries contested an area in the Pamir Mountains,
but in 2002 they reached a compromise and completely resolved the issue.
The "East Turkestan" movement is less active in Tajikistan, and the Chinese-
Tajikistan border along towering mountains makes passage very difficult;
hence the problem of "East Turkestan" is weak in Tajikistan. Economic ties

Table 3.7

Trade Between China and Turkmenistan, 1992–2006
(in tens of thousands of U.S. dollars)

Year	Total Trade Volume	China's Exports to Turkmenistan	China's Imports from Turkmenistan
1992	450	409	41
1993	465	385	80
1994	1126	366	759
1995	1759	1126	632
1996	1146	845.2	301.5
1997	1524	1163	361
1998	1252	1029	222
1999	949	747	202
2000	1616	1210	406
2001	n.a.	n.a.	n.a.
2002	8752	8678	74
2003	11300	10900	371
2004	9874	8485	1389
2005	10987	9088	1899
2006*	10520	9595	925

Source: Chinese General Administration of Customs. Quoted in http://www.fmprc.gov.cn/chn/wjb/zzjg/dozys/gjlb/1781/default.htm.

The figures of 2005–6 are according to the statistics of the Ministry of Commerce of PRC. http://ozs.mofcom.gov.cn/aarticle/date/200601/20060101402644.html, http://ozs.mofcom.gov.cn/aarticle/date/200611/20061103821313.html.

   * January–October 2006.

and trade cooperation is limited. Chinese investment is also small. The main barrier to economic ties and trade is transportation: there are no direct road or rail connections, and all cargoes must transit through Kazakhstan or Kyrgyzstan, thereby increasing costs. In December 2003 the Karasu Pass opened the first highway frontier port, giving China and Tajikistan their first direct land transportation tie. This port, however, can only operate during summer months. China provides some economic assistance to Tajikistan.

Turkmenistan

Turkmenistan is a special country in Central Asia. It adheres to neutrality in foreign relations, abstains from any regional organization, does not belong to the SCO, and keeps its distance from all countries. China's relations with Turkmenistan are therefore not as close as with other countries in Central Asia. Nevertheless, China does have normal, friendly relations with Ashgabat. Turkmenistan has rich reserves of natural gas; it is also the only route from Central Asia to West Asia, the Middle East, and Europe (via Iran), making

Turkmenistan very important in terms of energy and transportation links. Hence China seeks to develop good relations with Turkmenistan, especially with regard to trade and energy. The two countries have engaged in some cooperation in the energy field: in 2000 CNPC and the Oil Ministry of Turkmenistan signed a memorandum of understanding to cooperate on oil and natural gas. In April 2006, during Turkmenistan President Niiazov's visit to Beijing, China and Turkmenistan signed an agreement that Turkmenistan will sell 30 billion cubic meters of gas to China annually from 2009 to 2039. China's participation in energy exploration in Turkmenistan is also active. All that reflects China's hope of obtaining energy from Turkmenistan in the future.

Chinese Relations with Russia and the United States

The relations between China and other great powers—Russia and the United States—are an integral part of its policy toward Central Asia. In addition, a number of other countries—European states (and the EU), Turkey, Iran, India, and Japan—have also established a presence and influence in the region.

It is generally thought that the unique geopolitical position and rich energy deposits are two principal reasons for the involvement of global and regional powers in Central Asia. A further reason is the weakness of these newly independent states, which enables outside powers to play a prominent role in the region.

From China's perspective, these external powers can be divided into three categories in terms of importance: a top level consisting of Russia and the United States; a second level with India, the EU, and Japan; and a third level with Iran, Turkey, and miscellaneous other countries. The focus here will be China's relationship to the countries in the top category—Russia and the United States.

China and Russia in Central Asia

Sino-Russian cooperation in Central Asia is grounded in a strategic partnership, the fundamental principle of their bilateral relations. In short, the basic premise of Chinese policy toward Russia in Central Asia subsumes strategic cooperation and makes this central to strengthening their bilateral relations.

Sino-Russian cooperation here began with a mutual reduction of military forces and with the establishment of military trust along their border regions. Given Russia's close ties to Kazakhstan, Kyrgyzstan, and Tajikistan, the cooperation between China and Russia was naturally extended to Central Asia. Security and military trust in border regions will remain a key part of Sino-Russian cooperation in Central Asia for a long time to come.

The institutional framework for cooperation there is the SCO, consisting of China, Russia, Kazakhstan, Kyrgyzstan, Tajikistan, and Uzbekistan, with a geopolitical focus being Central Asia. Sino-Russian cooperation in the SCO underpins their cooperation in Central Asia. Ten years have passed since its original foundation as the "Shanghai Five" in 1996; this decade also marks a period of Sino-Russian cooperation in the region.

China recognizes Russia's special relationship to Central Asia and its special interests and welcomes the consolidation of Moscow's position there. Chinese policy pays heed to Russia's interests and seeks to avoid provoking dissatisfaction. China has never attempted to compete with Russia in Central Asia and makes every effort to avoid giving such an impression.

China and Russia: Common Interests in Central Asia

China and Russia are both neighbors of the Central Asian states. Both have many common concerns and interests that constitute the basis for their cooperation in the region.

One common interest is the goal of safeguarding border security. That is the specific focus of the Treaty on Deepening Military Trust in Border Regions and the Treaty on Reduction of Military Forces in Border Regions, which were signed by China, Russia, Kazakhstan, Kyrgyzstan, and Tajikistan. Although the border of China and Russia in the section between Mongolia and Kazakhstan is less than 50 kilometers, these two countries are the most important signatories to the two treaties and share the responsibility of safeguarding borders under these two treaties.

Terrorist, separatist, and extremist activities in Central Asia pose a security threat to both countries and constitute an important common interest. Given the weakness of the new Central Asian states, for a considerable time to come they will not be able to extirpate these three evils from the region. China and Russia are willing to help combat these threats. The threat to Chinese and Russian national security has varied in intensity, being sometimes greater and sometimes less. Given that this threat will not soon disappear, China and Russia have common interest in fighting these evils and bolstering security in the region.

By extension, China and Russia have a common interest in ensuring regional security and stability. The turbulence and chaos in Central Asia may unleash terrorist, separatist, and extremist forces that could not only destabilize the region but affect Russia and China.

These two states also have a common position on the issue of a long-term American military presence in Central Asia in the wake of 9/11. To be sure, the American bases have significant geopolitical implications and cannot fail to arouse concern in Moscow and Beijing. However, before 2005, neither China nor Russia raised objections; indeed, in operations against Taliban, both cooperated with the United Stats to varying degrees.

That response was based on several considerations. First, given the events of 11 September 2001, the deployment of American forces to conduct antiterrorism military operations had an incontrovertible moral basis. Second, China and Russia believed that the American overthrow of the Taliban regime served their own interests in combating Islamist extremism. Third, China and Russia have no realistic capacity to block American intervention and deployment of military forces. Fourth, China and Russia did not want to harm their relations with the United States.

Nevertheless, both countries oppose a long-term American military presence in Central Asia and regard it as a potential geopolitical threat. They do not, however, intend to form an anti-American alliance in Central Asia. To judge from the relations of these three powers, China and Russia regard their relations as more important than their relations with the United States.

Initially after 9/11, some analysts expected a change in these relations, claiming that changes in Russian-American relations were reminiscent of World War II and making optimistic predictions about the probable development of their relations.[20] Subsequent events, however, showed such predictions to be unwarranted: after a brief warming, relations returned to their earlier level, and their close cooperation in Central Asia proved short-lived. When American military forces established bases in Central Asia, K. Tozskii, Director of the Russian Federal Border Service, declared that Russia would accept such bases only to combat terrorism in Afghanistan, but not over the long term.[21] Tozskii's remarks were prescient. With the continuation of an American military presence in Central Asia and with the United States expanding its involvement in the region's domestic politics, tensions between Washington and Moscow have become increasingly apparent. Those tensions, in turn, have served to bolster Sino-Russian cooperation in the region.

The outbreak of the colored revolutions in several former Soviet republics and their spread to Central Asia has served to reinforce cooperation between China and Russia. Professor Stephen Blank has described this as the formation of a common ideological objective of the two countries.[22] China, Russia, and the United States have fundamental differences in principle, with China and Russia on the one side and the United States on the other. China and Russia oppose the policy of forced "democratic transformation" in Central Asia being promoted by the United States. They warn that American policy there can destabilize the whole region, not only bringing turbulence to Central Asian states but having direct negative consequences on themselves. This common ideological-political perspective has reinforced the perception of their common interests, but only time will tell whether this common perception and policy will survive over the longer term.

China and Russia: Areas of Competition

China and Russia not only cooperate but also compete. Many analysts, especially outside China, predict that the two countries will inevitably recognize the contradictions in interests and turn from cooperation to competition. Some even hold that Central Asia may be the apple of discord, as differences on regional issues lead to growing confrontation between China and Russia.[23]

The complexity of Sino-Russian relations in Central Asia lies in their special geopolitical structure. The two are neighboring large powers. From the perspective of traditional geopolitical logic, they have special geopolitical relations, including an element of competition. This geopolitical competitiveness should also affect their relations in Central Asia: situated between China and Russia, the region bears similar geopolitical import for both countries and naturally evokes an attempt by both powers to establish their influence. As traditional geopolitical logic deduces, China and Russia inevitably encounter each other in this region, as each tries to expand its control over the region and to expel its adversary. Competition between the two countries is unavoidable.

Historically, Central Asia was a site of competition and confrontation for Russia and China. That past doubtless casts a long shadow over their relations. The past is past, but historical memory survives—with important, if elusive, consequences for the present. For example, the famous Russian Sinologist, V.G. Gelbras, asserts that China's goal in Central Asia is to recover territory once belonging to China (namely, territory south of Lake Balkhash, including parts of Kyrgyzstan and Kazakhstan territory) and that every Chinese official openly admits this.[24] That assertion controverts the facts; it is not based on realistic, rational analysis, but merely reflects a certain *idée fixe* and fails to transcend historical memory and deal with modern realities.

For more than a century, Central Asia was a part of Russia, but the situation is now different: these countries are now independent, and China has reentered the region. From a long-term perspective, China's presence and influence will gradually increase. That does not mean, however, that Russian influence will disappear and that China will displace Russia. To be sure, compared with the earlier situation, Russia's influence has waned while that of China has grown. But this does not mean that either will achieve absolute dominance. For the foreseeable future, at least, Russia will remain the dominant influence in the region. It should be said that China's own estimate of its power is more conservative than that of Western scholars.[25]

The key to Sino-Russian relations in this region is not China's attitude toward Russia but vice versa: How will Russia respond to the rise of China's presence and role?

Russia is still experiencing the pain of having lost its historical empire, and that process will pass neither quickly nor easily. After the breakup of the Soviet Union, Russia still regards the countries in the CIS as within its sphere of influence and has even made attempts at reintegration. Although the government has not expressed any intention of seeking to reestablish the old empire, the "imperial complex" has deep historical roots and will not quickly disappear, especially in the elite.[26] This nostalgia is natural. So far as Central Asia is concerned, all this reinforces Russian doubts and suspicions toward the presence of other great powers in the region—which raises a few important questions: although Russia recognizes China's presence in Central Asia and the value of cooperation, is there a limit to its willingness to accept an increase in Chinese influence here? Will Russia continue to regard China as its partner if the latter's influence rapidly rises? If Russia recovers its former power, will it change its view of China's role in the region?

The Russian elite is viscerally opposed to the influence of other major powers in Central Asia, but its attitude toward China is more complex. Notwithstanding the fact that China and Russia have reached a strategic partnership to cooperate in Central Asia, the Russian elite remains critical of China's role in the region. In 2004 Viacheslav Trubnikov, former first deputy foreign minister and director of the Russian Foreign Intelligence Bureau, declared outright in an interview that it is impossible for Russia to look favorably on the presence of any major power, whether the United States or China, in Central Asia: "Central Asia is a region of vital importance to us and is the direction to which we give priority. Of course it does not please us to see the presence of major powers from outside the region."[27] His comment reflects the views of a considerable number of Russian elite; the latter cannot accept the full independence of Central Asian countries and still entertain high hopes of returning this region to Russian control. They psychologically resist the presence of other countries there and deem it a violation of Russia's natural sphere of influence. They regard China on the same level as the United States and are psychologically exclusive to China's presence in Central Asia.

China, however, does not regard itself as an "outsider" in Central Asia. It has deep historical roots here, with a long history of interaction that far antedates any Russian ties to the region. From multiple perspectives (history, geography, culture, political reality, economic ties, and security), China is a power with close connections to the region. It is both natural and essential that China become engaged in Central Asia and develop closer relations with the countries here. And Gelbras is wrong to assert that China seeks to recover territory here. To the contrary, China seeks to consolidate, not undermine, the legal basis of the current border. Given the conditions of modern international relations, it is impossible for Central Asia to return to the border status that prevailed in the nineteenth century. Hence it is simply impossible for China to entertain any fantasies about recovering lost territories; it has no intention of indulging in such unrealistic policies.

Although it is possible that China and Russia could compete in some matters, it is neither necessary nor inevitable that they become embroiled in confrontation and conflict. The predictions of such a conflict come from geo-political theory and the assumptions of political power as a zero-sum game. In the post-Cold War period geopolitics is one, but not the only law govern-ing international relations; even in the geopolitical framework, the model of international relations has many options and variants; and the zero-sum logic no longer conforms fully to international relations.

In the post-Cold War period, it is generally assumed that countries have the right to develop relations with whatever countries they choose. Blocs and alignments have lost their sway. This applies as well to Central Asia, which, following the dissolution of the Soviet Union, became an independent geopo-litical region. Although it maintains especially close ties with Russia, modern international relations do not give Russia any exclusive rights and empowers the states of Central Asia to develop relations with other powers. Hence it has become almost impossible for Russia to treat Central Asia as its special sphere of influence from where other countries should be excluded.

The Russian conception of its traditional sphere of influence has also undergone change. Russia recognizes the substantial changes taking place in its relations with former parts of the Soviet Union; that relationship is ceas-ing to be extraordinary and special.[28] This new conception (which applies to Central Asia as well) will help to reduce the visceral opposition to China's presence in the region.

Sino-Russian relations in Central Asia are different from those of any earlier period, for they reflect a relative balance of power between the two countries. Although China's influence in Central Asia is increasing, for the foreseeable future neither Russia nor China will have overwhelming superiority and the capacity to drive the other from this region. This relative balance of power will facilitate a strategic compromise and recognition of mutual rights and interests. Accordingly, China seeks strategic cooperation, recognizes Russia's special interests and position, and avoids affronts that could evoke resistance and conflict. The central objective is to avert unnecessary competition and confrontation.

China has relied mainly on economics to increase its influence in Central Asia. This growing influence is gradual; it does not precipitate dramatic, sudden changes in the relations between major powers. Nor does China have any intention of increasing its power in the region by seeking a military presence. In May 2005, to rebut rumors that China planned to station troops in Kyrgyzstan, China's foreign ministry immediately issued a categorical denial. Russian media speculated, however, that this had all been a trial balloon to test the reaction of the international community, but such conjecture is utterly unfounded.[29] Still, one cannot altogether preclude the possibility that China could become involved militarily, but it would do so only as part of a multilateral undertaking and would not establish military bases. China has in principle invited Central Asian and Russian states to participate in military exercises on its territory; these parties may extend a similar offer to China. Moreover, China has contributed troops to international peacekeeping activities, and, theoretically, it could do the same for similar undertakings in Central Asia.

The American presence, especially its military bases, has attracted the attention of both China and Russia and made the United States a principal object of concern. To some extent, the American challenge may reduce the possibility of competition between Russia and China as they coalesce to oppose the American intrusion. Given that the American presence is unlikely to diminish any time soon, it will probably be a long-term factor in shaping Sino-Russian relations in the region.

In short, there is potential for both cooperation and conflict between China and Russia in Central Asia. Currently and at least for near future, the factors favoring cooperation outweigh those generating conflict. It implies that China and Russia are much more driven to cooperation than conflict. In addition, it seems both China and Russia are clear that cooperation will bring much more gains and conflict would make both of them losers in general sense. This fact also positively affects China and Russia in preventing them from getting into conflict.

The Russian Military Presence in Central Asia: The View from Beijing

China obviously opposes a long-term American military presence in Central Asia. Given that, Western scholars ask about Beijing's attitude toward a Russian military presence in the region. Is China more inclined to oppose American than Russian bases? If so, why? These are delicate questions.

In October 2003 Russia deployed forces at the Kyrgyz air base at Kant (near Bishkek). It was the first Russian military base to be established in Central Asia since the dissolution of the Soviet Union. In October 2004 Russia commenced operations at a second military base in Central Asia, this time in Tajikistan. Both of those arrangements are long-term.[30] Kyrgyzstan and Tajikistan are neighbors of China; hence the Russian bases are near the border with China. In November 2005 Russia and Uzbekistan announced the establishment of an alliance that stipulates the right of each signatory to use the military installations on the other's territory if necessary. That gives Russia military access to Uzbekistan and may also imply the possibility of a Russian military presence in Uzbekistan.[31] It is entirely possible that Russia will continue to strengthen its military presence in the region.

China made no public statement regarding the Russian military presence in Central Asia. It has expressed neither approval nor disapproval. From the perspective of traditional geopolitical logic, Beijing cannot like any major power to establish a military base in neighboring countries; nonetheless the Chinese response to Russian bases in Central Asia has been different. One reason is history: Russia has had a military presence there for more than a century, even after the proclamation of independence in 1991 (e.g., Russia's 201st motorized division in Tajikistan). Hence the Russian bases represent the status quo, not a radical break from the past or a threat. A second reason is the strategic partnership that underlies the cooperation of the two powers. A third reason is the simple fact that, at least for some time to come, Russia will not pose a strategic threat. For all these reasons China takes a very different view toward the Russian than toward the American military presence in the region.

Chinese-American Relations in Central Asia

China has neither issued a formal statement on the American presence in Central Asia nor raised the issue directly with the United States. There are several possible explanations for such restraint. One is that China has no clear policy; another is that China deliberately pursues ambiguity; a third is that China does not see sufficient urgency or need to formulate a special policy. Whatever the explanation, China plainly has difficulty defining a clear position. Several factors underlay this difficulty.

One is the Chinese quandary: the United States appears to be neither partner nor rival, neither friend nor enemy. China finds it difficult to ascertain America's precise role and intent in Central Asia, particularly with respect to China itself. Still, since the United States is not an archenemy, China has no desire to turn Washington into an overt adversary.

Another difficulty is the different policies pursued by China and the Central Asian countries toward the United States in this region. Chinese policy must take into account the aims and policies of the countries in the region. And these countries seek to develop good relations with Washington and reap various benefits, such as economic assistance, guarantees for regional security, a counterweight to the other major powers, and a feeling of greater domestic stability for the regimes themselves (because of American support). This goal of closer relations with the United States is entirely reasonable for Central Asian states; and the decision to allow American military bases on their territories is not directed at China. Nevertheless, the difference in policies does generate some friction. China should show an understanding of the position of the Central Asian countries and respect their interests. Still, China must protect its own interests and react to the American military presence on the basis of its own needs. This tension—between recognizing the interests of Central Asian states and defending its own—makes it difficult to formulate a policy on the U.S. role in the region.

The Chinese and American interest structures in this region are quite contradictory: in the nontraditional security field, they share common enemies and common objectives, but have very different interests in the traditional security field. All this makes for very complicated relations. Although the two parties can cooperate in combating terrorism in Central Asia, for this conforms to their mutual security interests, the American military presence in Central Asia is a cause of concern in Beijing. This is the essence of the complex relations between China and the United States: they both seek to combat terrorism as a threat to security and stability, but that very cooperation generates a contradiction with respect to traditional security conceptions. This contradiction between realism and geopolitical logic is implicit in the structure of post-Cold War relations. The result is uncertainty and fluctuations in decision making and policy.

There is one other reason why China has difficulty defining its policy on the American presence in Central Asia: Sino-American relations in the region deviate from the more general pattern of a steady improvement in ties since 2001. China assigns great importance to good relations with Washington: this is important for Chinese economic development and for maintaining stability in the Taiwan Strait situation. Therefore China wants to avoid unnecessary conflicts with Washington. In Central Asia, however, that is not easy to do. China is uncertain about American policy and objectives in the region, has natural concerns about the long-term presence of U.S. military bases, and therefore remains ambivalent regarding the extent to which it should cooperate with Washington in this region.

The American Military Presence in Central Asia: The Chinese View

How does China assess the impact of a long-term American military presence in the region? What countermeasures should China adopt?

Assessments of the American military presence vary within China itself. Some believe that it poses no threat, for these military forces are too limited to pose a serious threat to China. Others argue that the American bases here do pose a serious threat and danger. Neither represent a majority. Most people in China believe that the American military presence is harmful to Chinese interests, but is of a more potential threat than an immediate and mainly affects strategic posture. The American military presence has both positive and negative elements. Destruction of the Taliban regime and resolution of the Afghanistan issue contribute to security in the region and therefore serve Chinese interests. However, the establishment of U.S. military bases in Central Asia has broader strategic implications: in the event of a Chinese confrontation over Taiwan or other issues, Washington could use its presence in Central Asia to pose a threat to the Chinese rear. Nor does Washington seem to understand that its military encirclement of China from different directions cannot fail to arouse a feeling in Beijing of being surrounded. The U.S. bases in the region have stimulated military competition, intensified tendencies of militarization, increased pressures for other major powers to have their own military forces—all of which China opposes.[32] While China believes that the United States often has a dual standard on such issues as fighting terrorism, Beijing is confident of American dual standard on the issue of "East Turkestan" separatism.[33]

Another consideration is the exploitation of Central Asia's energy resources. As already noted, this region will soon become a key source of energy for China; the oil pipeline from Kazakhstan to China is in operation. Importing energy from Central Asia is highly advantageous: transportation is overland and immune to interdiction by other countries. The American military presence in Central Asia has made this advantage problematic. China cannot agree to a long-term U.S. presence in a region of vital importance for its energy supply and its delivery. Finally, Sino-American relations suffer from absence of strategic understanding. It also underlines all the mistrust and doubts of China toward the U.S. military presence in the region.

The positive and negative roles of the American military presence in Central Asia, from China's perspective, are interwoven and inextricable. In general, the positive role is decreasing, while the negative role is growing in its potential. The positive role is relatively short-term; the negative role may be long-term. Therefore, from a long-term Chinese perspective, the disadvantages of the American military presence in Central Asia outweigh the advantages.

Chinese Policy Toward the American Presence in Central Asia

China does not welcome a long-term American military presence in Central Asia, but it regards the threat as potential and does not regard it as especially grave or urgent and some foreign analysts hold similar judgements.[34] China therefore has responded calmly and pursues a low-key policy. On 17 January 2002, for the first time, China issued a public statement on the issue of American bases in the region. In response to a question about this matter, a spokesperson of China's Foreign Ministry cited the repeated assurances from the United States that it does not seek a long-term military presence in Central Asia. China holds that stability and development in Central Asia not only conform to the fundamental interests of the region and its neighbors but also promote global peace and stability.[35] In 2003 China made a slight change in its rhetoric, adopting as its standard response the following:

> Peace and stability in Central Asia involve all the countries in the region. We have also noticed that the United States has said repeatedly that it has no intention of long-term deployments in Central Asia. We hope all parties will jointly commit themselves to maintaining peace and stability in the region. Only doing so will be beneficial to the regional peace and development.[36]

In a November 2003 interview with the German weekly *Der Spiegel*, China's foreign minister Li Zhaoxing noted that the Americans had clearly denied any intention of seeking a long-term military presence in Central Asia. He affirmed that China welcomed an improvement in American relations with South Asian countries; he also expressed the hope that the United States would play a constructive role in Central Asia, South Asia, and the Asia-Pacific region as a whole.[37] Hence China hopes that the United States will not maintain troops in Central Asia for a long period. Beijing's moderate response shows that it seeks to avoid any provocation. In short, China has changed its attitude toward American forces in the region: instead of vigilance and suspicion, it adopted a more open-minded attitude and welcomed a constructive role for the United States.

On 5 July 2005 the SCO held a summit in Astana, Kazakhstan, where it adopted a formal declaration affirming the necessity for its members to set a final deadline for their temporary stationing of foreign military contingents on their territories.[38] That declaration raised new doubts in Washington about Chinese policy; the American secretary of defense attributed the declaration to pressure being exerted by the two major powers—Russia and China—while others made China responsible for initiating the SCO decision.[39] The Astana declaration did reflect China's consistent opposition to a long-term American military presence in Central Asia, but it does not demonstrate that China abruptly changed its position and became uncompromising. The real factor behind the SCO declaration was dissatisfaction among the Central Asian states about American policy toward the region—a direct consequence of the colored revolutions in the former Soviet republics. Georgia, Ukraine, and Kyrgyzstan all experienced this type of generally peaceful revolution—regime changes in which the United States played a role as an external sponsor. The leaders of Central Asia, especially Uzbekistan, became anxious that the United States was promoting colored revolutions in the region. The request that the United States set a deadline for closing its military bases was one way of voicing their displeasure with Washington.

The Central Asian countries, especially Uzbekistan, determine their attitude toward the United States, and neither China nor Russia can exert much influence on them. China has supported, but has not, in fact, attempted to put pressure on Central Asian countries. The American military bases were on the territories of Central Asian countries and any Chinese request for the withdrawal of American forces would have been tantamount to making demands on Central Asian countries. China does not make such demands, whether because of its basic principle of keeping a low profile, its unwillingness to make a bad impression, or its tendency to follow the tradition of the golden mean in Chinese diplomacy. Making demands is contrary to the Chinese approach. Rather, China preferred not to exacerbate the issue of American bases in Central Asia and not to allow this issue to burden the development of Sino-American relations.

China defines its attitude toward the U.S. presence in Central Asia from the perspective of overall Sino-American relations, and Central Asia, from Beijing's perspective, is not a central component in the two countries' relationship. Central Asia depends on general U.S.-China bilateral relations, not vice versa. Hence, if Sino-American relations are generally good, it is easier to deal with the question of Central Asia; if the general relations are strained, then the Central Asian question becomes more difficult to resolve. China, at least, is hopeful that the Central Asian question will not sour bilateral relations with the United States more generally. As noted, China has several reasons for seeking to develop relations with Washington—to advance the country's economic interests, to ensure stability in the Taiwan Strait, and to reinforce a secure strategic environment. From the Chinese perspective, any harm to overall bilateral relations because of Central Asia would far outweigh the gains.

China has a guiding ideology for its relations with the United States in Central Asia, but as stated above, China has no clear-cut policy. It regards the current phase as a transition, adopts what can be called a wait-and-see policy, and awaits change and finalization of various relations in the region, including the Afghanistan situation, U.S. relations with Central Asian countries, and great-power relations.

In the triangle of China, Russia, and the United States, Chinese policy is to give priority to Russia, not the United States. That is because Sino-Russian cooperation provides the strategic framework for the triangular relationship and naturally extends to Central Asia. In that region, China and Russia have similar views and positions with respect to American bases there.

In general, however, China does not intend to play the "Great Game" in Central Asia and does not like the history of "Great Game" repeat in the region. Such competition and confrontation between great powers in Central Asia are contrary to China's interests and desire for peripheral stability. Hence China is willing to cooperate with the United States in this region and to form good, stable bilateral relations there—which it has many times reiterated.[40] China recognizes the many common interests it shares with the United States in Central Asia, and believes that the two countries can and should cooperate to combat terrorism, fight drug smuggling, defuse regional conflicts, and maintain regional stability and energy flows.[41]

From 9/11 to the Colored Revolutions

The terrorist attacks of 11 September 2001 and the colored revolutions are the two most important set of events in the past five years and have had a profound impact on the geopolitical situation and the interrelations of the major powers in Central Asia. These events have combined to trigger dramatic changes not only in the region, but have had significant (though differing) impacts on the three main powers in the region. In particular, these three powers have had very different responses to the colored revolutions.

Chinese scholars question the phrase colored revolution. Since in their view the word "revolution" denotes a change of system and brings historical progress, the events in the former Soviet republics, especially in Central Asia, cannot be called revolutions. As to the causes of the colored revolutions, this author can only express his own personal view.

From the early 1990s, a new political process has been at work in the former Soviet republics. This process has created new social forces, nurtured a new humanistic spirit, advanced new political appeals, and formed new space for political development. Fifteen years have elapsed since the formation of the newly independent states; twenty years have passed since the initiation of Mikhail Gorbachev's perestroika campaign. People under forty years of age constitute a new generation; they grew up against a new historical background and in a new social environment. Their weltanschauung and value system are different from the older generation; what they have seen is not progress and democracy, but a gap between reality and the ideal of democratic government. It is striking that youth organizations have played an especially active and resolute role in the colored revolutions. Georgia had a youth movement called Kmara ("that's enough"), Ukraine had Pora ("it is time"), and Kyrgyz-stan had KelKel ("road to reform"). These organizations served to mobilize, propagandize, and lead the charge forward. In commenting on the colored revolutions, former U.S. Secretary of State Zbigniew Brzezinski emphasizes that the rise of the younger generation with new political concepts and demands is characteristic of the colored revolutions.[42] In time, the older generation of leaders will withdraw from the political stage (for political reasons or physi-ological reasons), and that is a natural turning point for social change and power transformation.

The movements behind the colored revolutions gained such momentum in the former Soviet republics by mobilizing mass support from all strata of the population. The revolutions were initiated and organized by an opposition bearing the banner of democracy, but it was the mass of ordinary citizens who played the principal role. And the people were not necessarily motivated by a desire for democracy or pro-Western policies, but by poverty, dissatisfac-tion with the regime, and nationalist or ethnic consciousness. The opposition provided an opportunity to express this multifaceted discontent.

The discontent was generated primarily by poverty, polarization, corrup-tion, and social injustice. Poverty has been a universal problem in most of the former Soviet republics, but especially in the countries that had the colored revolutions. For example, the Georgian economy suffered a precipitous decline after the breakup of the USSR; by 1994 its GDP plunged by 72 percent, its industry by 84 percent, its agriculture by 46 percent, and its investment in capital construction by 95 percent (compared with 1990). In 1995 the Geor-gian economy began to recover, but at a slow pace. In 2003 its GDP had risen by 63 percent from 1994, yet was still below the level achieved prior to the dissolution of the Soviet Union. Poverty is ubiquitous there. According to a sample survey, by 2002 the income of 90 to 95 percent of Georgian families was beneath poverty line.[43]

Ukraine, once called the granary of the Soviet Union, has a solid industrial foundation and good agricultural conditions, but underwent sharp economic decline after gaining independence: between 1992 and 1999 its GDP dropped by 75 percent, and about 70 percent of the population lived below the pov-erty line. A country with a developed culture and saw millions leave their homeland and go to Russia and elsewhere abroad to find work. Complaints from the masses were heard everywhere. According to Ukrainian scholars, the Ukrainian economy is the least successful of all the CIS countries in the background of its more developed industrial and agricultural infrastructure.[44] Although the Ukrainian economy has began to recover since 2000, the ac-cumulated problems will require many years to resolve.

Kyrgyzstan, one of the least developed Soviet republics, suffered economic recession and acute social distress during the first years of independence. By 1999 people under the poverty line accounted for 60 percent of a country of 5 million residents. Kyrgyzstan has since begun a slow recovery, but by 2002, people living below the subsistence minimum still comprised 52 percent of the population. Its level of industrialization is lower; 66 percent of the people live in the countryside, where poverty is particularly intense. In some regions, such as Naryn province, the poverty rate is over 80 percent; in Talas province it is 72 percent. Indeed, of all the former Soviet republics, poverty rates are the highest in Kyrgyzstan and conditions are bleak, especially in the villages. Seventy percent of the villages lack running water and 41 percent do not have a hospital or clinic. Wages are extremely low; the monthly average is between 20 and 30 U.S. dollars, but sometimes even below 10 U.S. dollars. At the very bottom of the social ladder are 13 percent of the residents, whose income suffices only to buy the basic necessities.[45]

Amidst this dire poverty a strata of nouveau riche has appeared, with a steady growth in the polarization between rich and poor. Former state and party officials have become capitalists and businessmen, forming a new wealthy elite. In Georgia, the income of the top 10 percent of the population is 2,530 times that of the bottom 10 percent.[46] Almost all the heads of large Ukrainian banks are former party or komsomol officials. From the popular perspective, politicians are not statesmen but transients intent on reaping maximum profit as quickly as possible. The government is rife with corruption, nepotism, and personal enrichment—which can only provoke the animosity of the general citizenry. Commenting on the revolution that he led, Kyrgyz opposition leader Kurmanbek Bakiev called corruption the source of many social and economic problems and the main cause for popular anger.[47] Western scholars also generally agree that these social factors were central to the Kyrgyz revolution.[48]

Regional and ethnic opposition also played a special role in the colored revolutions, especially in Ukraine and Kyrgyzstan. In those two revolutions, the lines between opposing sides were drawn not only by power and adherence to democracy, but also by complex regional and ethnic ties.

Another factor in the colored revolutions is the United States, which has sought to promote Western democracy and values throughout the world. This policy of supporting democratic transformation in the former Soviet republics has geopolitical implications. In Brzezinski's view, the colored revolutions indicate the appearance of a pluralistic configuration in the CIS—in other words, the configuration centered around Russia has been broken.[49] That is the American objective in Central Asia.

However, the colored revolutions were not solely due to American support and assistance. These revolutions, were there not the requisite domestic conditions, would not have occurred; these domestic factors are the most fundamental and principal reasons for the revolutions there. Nevertheless, without the long-term preparations and the support and assistance of the United States, the colored revolutions would not necessarily have occurred at these particular times and with such success. Josef Bandsky observes that, while discontent was rife in the affected countries, it would not have turned into a crisis and regime change without foreign support and financing.[50] The *Guardian* observes that the Orange Revolution in Ukraine was the creation of Americans through a well-conceived plan akin to the mass marketing and promotion of Western brands.[51] The former president of Kyrgyzstan, Askar Akaev, claims that the revolution in his country was the handiwork of the United States.[52] In short, the United States has played an important role in the colored revolutions.

The Colored Revolutions: Impact on Great-Power Relations in Central Asia

The colored revolutions have had a negative impact on American power in the region and diminished what Washington achieved in the wake of 9/11. These revolutions have precipitated pressure on the United States to close its military bases in Central Asia, which had been one of Washington's key gains. Despite assurances, the United States evidently intends to maintain these "temporary" bases for a long time to come. The colored revolutions precipitated new opposition from regional leaders and the SCO declaration of July 2005, which demanded a timetable on the withdrawal of American military bases from Central Asia. Shortly afterward, on 29 July 2005, Uzbekistan officially gave the United States six months to leave its military base in Karshi-Khanabad. Although Kyrgyzstan agreed to the continued presence of the American base at Manas, it did so only after the U.S. secretary of defense made a personal plea and agreed to pay a higher price.[53] On 21 November 2005 the United States closed its military base in Uzbekistan, so the small country of Kyrgyzstan became the sole Central Asian country to have an American military facility on its soil. However, because its neighbors neither have nor want an American military base, and because Kyrgyzstan has close ties to Russia, Bishkek must feel embarrassed by its decision to allow the stationing of U.S. forces on its territory. It is fair to surmise that the long-term American military presence in Central Asia is bound to encounter difficulties.

The relations between the United States and the countries of Central Asia had improved after 9/11, but have more recently deteriorated. That is especially true for Uzbekistan, which had been Washington's most important partner and the strategic fulcrum of its Central Asian policy. In March 2002 the two countries announced the formation of a strategic partnership that, in part, said that the United States "affirms that it would regard with grave concern any external threat to the security and territory integrity of the Republic of Uzbekistan." But the spread of colored revolutions undermined that relationship, and the Andijon incident of May 2005 had a significant negative impact on their bilateral relations. Indeed, the strategic partnership was almost purely nominal. The colored revolutions also aroused the concern of other Central Asian countries and harmed their ties with the United States. The American ambassador to Tajikistan, Richard Hoagland, offered the ironic observation that he was the ultimate victim of the colored revolutions, since he now aroused universal suspicion in Tajikistan.[54] That is no less true of American relations with the other Central Asian countries.

After 9/11, the United States might have become one of the important security assurance mechanisms in Central Asia and even replaced the SCO and the Collective Security Treaty Organization. That possibility, however, is now diminished. The American strike against the Taliban and Al Qaeda in Afghanistan was an act of vengeance; it bore no coherent policy and plan to provide a security guarantee for the region. Still, the American bases increased the sense of security. The colored revolutions undermined that assumption and increased each regime's sense of insecurity. With the closing of the American military installations in Uzbekistan, the U.S. presence and security assurance will obviously decrease.

While U.S. predominance has largely disappeared, Russia continues its attempt to recover lost position and to increase its influence in Central Asia. Although the American support for a democratic transformation initially appeared to weaken Russian influence, the net effect was just the opposite: the colored revolutions have tipped the scales in Russia's favor. Central Asian countries now rely more heavily on Russia for security and favor Russian military presence. Russia, in turn, has increased its political, economic, and military involvement. After the new president of Kyrgyzstan, Bakiev, took office, his first act was to visit Russia. In September 2005 the two countries signed a new cooperative agreement on military technology. Bakiev said that Russia was and will be his country's main strategic partner in politics, military technology, economics, culture, and humanitarian sphere.[55] The development of relations between Russia and Uzbekistan is still more striking. In September 2005 the two countries held the first joint military exercises since the dissolution of the Soviet Union. That same month Russia and Uzbekistan signed an agreement on ensuring flight security for civilian aircraft. Although the contents of the agreement were not disclosed, one analysis holds that this is Russia's first step toward bringing Uzbekistan into the CIS collective air defense system.[56] Uzbekistan is thus making Russia, not the United States, its strategic partner.[57] In October 2005 the Central Asian Cooperation Organization and the Eurasian Economic Community were merged; this will bring Uzbekistan into the integration process of the Eurasian Economic Community. On 14 November 2005 Russia and Uzbekistan announced the formation of an alliance—a dramatic contrast to the closing of the American military base in Karshi-Khanabad a week later.

The colored revolutions have also facilitated closer Sino-Russian cooperation in Central Asia and have reinforced Russia's strategic interests in the east. The revolutions pose the same challenge to China and Russia, which have similar interests, similar concepts, and identical positions on this issue. American scholars contend that the colored revolutions added an ideological dimension to the differences between the Sino-Russian side and the United States, which actively promotes democracy and human rights in Central Asia.[58]

The colored revolutions have created a dilemma for American policymakers, for these changes have made it difficult for the United States to continue its original policy. Continued promotion of democratic transformation in Central Asia may further erode U.S. influence in the region. But Washington cannot renounce democratic transformation of the region, because the concept is fundamental to the U.S. understanding of its diplomacy and interests. Any overt retreat from support for democracy and human rights—after the Andijon incident—would encounter fierce criticism from conservative forces in the United States. The contradiction between the realistic interests and the ideological program recur often in U.S. diplomacy; and they have appeared yet again in its Central Asian policy, with the corresponding negative consequences.

The constellation of great-power relations in Central Asia are shifting in favor of Moscow and adversely for Washington. This rise in Russian influence and decline in American power are characteristic of the change in great-power relations in the region. Martha Brill Olcott affirms that the United States has lost the influence it exercised in the wake of 9/11.[59]

The main impact of the colored revolutions on great-power relations is the attitude of Central Asian states toward U.S. policy—which, to them, means instability and "regime change." The leaders of the Central Asian governments, naturally, oppose anything that might lead to political and social instability, and the United States is universally regarded as the most important external factor acting to promote the colored revolutions. The Central Asian governments universally condemn American intervention to support democratic transformation and have modified their erstwhile support for close ties to Washington. Central Asian states used to see the United States as the guarantor of security and economic interests, and the counterweight to the other great powers. The political threat of democratic transformation erased these advantages. Some American analysts in academic and political circles blame China and Russia for U.S. setbacks in Central Asia and demands for troop withdrawals.[60] In fact, however, this change is not due to Russian or Chinese pressure. Uzbekistan was favorably disposed toward the United States and suspicious of Russia; it has now reversed that orientation.

The realignment of great-power relations in Central Asia, however, does not mean an end to American influence in the region. The United States will remain a very important international player; its presence (not necessarily military) will be long lasting; its strategic influence will continue to be considerable. The change in Central Asian attitudes toward Washington after the colored revolutions also does not mean a radical deterioration in relations. The states of Central Asia will still pursue a multidirectional policy, be open to relations with Washington, and seek a balance among the major powers.

The current relations of the great powers in Asia are dynamic and subject to change or reversals. Of the many vagaries in great-power relations in Central Asia, two are particularly salient: one is change in Central Asia itself, and the other is a readjustment of the American policy toward this region. These two factors may have a new impact on the relations of the great powers in this region.

Change in Central Asia could take many forms. One is another colored revolution, which cannot be ruled out. The second is a political reversal after a colored revolutions—that is, the new regime cannot effectively govern, promote economic development, eliminate corruption, and practice democracy. All that can culminate in a political reaction against the colored revolutions and destroy their political benefits.[61] A third possibility is turmoil in the form of political struggle, social conflict, or perturbations in the relations between Central Asian countries.

China: Challenges of Colored Revolutions

The colored revolutions pose challenging issues to China, eliciting its attention and serving as a cause of concern.

The colored revolutions have brought uncertainties to the relations between China and Central Asian countries. Regime change brought about by a colored revolution may impact bilateral relations and require China to adjust accordingly. China must understand the new regime and its domestic and foreign policies, must endeavor to maintain the previous level of bilateral relations, and must uphold earlier agreements.

The colored revolutions bear a distinct ideological bent but also, insofar as the new regime gained power with the support of the United States, have a pro-American and pro-Western affinity. The new regimes may therefore re-calibrate their foreign policy in favor of the United States and the West. This is true for Georgia and Ukraine. If that recurs in Central Asia, it would naturally arouse concern in Beijing. A regime change can reconfigure international relations, realign the position of the great powers in Central Asia, and aggravate their competition in the region.

The colored revolutions may also have a negative impact on the internal unity and stability of the SCO. Any member state that undergoes a colored revolution may reduce its commitment to the SCO, reduce its participation, and raise objections to SCO policies and activities. This would make it more difficult for the SCO to reach a consensus on policy. The colored revolutions might also weaken the political identity of SCO members; if the new regimes espouse Western democratic transformation and the others do not, the result would be basic differences on political precepts and values. This would vitiate the internal unity and solidarity of the SCO and might even lead to an internal split.

From China's perspective, the Central Asian situation is fraught with many contradictions, and terrorist and extremist forces have much influence. Once colored revolutions occur and masses of people take to the streets, countries could dissolve into chaos that terrorist and extremist forces could exploit. Hence the colored revolutions may lead to destabilization, not democratization. The Tulip Revolution in Kyrgyzstan in March 2005 and the Andijon incident in Uzbekistan in May 2005 show how popular antigovernment movements can spiral out of control and ignite violent conflicts and regional turbulence. Destabilization of Central Asia could impact China's security environment, its economic and trade activities, and the personal safety of Chinese businesspeople. During the Kyrgyz upheaval of March 2005, some Chinese businesspeople were attacked, goods were plundered, and trade with Kyrgyzstan was disrupted.

If another colored revolution were to occur in Central Asia, it would confront China and the SCO with a difficult dilemma. China as a great power has important strategic interests in Central Asia, yet could not effectively intervene in the event of social and political turmoil. The same would be true of the SCO. Although the SCO makes security a principal concern, it would not intervene in the internal affairs of states in the region. If any dangerous situation were to arise, the SCO would confront a difficult choice. If it did not intervene, Central Asia could be destabilized, with a negative impact on the SCO, its authority, and its prestige. After the Osh disorders in Kyrgyzstan (where the Tulip Revolution began), and the Andijon incident, some argued that, since the SCO could not guarantee security, it could not be regarded as an important regional organization. If, however, the SCO were to intervene, it would violate its basic principles and become embroiled in the political crisis. This is the challenge that the colored revolutions pose for China and the SCO; whatever their choice, it is fraught with negative consequences.

Hence China neither likes nor welcomes the colored revolutions in Central Asia. Its basic position is that Central Asian countries should conduct political and economic reforms and choose their political and economic models on their own—without any pressure from external forces to adopt their models. Chinese academic circles contend that the political change in the former Soviet region has its objective necessity rooted in the regional politics, economy, and society that developed after the dissolution of the Soviet Union. The former Soviet republics are countries in transition—that is, subject to continuous development and change. That, however, does not make a colored revolution inevitable in every former Soviet republic. It is only one form of political change; although these may continue to occur (given the presence of the preconditions), there is no adequate reason to assume that this is the only potential form of political change. In any case, China holds that the inevitable transformation in Central Asia should be done in an orderly and legal way.

China places a top priority on stability in Central Asia. Only stability can enable political reform, economic development, trade, and regional security. Hence stability serves the interests of both Central Asia and China. The difference between the Chinese and American perspective is not only a matter of understanding, but also of values: whereas China deems stability most important, the United States makes democratization its primary political objective. China holds that stability is a precondition for the development of democracy; the United States believes that democracy is a precondition for stability. China regards stability even under an imperfect regime as better than chaos under a perfect regime; the United States deems stability under a centralized regime unimportant and installation of a democratic government as a top priority.

China: Opportunities and Challenges in Central Asia

In China's view, for the next five to ten years it will face a Central Asia that will remain unstable with respect to its politics, economy, security, and social relations.

After the defeat of the Taliban regime and Al Qaeda, the security situation there has undergone substantial change and the threat to Central Asia was largely eliminated. Nevertheless, Afghanistan remains the most important external threat to regional security and stability: the Afghan domestic situation remains volatile, the control capability of the central government limited, and the tribal forces powerful. Remnants of the Taliban and Al Qaeda, under certain conditions, may still stage a comeback. Afghan reconstruction will require considerable time; in the foreseeable future, one should not expect complete stability to prevail in the country. As long as Afghanistan remains unstable, it will be a threat to Central Asia. Afghanistan also poses another threat: the drug trade. That threat has indeed increased since the fall of the Taliban and has not only caused social problems but also serves to fund terrorist activities. Narco-business has therefore increasingly aroused the concern of Central Asian countries.

Given the potential dangers of the Afghan situation, China holds that the international antiterrorism coalition should not withdraw from Afghanistan and should remain there to ensure stability. Withdrawal could cause a deterioration in the situation there. However, China also believes that Afghan stability depends on the country itself. Other countries cannot provide security guarantee over the long term. Only the establishment of domestic unity and effective state power can bring stability to Afghanistan. To eliminate terrorism, comprehensive antiterrorism measures (including, in particular, economic development and higher living standards) are essential.

Over the next five or ten years, China believes that "three evil forces"—terrorism, separatism, and extremism—will remain a menace to Central Asia. These forces develop because of both external and internal factors, neither of which can be easily or quickly eradicated. Since 2001 authorities have made a full-scale assault on terrorist forces, which have either been crushed or dispersed and immobilized. The Islamic Movement of Uzbekistan still exists, but has undergone some change. Its role in the terrorist explosions in Tashkent and Bukhara (March–April 2004) cannot be conclusively proven, but these events do demonstrate the gravity of the terrorist threat. The Islamic Party of Liberation, or Hizb ut-Tahrir, the main religious extremist organization in Central Asia, is active and growing in size. Despite claims to be nonviolent, it adheres to extremist religious beliefs, seeks to establish an Islamic state, which goes against the laws of their states and will finally leads to political and social confrontation. According to some sources, Hizb ut-Tahrir also shows a proclivity to engage in violence. Some in the Uzbek government believe that Hizb ut-Tahrir were involved in the Andijon turmoil. There are also other extremist religious organizations in Central Asia. From the Chinese perspective, the terrorist threat in Central Asia varies in intensity, but appears to pose a long-term problem, with interludes of sudden and unforeseen outbursts of violence.

China regards economic development as very important—both because it is a high priority of Central Asian countries and because it is a means to facilitate the resolution of other issues. The Central Asian economies began to recover in the late 1990s, but under adverse conditions: its starting point was low, its basis weak, and its structure fraught with inherent weaknesses. Economic development there is imbalanced, with some countries developing much more rapidly than others, but with a general pattern of backwardness. Hence living standards are low; the question of pauperization is acute—no doubt an important cause of other problems, such as social tensions, terrorism, and religious extremism. Hence the governments there must seek to promote not only economic growth but also social equity and justice.

Political stability remains an important issue in this region. The mechanism for regime change is fragile, without a stable institutional character. Amidst the volatility of regime change, acute political conflicts can easily occur and unleash social disorders. And the coming years are bound to witness regime change; the question is whether this will lead to rejuvenation or collapse of the existing order. Circumstances vary, with the situation of Kazakhstan apparently being the clearest. In December 2005 Kazakhstan held presidential elections; the term of the newly elected president will expire in 2012. Kyrgyzstan had a new regime take power in July 2005; presumably it will not soon face the question of regime change. Uzbekistan will conduct presidential elections in 2007; although President Islam Karimov has not declared his intent, and although there appear to be no other major candidates, the United States will certainly do its utmost to block Karimov and support the opposition. Tajikistan held presidential elections in November 2006, in which president Rakhmonov was reelected for his next seven-year term. Turkmenistan faces an uncertain future in the wake of President Niiazov's sudden death. It is difficult to forecast post-Niiazov scenarios.

Bilateral relations within Central Asia, especially between Uzbekistan and Kyrgyzstan and between Uzbekistan and Tajikistan, could destabilize the region. In these two cases there are serious issues of borders, ethnic minorities, and water resources, all of which are critically important for Central Asian security and stability.

China may face some political challenges in Central Asia in the short- and medium-terms, but not grave crises. Relations between Beijing and the Central Asian countries do not entail major political problems, given the resolution of border issues and institutional guarantees for security. Although a great power, China treats Central Asian countries as equals and strictly adheres to the principle of nonintervention in internal affairs. Beijing also provides economic assistance and plans to increase such aid to Central Asia in the future. As for security, China seeks to cooperate closely with the Central Asian states to combat terrorism and the drug trade. Hence the Chinese policy emphasizing friendship, moderation, and cooperation will help to bolster bilateral relations.

China takes a flexible, pragmatic approach to Central Asia and eschews direct political pressure in the domestic political process. China will calmly accept any political change and is willing to develop bilateral relations with any legal regime. Hence Chinese policy there reflects the flexibility that has been a hallmark of traditional Chinese diplomacy. To be sure, some domestic political factors may cause the government to invoke ideology, but pragmatic thinking and policy will finally prevail. That was evident in its response to the collapse of the USSR and the subsequent "colored revolutions."

China may adjust its policy to deal with developments in Central Asia. The goal is, however, to build bilateral relations on the solid basis of common interests, establish pragmatic relations, and reduce the role of ideology and rhetoric. China will assign more importance to cultural and humanistic exchanges, project a more positive image, expand its cultural influence, and take steps to enhance popular understanding of its policies. Concrete measures include supporting Chinese language instruction in Central Asia, accepting more Central Asian students to study in China, training experts on Central Asia, stimulating the development of education, culture, and tourism, and so forth. In July 2005 China announced that it would provide funds to train 1,500 experts for the member states of the SCO in three years.[62] Also, in 2005 China established the Confucian College in Uzbekistan and the Chinese Cultural Center in Kazakhstan; it will open similar centers in the future to promote language instruction and the spread of Chinese culture.[63] In short, China will increase the quotient of "soft power" in its policy toward Central Asia.

Given China's policy of promoting friendly relations, the Central Asian states—even if they undergo political change—unless extremist forces take power can hardly adopt a hostile posture toward Beijing. China is more powerful than the Central Asian states; it would be unwise for Central Asian countries to provoke China. Rather, the sensible policy is to seek good relations with a neighbor that shares a border of some 3,000 kilometers, that is an important economic partner, and that is an important player among the great powers involved in the region. Cooled relations with China also reduce their maneuvering room and the possibility of choices among great powers. In short, an unfriendly policy toward China on the part of the Central Asian states would run counter to their own fundamental, long-term interests.

The uniqueness of Central Asia, however, may give rise to new issues and challenges to Chinese policy toward the region.

One issue is whether China should station troops in Central Asia. After the Tulip Revolution in Kyrgyzstan in 2005, the media reported that China might station troops in Kyrgyzstan—a report that aroused much attention inside and outside China. Although this report later proved inaccurate, it did raise an issue requiring serious consideration for China. Some in China argue, contrary to traditional policy, that China should station some troops abroad in regions of strategic interest. They argue that the goal of deployment of troops abroad for China is totally different from the Cold War period. It is not aimed at any other states but tries to combat terrorism and defend regional stability. In the first instance that would be Central Asia, partly because it is a peripheral region, but more importantly because it is a region from where comes direct terrorist threat; besides, it is a region that is much more open to a foreign military presence. Given China's strategic interests, it should have the same right as Russia and the United States—which have already deployed forces in the region.

Another, related question is whether China should intervene in the event of a destabilization of Central Asia. Noninterference has traditionally been a cardinal principle of China's diplomacy. But Central Asia, which is critical to the security of northwestern China, will force Beijing to reconsider that precept if chaos and crisis were to develop in that region. In that event, should China adhere to the principle of noninterference if the emerging situation threatens to harm China, or should it take a more proactive policy and avert a deterioration in the situation? This will also be a serious challenge for China. If Beijing declines to intervene, its interests will be damaged, its safeguard of Central Asian stability suspect, and its prestige tarnished. If, however, China were to intervene, it would not only be deviating from its traditional diplomatic principles but also incur political risk, including entanglement in the internal political power struggles, the alienation of some indigenous political forces, and complications in its relations with other Central Asian states and the great powers.

From the short- and medium-term perspective, China will not fundamentally change its policy of stationing its troops abroad. Such a policy shift would entail a radical shift in China's concepts of diplomacy, which would be very difficult and complicated. Such a deployment would require the approval of local governments, but these have made no such requests. Nor is such a deployment in China's interest, given the attendant risk and high cost. Those costs are not only financial but also political: such military intervention would only redouble regional fears and anxieties about China's power and intentions. Another negative consequence would be a rise in Russian dissatisfaction and vigilance. In sum, the dispatch of Chinese troops to Central Asia could become a serious diplomatic burden.

In theory and practice, however, China may adopt a more open, proactive foreign policy in the future. It may seek, for example, a more flexible policy in the political and security fields. While China will not station troops in Central Asia, it may consider participating in multilateral military operations and in joint military exercises. Beijing has invited Russia and Central Asian countries to participate in military exercises on Chinese territory, which implies that

China has the right to participate in similar activities on the territories of the Central Asian countries.

China will become more active in Central Asian affairs. It will not directly intervene and support one group against another, but it will not ignore events that threaten regional stability. For example, during the Kyrgyz parliamentary election in March 2003, China sent a delegation to observe the electoral process—a first such move for China. During the Kazakh presidential elections in December 2005, China also sent observers. China has done so again during the Tajikistan presidential elections in November 2006. This shows that China has turned from complete abstention to selective involvement, a sharp change from past policy and tradition.

In the next five to ten years, China's primary opportunity in Central Asia is in the economic sphere. This is what makes China most attractive to Central Asian countries and constitutes its principal diplomatic resource. Hence economic relations will be the main factor in bilateral relations. This economic factor will, above all, depend on the Chinese economy itself, and thus far it has maintained a rapid rate of growth. This economic development can power an expansion of trade with Central Asia, strengthen China's investment in the region, and increase Chinese economic assistance to the region. Since the late 1990s the economy of Central Asian countries has entered a phase of recovery and growth, but still has fragile foundations. Sustaining that development will be a central task. The Central Asian economies require structural change, major rebuilding of the infrastructure, and large-scale investment—all of which means that Central Asian interest in China will increase, not diminish. In the past decade their mutual relations have shown considerable progress. China trade volume with Central Asian countries (excluding Turkmenistan) was slightly more than 500 million U.S. dollars in 1992, increased to 2.3 billion U.S. dollars in 2002, and by 2005 amounted to 8.7 billion U.S. dollars. That growth can be expected to increase substantially in coming years.

However, changes in the economic and trade environment in Central Asia pose new issues for China. For more than a decade, trade with Central Asia has been nongovernmental and has concentrated on commodities. This trade flourished under a specific environment that involved low-quality, cheap goods, operated through large markets, and met the demand of low-income residents. This played an important role in helping many low-income families to survive difficult times. While this private trade will continue, its potential has been largely exhausted for two reasons. First, with the growing imposition of state restrictions and the standardization of requirements, the price of Chinese goods on Central Asian markets through nongovernmental channels will inevitably increase. Chinese goods do not enjoy much prestige in Central Asia; they are successful only because of their cheap prices. A price increase would reduce the competitiveness of Chinese goods. Second, as the economic situation in Central Asia improves, the higher standard of living will mean a decrease in demand for cheap Chinese goods; that change is already being felt. This contraction in private trade will significantly impact China's presence on the Central Asian markets.

The response of Central Asian countries to China's rapid economic development is complex and multifaceted: China's growth provides opportunities, but also poses challenges for the Central Asian countries. The principal concern is that Chinese economic power will turn Central Asia—given its economic backwardness, underdeveloped industry, and scientific and technological level—into a mere supplier of raw materials. Given China's economic might, Central Asia fears that it will become marginalized and reduced to a mere supplier of primary goods. The economic and trade structure of Central Asian states, it bears noting, is due not to China but to the policies and priorities of the Soviet era. This issue does not apply only to China; it is true as well of Western countries, which have also concentrated investment in energy and raw materials.

China must constantly adjust its policy to change and seek to optimize the structure of economic cooperation with Central Asian countries. In particular, apart from promoting private trade, China should give more emphasis to different forms of economic and trade cooperation, especially investment and joint ventures. This is an important way to raise the level of economic cooperation with Central Asian countries and to lay the basis for long-term bilateral economic relations. This is essential both for political and economic reasons.

There are many barriers to the development of investment and bilateral cooperation—in particular, the need for Central Asia to provide a more attractive investment environment and reduce the current level of risk. Capital naturally pursues material gain; if capital sees good prospects of profit, it will pour in. If the environment does not seem to engender profitability, capital will simply not appear. Thus a gradual improvement in the investment and business environment in Central Asia will lead to growing Chinese investment. Although China is not a large exporter of capital, a relaxation in Chinese restrictions will lead to a growth of investment in Central Asia. For example, the total investment in the Sino-Russian joint Suifenhe-Pogranichny frontier trade zone is estimated at 600 million U.S. dollars, with China providing 80 percent of that sum; the investment in the Shanghai project Baltic Pearl in St. Petersburg is estimated (by the Chinese side) to be 1.2 billion U.S. dollars. Other leading corporations, such as TCL, have also begun to develop business in Russia. China's economic relations with Russia are similar to those with Central Asia. To promote economic relations with Russia and Central Asia, the Chinese government previously made demands on enterprises that were tantamount to an administrative order or semi-order. As events have shown, this policy, which was contrary to economic and market laws, achieved little. Apart from direct interstate projects, the main function of the government is to provide information, consultation, proposals, and other services to reduce risks for an enterprise.

To expand economic cooperation with Central Asia, China needs to encourage more private capital and to involve its coastal provinces. Private enterprises account for half of the Chinese economy; private capital has enormous capacity, flexibility, high efficiency, and adapts more easily to the environment of transitional economies. China's border provinces are the main agents in trade and economic cooperation with Central Asia; they have favorable climatic, geographic, human, and other advantages in conducting trade with Central Asian countries. The coastal provinces are much farther removed, but have significant scientific and technological resources as well as greater investment ability.

It is also important to change the image of Chinese goods, which have an unfavorable reputation. Especially in the early 1990s, some Chinese imports to the CIS were of inferior quality and gave Chinese goods a bad reputation. Undoing that bad impression is a long process; customers must learn to distinguish between different grades of goods and not lump them all under the same rubric. The poor reputation of Chinese goods is due partly to their low production quality (resulting from low wages) and partly due to the limited purchasing power of Central Asian consumers (meaning a preference for cheap goods). Geography plays a role too: contiguity encourages participation by small businesspeople. As a result, hi-tech goods from China (e.g., electronics and electrical appliances), which enjoy a strong demand in the United States and in Europe, have a small share of the market in Central Asia. The main problem today for China is not the inferior quality of its goods, but their negative image. Hence the central task for China is to refurbish the image of its consumer goods.

For China, the SCO is both an opportunity and a challenge in Central Asia during the coming decade. As noted above, while SCO from China's perspective, serves the interests of all the state-members, it represents China's engagement in the region and advances its interests there. Hence development of the SCO will enable China to expand its role in Central Asia. If the SCO does not develop, however, the impact on China would be negative. The SCO has survived its initial phase; the key problem for China is its future development, a question that has several main dimensions: one is whether China can constantly advance the SCO; another is how China should do this; and a third concerns the proper direction of the organization. As the SCO expands its role, it must adjust to changes in the situation, reprioritize objectives, redefine functions, restructure its organizational tasks. As the SCO grows, it must address its many and complex choices.

Another important challenge over the next decade concerns China's relations with Russia: It does not imply that Sino-Russian relations are doom to crisis in the future. It just suggests that Russia, not the United States, will impact China's engagement most in Central Asia, both positively or negatively. If Sino-Russian relations are good, it can be very beneficial to China. If Sino-Russian relations are not good, it can bring more damage to China. Russia is the primary great power in Central Asia; the United States, after all, is far removed from the region and has no major geopolitical interests there. The tenor of Sino-American relations has affected Beijing's policy on Central Asia, but less so than have Sino-Russian relations. Therefore, Sino-Russian, not Sino-American, relations will significantly impact Beijing's policy toward Central Asia in the next five to ten years.

It therefore bears emphasizing that China and Russia not only share some common interests but are also competitors in Central Asia. When the common interests outweigh the competition, as is now the case, this serves to facilitate cooperation. If, however, competition comes to predominate, then the cooperation will accordingly diminish. Although cooperation has generally prevailed, the central task is to ensure it continues to do so. The coming decade will be crucial in determining whether China and Russia will lay the foundations for long-term, effective cooperation in the region.

The next decade will witness a growth in the role of both China and Russia in the region. Apart from China's growing economic, political, and security role, one must also anticipate an increase in Russia's influence, as it regains its former strength and seeks a greater role in post-Soviet space. That is especially true for Central Asia, which depends heavily on Russia in politics, economy, and security and which is the most receptive among the former Soviet republics to a resurgence of Russian influence. The waxing role of these two powers will lead to more extensive contacts and more direct competition, even conflicts of interest.

Russia will be faced with a strategic reorientation toward an expanding Chinese role in the region. It must, in essence, decide whether to regard China as its partner or its competitor. How Russia answers this question will directly affect Chinese policy. If Moscow chooses partnership, the two countries will maintain the strategic framework of cooperation; if Moscow chooses competition, then strategic cooperation will recede. China will modify its strategy accordingly.

China and Russia will face structural problems in promoting the economic integration of Central Asia. The two support this process, but envision different institutional frameworks: China proposes to use the SCO and Russia the Eurasian Economic Community. These frameworks subsume different political and economic conceptions. Namely, the SCO includes China, Russia, and

Central Asia; it may also expand to incorporate southern and western Asia. China favors the SCO framework mainly for economic reasons (viz., directing Central Asian economic development toward China and surrounding countries); this approach entails no clear-cut geopolitical objectives. The Russian goal is to integrate Central Asia in the Eurasian Economic Community, which was founded in October 2000 (as a successor to the Eurasian Customs League, which consisted of Russia, Belarus, Kazakhstan, Kyrgyzstan, and Tajikistan). In October 2005 the St. Petersburg summit of the Central Asian Cooperation Organization adopted a resolution to merge participants (Kazakhstan, Uzbekistan, Kyrgyzstan, Tajikistan, and Russia) with the Eurasian Economic Community. This step bore transparent geopolitical meaning; it represents a process of economic integration of former Soviet republics under Russian aegis. This model has a clear rationale (based on the special economic ties of former Soviet republics), but that selectivity imposes its own constraints and limitations. Thus there is a basic divergence between the Russian and Chinese approaches toward economic integration in Central Asia; while, at present, the difference is muted, it could evolve into a difficult problem.

Another issue concerns the development of the SCO: Will these two powers share a common conception about the future of this organization? How will they resolve any disagreements? Although contradictions are not inevitable and will not necessarily paralyze the SCO, they could pose problems that the two powers will have to resolve. How effectively China resolves these problems will determine whether it obtains new development resources—or new challenges—in Central Asia.

In general, over the coming decade China will have important opportunities and challenges in Central Asia. The opportunities, especially in the economic sphere, outweigh the challenges: China may substantially increase its investment, expand trade, and construct new transportation networks. In particular, China will develop significant ties to the Central Asian energy sector; the China-Kazakhstan oil pipeline will go into full operation; China and countries in the region will become strategic energy partners. All these factors accentuate closer relations and common interests, with corresponding implications for the political sphere. All the dynamics point toward a significant increase in China's influence in Central Asia over the coming five to ten years.

Notes

1. Almaty Joint Statement of Kazakhstan, China, Kyrgyzstan, Russia, and Tajikistan, 3 July 1998.

2. Li Qi, *Uygurs in Central Asia* (Urumqi: Xinjiang People's Publishing House, 2003), 189.

3. See Ma Dazheng, *National Interests the Highest* (Urumqi: Xinjiang People's Publishing House, 2002), 32.

4. The Information Office, State Council of China, "'East Turkistan' Terrorist Forces Cannot Escape the Responsibilities for the Crimes," *People's Daily*, 22 January 2002.

5. In October 2001 the Chinese government publicly addressed the issue of "East Turkestan" for the first time. The Chinese foreign minister, Tang Jiaxuan, declared that China had suffered grave harm from "East Turkestan" terrorism. On 11 November 2001, in a speech at the United Nations, Tang Jiaxuan said that "East Turkestan" separatists constituted a part of international terrorism and that China faced the threat of "East Turkestan" terrorism. On 22 January 2002, the Information Office of the State Council of China published a lengthy article titled "'East Turkestan' Terrorist Forces Cannot Escape the Responsibilities for the Crimes."

6. The "East Turkestan" organizations in Central Asia were mainly created by members of the movement who have fled from China to Central Asia. In the 1960s, against the background of Sino-Soviet confrontation, large numbers of China's Xinjiang residents were encouraged to flee to the Soviet Union and Central Asia and to establish "East Turkestan" organizations there. However, most of the Chinese fleeing to Central Asia were not members of "East Turkestan." In the 1980s and 1990s, Central Asia again became a refuge for adherents of "East Turkestan"; these are the core members of secessionist forces in Central Asia. Because of these changes in the "East Turkestan" organizations in Central Asia, accurate statistics are not readily available. Different sources cite different numbers regarding "East Turkestan" organizations active in Central Asia. According to Ma Dazheng's research, in 2002 there were eleven "East Turkestan" organizations in Central Asia, of which four conducted terrorist activities. See Ma Dazheng, *National Interests the Highest*, 193. The research of a Kazakhstani scholar, K. L. Syroezhkin, describes the activities of "East Turkestan" in Central Asia. See his *Mify i real'nost' etnicheskogo separatizma v Kitae i bezopasnost' Tsentral'noi Azii* (Almaty: Dark-press, 2003).

7. See Tian Churning, "Analysis of China's Oil Import and Export in 2002," *International Oil Economy*, 2003, no. 3, 26.

8. According to some sources, each year Russia will deliver 5 million tons of oil from Omsk to China via the China-Kazakhstan oil pipeline. See "Rossiia budet eksportirovat' v Kitai neft' cherez Kazakhstan" (http://www.strana.ru).

9. China's Xinjiang Province has seventeen frontier ports open to international business approved by the sate, of which eleven are oriented toward Central Asia, and others are local-level ports. Central Asia accounts for about 60 percent of the foreign trade volume of Xinjiang. In 2003, for example, Xinjiang's foreign trade volume was over 4.7 billion U.S. dollars; of that amount, over 2.5 billion U.S. dollars was with Central Asia. See Hu Hongping, "Vigorously Marching Towards Central Asian Market and Extending Economic and Trade Cooperation," *Russian, Central Asian and East European Markets*, September 2005, 28.

10. The Declaration of Heads of Member States of the Shanghai Cooperation Organization on 5 July 2005 stated: "Considering the completion of the active military stage of antiterrorist operation in Afghanistan, the member states of the Shanghai Cooperation Organization consider it necessary, that respective members of the antiterrorist coalition set a final timeline for their temporary use of the above-mentioned objects of infrastructure and stay of their military contingents on the territories of the SCO member states." See http://www.sectsco.org.

11. *Brief Account of China's Historical Geography*, ed. Zou Yilin (Shanghai: Shanghai Education Publishing House, n.d.), 101.

12. M. Ashimbaev, "Situatsiia v TsA posle 11-ogo sentiabria i razvitiia ShOC," in *Collection of Papers of the International Seminar on Central Asian Situation and the SCO* (Shanghai: Shanghai Institute for International Studies, 2003), 235.

13. Reported 22 August 2005 at http://finance.sina.com.cn.

14. Reported 19 October 2005 at http://finance.sina.com.cn.

15. See the Joint Declaration between the People's Republic of China and the Republic of Kazakhstan, 3 June 2003, at http://www.sina.com.cn.

16. Reported 15 October 2004 at http://sina.com.cn.

17. See the speech of Hu Jintao to the parliament of Uzbekistan on 16 June 2004 at http://www.sina.com.cn.

18. Reported 12 October 2005 at http://kz.chineseembassy.org/chn/xwdt/t216261 .htm. This figure is contradictory to the data cited above, reporting investments by China in Central Asia of more than 1 billion U.S. dollars. Both figures are official, however; the discrepancy may be due to the use of different statistical methods. The latter obviously excludes China's energy investment in Central Asia; the former evidently excludes the investment in China's purchase of PetroKazakhstan.

19. The Joint Statement on Establishment and Development of Strategic Partnership Between China and Kazakhstan, 4 July 2005, at http://www/.sina.com.cn.

20. For example, Alexander Konovalov, President of Russian Strategic Assessment Institute, said that "after the 9/11 incident, a unique window of opportunity to get close to the West appeared in front of Russia: You will get what you want, no matter whether partnership, integration or other desires." Reported 27 December 2001 at http://www.strana.ru.

21. *Nezavisimaia gazeta*, 18 December 2001.

22. Stephen Blank, "U.S. Strategic Dilemmas in Uzbekistan and Turkmenistan," United States Commission on International Religious Freedom and the Center for Strategic and International Studies, Briefing at CSIS, 27 July 2005 at http://www.csis.org.

23. For example, Cory Welt holds that it can be expected that Russia and China will be in constant competition for influence and resources in Central Asia. "U.S. Strategic Interests in Uzbekistan and Turkmenistan, Briefing at CSIS, July 27, 2005," at http://www.csis.org.

24. "China's Remote Areas, The Tenth Summit of Shanghai Cooperation Organization, An Interview with Sinologist Vilia Gelbras," *Novaia gazeta*, 11–13 July 2005.

25. It is generally thought in Western academic circles that in the future China will play a leading role in Central Asia. See, for example, Zbigniew Brzezinski, "China's New Journey to the West. China's Emergence in Central Asia and Implications for U.S. Interests. A Report of CSIS Freeman Chair," *China Studies*, ed. Bates Gill and Matthew Oresman, August 2003, vi. E. Wayne Merry with the American Foreign Policy Council also holds this view. See his "Moscow's Retreat and Beijing's Rise as Regional Great Power," *Problems of Post-Communism* 50, no. 3 (May–June 2003), 26.

26. Boris Rumer has given a detailed explanation on this topic. See *Central Asia at the End of the Transition*, ed. Boris Rumer (Armonk, NY: M. E. Sharpe, 2005), 45–55.

27. "Est' predel ustupkam Moskvy," *Nezavisimaia gazeta*, 12 May 2004.

28. In an interview in 2005, Russian Foreign Minister Lavrov declared that the post-Soviet space has never been Russia's hereditary territory, and hence there should be no case of vying with other countries for a sphere of influence. See the report of

29 April 2005 at http://www.America-russia.net. In August 2005, at the CIS summit in Kazan, Putin proposed to cooperate with the West in the CIS region, intimating that Russia had come to accept a Western presence in the region. RIV Novosti, 26 August 2005.

29. A Russian commentary attributes the denial by China's Ministry of Foreign Affairs to the passive response of Central Asian countries and Russia. In reality there is no official confirmation of reports that China may station forces in Kyrgyzstan. The Chinese foreign ministry has no plan to raise this issue; hence there has been no need for a response by the other countries involved. "Kitai gotov eksportirovat' voennye bazy. Odnako v Kirgizii, skoree vsego, garantii stabil'nosti stanut Rossiiane." See the report of 31 May 2005 at http//www.strana.ru.

30. According to the agreement between Russia and Kyrgyzstan, the time limit of the Kant base will be fifteen years, which can be extended. Russian military bases in Tajikistan have no terminal limit.

31. "Dogovor o soiuznicheskikh otnosheniiakh mezhdu Rossiiskoi Federatsiei i Respublikoi Uzbekistan." Reported 14 November 2005 at http://www.president .kremlin.ru/interdocs/2005/11/14/1934_type72066_97086.shtml?type=72066.

32. In a sense, Russia's establishment of military bases in Central Asia was closely linked to the deployment of American military forces in the region. During the first ten years after the Central Asian republics became independent, there were no foreign military bases in the region, though Russia's 201st motorized division remains stationed in Tajikistan after the dissolution of the Soviet Union; nor was there any reason for a foreign country to station troops there, since that could only provoke opposition from other countries. The establishment of American military bases set a precedent for other countries to follow. Even during the Taliban era, Russia had no military base in Central Asia; with the overthrow of the Taliban regime, the security situation in Afghanistan and Central Asia did improve. However, it was at that point that Russia reestablished its first military base in the region in 2002, i.e., the Russian Kant base in Kyrgyzstan (only a few dozen kilometers from the U.S. Manas base, Kyrgyzstan). U.S. military intervention obviously played an important role in precipitating the Russian response. There have been reports that even India is disposed to establish a military presence in the region.

33. Prior to 9/11 the American government was ambivalent about the "East Turkestan" issue, but the terrorist attacks induced Washington in April 2004 to list the "East Turkestan" Islamic Movement as a terrorist organization. In September 2004, however, Washington tacitly allowed the establishment of the "East Turkestan Government in Exile" in the United States itself. That caused great displeasure in Beijing, which also requested the extradition of fifteen members of East Turkestan held in detention at the U.S. base on Guantanamo. Washington refused.

34. For example, Jessica T. Matthews believes that the 11 September 2001 attacks brought some short-term benefits to China, but profoundly changed China's geopolitical environment and forced it to respond to a potential danger. See Jessica T. Matthews, "Carnegie Endowment, Policy Brief, Special Edition," no. 18 (2002).

35. Regular press conference of the spokesperson for the Foreign Ministry of China, 17 January 2002 (http://www.mfa.gov.cn).

36. Regular press conference of the spokesperson for the Foreign Ministry of China, 11 March 2002 (http://www.mfa.gov.cn).

37. Interview of the Chinese Foreign Minister in *Der Spiegel* (Germany), 2 December 2003, at http://www.mfa.gov.cn.

38. The Declaration of Heads of Member States of the Shanghai Cooperation Organization, Astana, 5 July 2005, at http://www.sectsco.org.

39. For example, Martha Brill Olcott contends that the Astana declaration may have been drafted by President Islam Karimov of Uzbekistan during a visit to China. See "U.S. Strategic Interests in Uzbekistan and Turkmenistan, Briefing at CSIS," 27 July 2005, at http://www.csis.org.

40. As early as the eve of Chinese President Jiang Zemin's visit to the United States in October 2002, Li Zhaoxing (Executive Deputy Foreign Minister) declared that China is willing to consult and cooperate with the United States on international and regional issues, including those pertaining to Central Asian. China's attitude has not changed. See the report of 13 August 2002 at http://www.cnradio.com.

41. China later raised the matter of Sino-American energy cooperation in Central Asia. There are indications that China paid increasing attention to such cooperation, including in Central Asia. One of the main topics in the Sino-American strategic dialogue starting in August 2005 has been energy cooperation.

42. Zbigniew Brzezinski, "Russian Roulette," *Wall Street Journal*, 29 March 2005.

43. Teimuraz Beridze, Eldar Ismailov, Vladimir Papava, *Tsentral'yi Kavkaz i ekonomika Gruzii* (Baku: Nurlan, 2004), 58–61.

44. Professor B. Shchedev, Director of Asian Studies Center, Ukrainian Institute for World Economy and International Relations, holds this view (interview with the author on 24 September 2002).

45. *Problemy bor'by s bednost'iu v stranakh Tsentral'noi Azii v usloviiakh globalizatsii* (Almaty: Institut mirovoi ekonomiki i politiki pri Fonde Pervogo Prezidenta RK, 2004), 144.

46. Beridze et al., *Tsentral'nyi Kavkaz*, p. 61.

47. Kurmanbek Bakiev, "Vo vsem vinovata korruptsiia," *Nezavisimaia gazeta*, 8 April 2005.

48. Justin Burke argues that the Kyrgyz revolution cannot be included in the list of "velvet revolutions" but rather has more in common with revolution in the traditional sense. See Justin Burke, "Kyrgyzstan's Revolution: Be careful of What You Wish For," posted 25 March 2005 at http://www.eurasianet.org. The *Economist* also writes that the Kyrgyz revolution is a mixture of different elements, not just a brilliant victory for democracy. See "Kyrgyzstan: One Down, Four to Go. Revolution Reaches the Steppe," *Economist*, 2–8 April 2005.

49. Brzezinski, "Russian Roulette."

50. "Barkhatnye revoliutsii razvrashchaiut oppozitsiiu," posted 18 March 2005 at http://www.kabar.kg/rus.

51. "Za besporiadkami v Kieve stoiat amerikantsy," *The Guardian*, 26 November 2004, at http:/www.inosmi.ru.

52. A. Akaev, "Revoliutsiia tiul'panov—detishche SShA," *Nezavisimaia gazeta*, 31 March 2005.

53. On 26 July 2005, after the SCO summit in Astana, the U.S. Secretary of Defense Donald Rumsfeld visited Kyrgyzstan. President Bakiev later said that the United States could keep its air base at Manas, but must increase payments for its use. See "Kyrgyz Say U.S. Forces Can Stay if They Pay More," 21 September 2005, at http://www.eurasianet.org. There were also reports that Washington promised to increase financial aid to 200 million U.S. dollars, but Kyrgyzstan denied this. See "Rumsfeld's Visit May

Only Temporarily Relieve Pressure on U.S. Forces in Central Asia to Leave," 28 July 2005, http://www.eurasianet.org. According to the Kyrgyz government, Kyrgyzstan receives only 50 million U.S. dollars for the American military base.

54. "U.S. Envoy Says Russian Security Service Main Threat to Tajikistan," *Avesta*, 9 September 2005.

55. "Sergei Ivanov: Aviabaza v Kante—dolgosrochnyi proekt," 21 September 2005 at http://www.strana.ru.

56. "Rossiia vosstanavlivaet pozitsii v Srednei Azii," 23 September 2005, at http://www.strana.ru.

57. In June 2004 Russia and Uzbekistan declared that they were strategic partners.

58. Stephen Blank, "U.S. Strategic Dilemmas in Uzbekistan and Turkmenistan."

59. Martha Brill Olcott, "U.S. Strategic Dilemmas in Uzbekistan and Turkmenistan," Stephen Blank, "U.S. Strategic Dilemmas in Uzbekistan and Turkmenistan," United States Commission on International Religious Freedom and the Center for Strategic and International Studies, Briefing at CSIS, 27 July 2005 at http://www.csis.org.

60. For example, Richard Myers, chairman of the Joint Chiefs of Staff, holds that the SCO request for the withdrawal of American military bases in Central Asia was the result of intimidation of small countries by major powers—China and Russia. See "Russia and China Bullying Central Asia, U.S. Says, Pentagon Pressured to Pull out of Uzbek, Kyrgyz Bases," *Washington Post*, 15 July 2005.

61. The countries that experienced colored revolutions are faced with this issue in varying degrees. Ukraine is the most obvious: Once the new regime took office, it encountered a power struggle, grave corruption, and deterioration of the national economic situation. And all that led to the dissolution of the government in September 2005 and a new political crisis. After the colored revolution, Georgian economic and social development made no obvious progress and gave no cause for optimism. Kyrgyzstan shows signs of political instability, including a growing conflict between the new president and the parliament.

62. Hu Jintao's speech of 5 July 2005 ("Strengthening Solidarity and Cooperation and Promoting Stability and Development"), delivered at the SCO summit in Astana is available in a report of 6 July 2005 at http://www.sina.com.cn.

63. Central Asian countries have certain demands for Chinese language teaching and many young people from Central Asia hope to come to China for studies. Chinese support for such studies cannot meet the demand.

Index

About the Authors

Rajan Menon is Monroe J. Rathbone Professor of International Relations at Lehigh University and Fellow at the New America Foundation.

Eugene Rumer is a Senior Fellow at the Institute for National Strategic Studies at the National Defense University.

Dmitri Trenin is Deputy Director, Carnegie Moscow Center, and Senior Associate, Carnegie Endowment for International Peace.

Zhao Huasheng is a senior research fellow and Director of the Center of Russian and Central Asian Studies, and the Center of Shanghai Cooperation Organization Studies at Fudan University.